ELECTRONIC COMMERCE:

LAW AND PRACTICE

AUSTRALIA
LBC Information Services Ltd
Sydney

CANADA and USA
Carswell
Toronto

NEW ZEALAND
Brooker's
Auckland

SINGAPORE and MALAYSIA
Thomson Information (S.E. Asia)
Singapore

ELECTRONIC COMMERCE:

LAW AND PRACTICE

Michael Chissick

Field Fisher Waterhouse

and

Alistair Kelman

London
Sweet & Maxwell
1999

Published by
Sweet & Maxwell Limited of
100 Avenue Road,
Swiss Cottage, London NW3 3PF
(http://www.smlawpub.co.uk)
Typeset by Dataword Services Limited of Chilcompton
Printed in Great Britain by
Bookcraft (Bath) Ltd

A C.I.P. catalogue record for this book
is available from the British Library

ISBN 075200 6509

No natural forests were destroyed to make this product,
only farmed timber was used and replanted

To Diana

AK

To Don, Roz, Darren, Graham and Lev

MPC

PREFACE

Our thanks go to Edward Cheng for his invaluable assistance with respect to Chapters 3 and 4. Edward's contribution in both writing and research was instrumental in enabling this book to be written. Our thanks also go to Hayley Stallard and Graeme Nuttall, partners at Field Fisher Waterhouse, for contributing Chapter 8 on Webvertising and Chapter 9 on Tax respectively.

We give particular thanks to John Hartle and Peter Sommer for their constructive criticism of the various chapters as they evolved. Naturally all mistakes are our joint responsibility.

The law of electronic commerce is the most active branch of law; changes and new legal and technological developments occur constantly. It is therefore important that the reader should be in possession of the latest information as soon as possible and this book should be treated as a starting point rather than as a conclusive document. The book is no substitute for professional legal advice.

We have tried to restrict Web references to pages either to home pages or to pages which appear unlikely to be moved in the near future. However web sites do get redesigned and altered. Readers will find, over time, that the detailed web references at some future date may not always lead to the sought document. When this situation occurs we would recommend readers to put the text description of the web reference into a web search engine to find the reference's new location. We have found the Northern Light search engine (**http://www.northernlight.com/**) to be particularly useful in performing this task.

This law is given in this edition as it stood on *October 1, 1998* unless another date is given.

	Michael Chissick	Alistair Kelman
Practice Address	**Field Fisher Waterhouse** 35 Vine Street London EC3N 2AA	**Lancaster Buildings — Barristers in Cyberspace** UK Administration: Lancaster Buildings 77 Deansgate Manchester M3 2BW
E-mail	mail to: **mpc@ffwlaw.com**	mail to: **akelman@cix.co.uk** mail to: **A.Kelman@lse.ac.uk** mail to: **Alistair@urgentmail.com**
Telephone	+44 171 481 4841	+44 171 649 9872
Other Professional Address		**The LSE Computer Security Research Centre** Houghton Street London WC2A 2AE
Web Sites	http://www.ffwlaw.com/	http://www.lbnipc.com/ http://www.telepathic.com/ http://www.csrc.lse.ac.uk/

CONTENTS

LIST OF ABBREVIATIONS AND GLOSSARY OF TERMS

As with most technology the Internet is full of buzz words and jargon. Listed below are the most common words along with their plain English explanations.

Access provider
A company that sells Internet connection. Known variously as Internet access or service providers (**IAPs** or **ISPs**), *e.g.* Demon, CompuServe or America Online.

Anonymous FTP *server*
A remote computer, with publicly accessible file archives, that accepts 'anonymous' as the log-in name and an **e-mail address** as the password.

Archie
A program that searches Internet **FTP** archives by file name.

Applet
A small program which is embedded within another application — usually a web **Browser** — and which can run on any system that runs the other application.

ASCII
The American standard code for information interchange. A text format readable by all computers.

Asymmetric cryptography
An encryption/decryption system in which it is impossible to derive the decryption key from the encryption key or the other way around.

Authentication
Authentication is the process of validating the identity of someone or something.

Bandwidth
The term used to describe the amount of data which can be sent over a telecommunications link to the Net. The higher the bandwidth, the faster data can flow.

Baud rate
A measure of the bits per second (bps) that a device can communicates or the bps that can be carried on a given communications circuit. Commonly used to describe the speed of a **modem** when transmitting data.

BBS
Bulletin Board System. A computer system accessible by modem. Members can dial in and leave messages, send e-mail, play games, and trade files with other users.

Block Encryption   An encryption method that encrypts and decrypts data in blocks rather than one bit (or byte) at a time in a stream. Block encryption is typically associated with the use of a single **Symmetric cryptography** key for both encryption and decryption.

BlowFish   The 64-bit BlowFish block cipher developed by Bruce Schneier which uses a simplification of the principles used in **DES** to provide the same security with greater speed and efficiency than **DES** in software. BlowFish is the precursor to **TwoFish**.

Bookmarks   A Web **browser's** file used to store **URLs**.

Browser   A software program, such as Netscape Communicator or Microsoft's Internet Explorer, that allows you to read and **download** Web documents.

Bulletin board   One computer running software allowing multiple people to access the same information and to post information. Virtually all **bulletin boards** are text and graphics only, although they could become capable of displaying audio visual works.

Chat room   A section of an online service where interactive textual communication occurs amongst a collection of people.

Click   People click on a mouse button to instruct the cursor on screen to activate something.

CGI   Computer graphical interface.

CPU   The central processing unit of control of a P.C. which executes programs.

Cryptography   Cryptography is the science of keeping communications private. A central element of cryptography is encryption, which is the transformation of data into an unintelligible form. Encryption and decryption (the reverse of encryption) using computers require the use of some information, usually called a key. Some encryption systems use the same key to encrypt and decrypt (**Symmetric cryptography**), while others rely upon the two parties having different, but mathematically related keys (**Asymmetric cryptography**).

Cryptographic algorithm	A cryptographic algorithm is a mathematical function that takes intelligible information (plain text) as input and changes it into unintelligible cipher text.
Cyberspace	A term coined by science fiction writer William Gibson, referring to the virtual world which exists within the marriage of computers, telecommunication networks, and digital media.
Database	A computerised filing system for storing, arranging and retrieving information.
DES	The Data Encryption Standard. A block algorithm that has been endorsed by both the U.S. National Institute for Standards and Technology (NIST) and the American National Standards Institute (ANSI) as providing adequate security for unclassified sensitive information.
Dial-up	A term used to describe use of telephone lines or **ISDN** communication networks to connect a computer to the WWW.
Digital certificates	A digital certificate indicates the ownership of a public key by an individual or other entity. It allows verification of the claim that a given public key does in fact belong to a given individual. Certificates help prevent someone from using a phoney key to impersonate someone else. In their simplest form digital certificates contain a public key and a name. More sophisticated versions also contain an expiration date, the name of the certifying authority that issues the certificate, a serial number, and the digital signature of the certificate issuer. The most widely accepted format for certificates is defined by the X.509 international standard. Therefore certificates can be read or written by any application complying with X.509.
Digital signature	A digital signature verifies the contents of a message and the identity of the signatory. It also provides a way of ensuring that a document was in fact sent by a particular sender. This feature is known as non-repudiation. So long as a secure cryptographic hash function is used to generate the digital signature, there is no way to extract someone's digital signature from one document and attach it to another, nor is it possible to alter a signed message in any way. The slightest change in a signed document will cause the digital signature verification process to fail.

Direct connection

A connection, such as SLIP or **PPP**, whereby your computer becomes a live part of the Internet. Also called full IP access.

Domain

A part of the Internet name that specifies certain details about the **host** such as its location and whether it is part of a commercial, governmental, or educational entity. The address is written as a series of names separated by full stops.

Download

The transfer of a file from one computer to another.

E-Commerce

A broad term describing business activities with associated technical data that are conducted electronically.

Electronic Commerce

See **E-Commerce**.

E-mail

E-mail is a way of sending messages electronically to other people from your P.C.

E-mail address

The unique private Internet address to which your e-mail is sent. Takes the form of user@host.

Encryption

The mathematical processing of securing text or data by making it unintelligible to all but the intended recipient. Encryption is based on two components — a **Cryptographic algorithm** and a key.

Firewall

A collection of hardware and/or software components or a system that sits between the Internet and a network through which all traffic from inside to outside, and vice-versa, must pass through and which ensures that only authorised traffic, as defined by the local security policy, is allowed to pass through it. The firewall itself has to be immune to penetration.

Flame-mail

An inflammatory, aggressive, abusive or deliberately anti-social e-mail.

FTP

File transfer **protocol**. The standard de facto method of sending and receiving files over the Internet.

Gopher

A menu-driven system for retrieving Internet archives, usually organised by subject. It is a text-only service which is being supplanted by the www.

GUI Graphical user interface. A method of driving software through the use of windows, icons, menus, buttons and other graphical devices.

Hash function A hash function is a one-way mathematical function that takes a variable-length input string (sometimes called a pre-image) and outputs a fixed-length string (called a hash, hash value, hash word or message digest). The iterative process that computes a hash from a pre-image is termed hashing. Hashing is used in proving that electronic commerce messages have not been modified, corrupted or altered.

Home page Either the first page loaded by your **browser** at start-up, or the main Web document for a particular group, organisation, or person.

Host Your host is the computer you contact to get on to the Net.

HTML **Hypertext** mark-up language. The language used to create documents on the www.

HTTP Hypertext transfer protocol is the standard method of transferring **HTML** documents between **browsers** and **Web servers**.

Hypertext Text where any word or phrase may be linked to another point in the same or another document. These links trigger other documents to be displayed.

Internet A cooperatively run global collection of computer networks with a common addressing scheme: the **TCP/IP** protocols.

Intellectual property The legal rights which result from intellectual activity in the literary, artistic, industrial and scientific fields.

Intranet The deployment of Internet technology inside an organisation which uses the Internet protocols. An intranet needs no connection to the global public Internet.

I.P. Internet protocol. The most important protocol on which the Internet is based. It defines how **packets** of data get from source to destination.

ISDN   Integrated services digital network. A digital telephone network, ISDN can dramatically speed up transfer of information over the Internet or over a remote LAN connection, especially rich media like graphics, audio or video or applications. Out-of-band signalling is used to communicate information simultaneously, over fewer channels than would otherwise be needed. Typically an domestic ISDN line runs 128kb per second although far higher speeds are possible with commercial links.

ISP   Internet service provider. A company that sells access to the Internet and other online services.

Java   A computer language developed by Sun Microsystems. Java was designed to meet the challenges of application development in the context of heterogeneous, network-wide distributed environments. Paramount among these challenges is secure delivery of applications that consume the minimum of system resources, can run on any hardware and software platform, and can be extended dynamically.

Java applet   A small program written in Java which is embedded within another application — usually a web **Browser** — and which can run on any system that runs the other application.

JPEG   A graphic file format that is preferred by Net users because its high compression reduces file size, and thus the time it takes to transfer.

Key   A mathematical value (usually a large number) used by all modern cryptographic algorithms that determines the outcome of the encryption and decryption functions.

Key Escrowing/   A set of policies, procedures, and mechanisms that
Key Archiving   provides backup access to cryptographic keys necessary to decrypt data outside of a normal application. Key escrow in particular carries connotation of key storage with a third party, whereby law enforcement agencies might be able to acquire keys used to decrypt messages from suspected criminals. Key archiving more generally refers to the topic of key storage for the purpose of recovering encrypted data when the original decryption key is lost, stolen, or needed for some other purpose.

Key Generation	The creation of a key or a distinct pair of Public and Private keys.
Key length	Encryption strength is a function both of the algorithm and the key length used with the algorithm. As a rule, the longer the key length, the greater the security.
Key Management	The generation, storage, distribution, deletion, archiving, and application of keys in accordance with an established security policy.
Link	A connection between two items of **hypertext**.
Message Digest function	See **Hash function**.
MD5	MD5 is a Hashing algorithm (sometimes termed a Message Digest algorithm). It is used for digital signature applications where a large message has to be compressed in a secure manner before being signed with the private key. MD5 takes a message of arbitrary length and produces a 128-bit hash or message digest. A message digest or hash can be considered a digital fingerprint of the larger message.
Modem	Modulator/demodulator. A device that allows a computer to communicate with another over a telephone line, by converting the digital information into analogue signals and vice versa.
Netiquette	The etiquette of using the Internet.
Newsgroup	**Bulletin boards** on the Internet covering every conceivable subject (see **Usenet**).
Online	A network connection to another computer.
Packet	A unit of data. In data transfer, information is broken into packets, which then travel independently through the Net. An Internet packet contains the source and destination addresses, an identifier and the data segment.
PGP	See **Pretty Good Privacy**.

PIN

A Personal Identification Number. Used similarly to a password to access and manipulate information electronically.

PKI

Public Key Infrastructure. See **PKIX**.

PKIX

(Public Key Infrastructure X.509): This is a working group of the Internet Engineering Task Force (IETF) concerned with defining standards for interoperability of public key infrastructure components such as security administrators, certification authorities, users, and directories.

POP

Point of presence. An access provider's local dial-in points to reduce the cost of telephone charges for customers dialling in.

PPP

Point to point protocol. A protocol which allows your computer to join the Internet via a modem. Each time you log in, you are allocated a temporary **I.P.** address. It is a more efficient system than the old SLIP connections, and easier to configure.

Pretty Good Privacy (PGP):

PGP or Pretty Good Privacy is a high-security cryptographic software application that allows people to exchange messages in privacy.

Private Key

A key for encryption and decryption that is paired with a **Public Key** and is kept secret by its owner.

Protocol

An agreed way for two network devices to talk to each other.

Public Key

An encryption or decryption key that is paired with a **Private Key** and is publicly known.

Public-key cryptography

Another name for **Symmetric cryptography** which is sometimes shortened to PKC.

RC4

RC4 is a **Symmetric cryptography** cryptosystem designed by Ron Rivest of RSA Data Security. It is a variable key-size operation that runs very quickly in software. While the algorithm is confidential and proprietary to RSA Data Security, Inc, it has been scrutinised under non-disclosure conditions by independent analysts and it is considered secure.

Robot	A 'crawler' program that trawls the Web to update search **databases** such as InfoSeek and Lycos.
Router	A special-purpose computer (or software package) that handles the connection between 2 or more networks. Routers spend all their time looking at the destination addresses of the packets passing through them and deciding which route to send them on.
RSA	RSA is an **Asymmetric cryptography** cryptosystem for both encryption and authentication invented in 1977 by Ron Rivest, Adi Shamir and Leonard Adleman. RSA's system uses a matched pair of encryption and decryption keys, each performing a one-way transformation of data.
Search engine	A computer program that utilises key word identification to find websites and establish **hypertext** links to them.
Server	A central computer which provides multiple users simultaneous access to data and services.
SMTP	Simple mail transfer protocol. The Internet protocol for transporting mail.
SPAM	An inappropriate attempt to use a mailing list, or USENET or other networked communications facility as if it was a broadcast medium (which it is not) by sending the same message to a large number of people who did not ask for it. The term comes from a Monty Python sketch which featured the word "spam" repeated over and over.
SET	The Secure Electronic Transactions (SET) protocol is being developed by a consortium including VISA, Mastercard, Microsoft, Netscape, IBM and others. It aims to establish a single technical standard for protecting credit card purchases made over the Internet.
SSL	Secure Sockets Layer: A protocol designed by Netscape Communications to enable encrypted, authenticated communications across the Internet. SSL is used mostly (but not exclusively) in communications between web browsers and web servers. **URL's** that begin with 'https' (rather than 'http') indicate that an SSL connection will be used.

Symmetric cryptography   An encryption/decryption system in which knowledge of the encryption key is equivalent to knowledge of the decryption key.

TCP/IP   Transmission control protocol/Internet protocol. The protocols that drive the Internet, regulating how information is transferred between computers.

Telnet   A remote Internet log in service. It allows users to access another Internet site as if they are directly connected.

Trojan Horse   A program used to capture unsuspecting people's log on and passwords.

TwoFish   The U.S. Government, has sought public submissions of an improved block cipher which would serve the specific purpose of protecting the unclassified communications of the U.S. Government. The block cipher that is accepted will be called the AES, for Advanced Encryption Standard and will replace **DES.** TwoFish developed by Bruce Schneier as a successor to his 64-bit **BlowFish** block cipher is the leading candidate for the AES.

URL   Uniform resource locator. The standard addressing system for the World Wide Web.

Usenet   User's network. A collection of networks and computer systems that exchange messages, organised by subject into over 27,000 discussion areas, called **newsgroups.** About half the Usenet machines are on the **Internet.**

Web   The World Wide Web or WWW the generic terms for a network of graphic/hypermedia documents on the Internet that are interconnected through hypertext links.

Website   A collection of Web pages about a particular subject or organisation.

Web server   A computer on the Internet that stores Web pages and sends them to Web **browsers.**

X.509   A standard which specifies the format of **Digital certificates,** to provide a way to securely tie a name to a **Public Key.**

— • 1 • —

ELECTRONIC COMMERCE UNLEASHED

> "By the end of this Parliament I want the U.K. to be globally recognised as the best environment in which to trade electronically"[1]

INTRODUCTION

Everybody agrees[2] that electronic commerce[3] is going to revolutionise spending habits and change the way business is conducted. The reasons are many and varied:

1.01

> globalisation and the dismantling of trade barriers;
> the deployment of smart cards;
> the Internet; and
> the *de facto* emergence of English as the global language.[4]

Yet the certainty is tinged with concern. Predicting how fundamental technological change will affect society is fruitless since nobody's imagination can cover all the interactivities that follow on from a radical cost shift. In the nineteenth century the development of the railways affected commerce by reducing ten fold the cost of shipping a ton of goods when compared to transportation by wagon or canal barge. The Victorian railways meant that local goods could be sold nationally instead of regionally and gave support to the creation of a national system of trade marks and trade reputation. But the railways also led to the creation of national daily newspapers, weekend holiday trips and improved the nation's health by making perishable goods such as fish and fruit more widely available. It is this latter type of changes which

---

[1] The Rt Hon. Peter Mandelson, Secretary of State for Trade and Industry (September 8, 1998). In the same speech Mr Mandelson also pledged to use the Government's market power to boost electronic commerce and promised early legislation on encryption and digital signatures.
[2] In the course of extensive research over eighteen months the authors have not found a single dissenting opinion.
[3] See the Glossary for definitions of all terms of art.
[4] This opinion is supported by the fact that many meetings on scientific subjects in European Commission funded projects now take place in English even if English is not the language of any of the participants.

dominate our modern perception of the power of railways rather than the economics of train travel. Yet it is the economics that rebuilt the nineteenth century world.

Electronic commerce repeats this process at the close of the twentieth century by effectively eliminating the cost of transportation of information. By doing so it speeds up a fundamental economic change which has been underway for some time — the globalisation of the world economy based on free trade without tariff barriers. We can measure and predict the direct economic impact of these changes without too much trouble. But we cannot predict the secondary effects which, in the long term, are likely to be far more significant.

1.02   It must also not be forgotten that electronic commerce is also a battle of technology standards. Like the VHS/Betamax confrontation in early video recorders which was finally won by VHS, the electronic commerce marketplace is littered with competing technologies all of which are striving to become accepted as the single global standard for electronic commerce. Many countries have their national champions and government support for particular electronic commerce technologies is often rooted in partisan national interests rather than technical superiority or genuine risk. The most well-known standards battle involves the Secure Electronic Transaction (SET), a technical standard for safeguarding payment card (debit and credit card) purchases made over open networks. The SET protocol was developed jointly by VISA and MasterCard and requires the use of public key certificates to authenticate the parties to each other at every step along the way. But SET may not be the eventual winner in electronic commerce. Some would say that it is an overcomplicated solution to a problem which is adequately addressed for consumer purposes by the Secure Hypertext Transfer Protocol (SHTTP) and Secure Socket Layer (SSL) technology. If electronic commerce takes off on non-SET systems then there will be no reason for companies to incur the additional overheads imposed by SET.[5] Unless governments decide to interfere.

1.03   Over the next few pages we outline some of the immediate potential problems which face governments all over the world. These problems are not barriers to the technology being deployed; rather they indicate that governments will act in concert to protect their revenue bases and may need to establish sensible security standards to protect national economies from being riddled with commercial racketeering and criminality. The transition between well understood conventional commercial systems and their jargon (Letters of Credit, Bills of Exchange, INCOM terms etc) to secure electronic commerce and its jargon (digital certificates, Trusted Third Parties, DES, TwoFish etc) will require the world economy to pass through a short period of vulnerability to fraud until the risks are well understood and controlled.

We make no apology for including this speculative analysis of the future regulation of electronic commerce environment in a textbook which is mainly intended for use by commercial lawyers. Moneylaundering legislation impinges upon everyone (including solicitors and accountants acting for clients) and it is essential that practitioners are aware of the dubious and doubtful uses of electronic commerce so that they can protect both their own and their clients' interests. Lawyers also need to know not only the

---

[5] A explanation of these emerging technologies is set out in Chapter 5: "Payment Mechanisms: Encryption and Digital Signatures".

current state of the law but also how it is likely to evolve. English lawyers are slowly coming to terms with the purposive approach to the interpretation of U.K. legislation to give effect to the U.K.'s obligations under European directives, even if this involves a departure from the strict and literal application of the words used in the U.K. legislation.[6] With highly technical subjects such as control over encryption and digital signatures, it is essential for the lawyer to understand the law of electronic commerce in context. Governments will undoubtedly implement new directives and regulations to regulate the use of electronic commerce in moneylaundering and to maintain national tax revenues.

GLOBALISATION AND THE DEMATERIALISATION OF TRADE

The way that pop stars and politicians are marketed and sold as commodities has undergone a revolution in the closing decades of this century. Complex commercial synergies arise in blockbuster films — product placements are reinforced by tie-in merchandise associated with music albums and videos. Media campaigns by politicians at election times enjoy similar choreography and media planning.

1.04

But what of the future? Today, every pop star and political campaign has a promotional website. Some of these already sell tie-in merchandise. How soon will it be before we have global political parties selling books, speeches, videos, CD–ROMs from websites to fund political campaigns and voter registration programmes in selected nations?[7]

These visible changes reflect the rise in importance of intellectual property rights, particularly trade marks. In a global market place, pop stars and political parties need to protect their "brands". In the post GATT-Trips world, every country has undertaken to strengthen and unify their protection of intellectual property rights. By the early years of the next century all nations should have fulfilled their treaty obligations with improved reciprocal enforcement of rights.

The trend towards better enforcement of intellectual property rights will have a positive effect on global trade in commodities containing intellectual property (videos, CD–ROMs, microprocessors, books etc.)[8] But problems are already arising in dematerialised commodities, such as software, which are sold over the Internet. Should sales tax or VAT be paid on these sales or should everything sold in cyberspace be tax free? Is it unfair to European Internet Service Providers for non-European Internet Service Providers to offer Web space to European customers and not levy VAT on their invoices?[9]

1.05

---

[6] The House of Lords recognised this approach to construction in *Pickstone v. Freemans* [1989] 1 A.C. 66 and *Lister v. Forth Dry Dock and Engineering Co. Ltd (In Receivership)* [1990] 1 A.C. 546.

[7] We are already getting cross-over between political speeches and commercial advertising. The South African restaurant chain "Nando's" has had a very successful radio campaign in Australia based around the right-wing politician Ms Pauline Hanson whose extreme racial views have made her subject to death threats. The campaign featured a soon-to-be grilled chicken parodying a recording made by Ms Hanson to be played in the event of her assassination.

[8] But *pace* the problems with trade marks, copyright and exhaustion of rights — See Judgment C–355/96 *Silhouette International Schmied GmbH & Co. KG v. Hartlauer Handelsgesellschaft mbH* July 16, 1998) **http://europa.eu.int/cj/en/cp/cp9849en.htm.**

[9] This matter is now partly addressed by revised VAT legislation in the U.K. which took effect from July 1, 1997 relating to telecommunications services. These measures are only temporary and will be replaced by definitive changes to the Sixth Directive (77/388/EEC) before the end of 1999. For further information see Chapter 9.

At the moment, these concerns are not of major importance to governments. But as world trade moves into cyberspace and there is a general loss of government revenue, the entire basis of commercial taxation may have to be reviewed with new directives and legislation.

WHERE THE SMART MONEY IS HEADING

1.06   The concept of a credit-card sized piece of plastic which will contain digital cash is already familiar; several systems are just about to be launched onto the European, American and Asian markets having had extensive trials in towns and communities. At the moment, these remain interesting local experiments. Once a significant amount of commercial activity is conducted using digital cash, a number of economic effects are likely to be felt, all of which will have to be addressed by legislation or bank regulation. Digital cash will ultimately replace a significant part of the legal tender issued by the central banks, which will have implications for their own revenues and activities. It must not be forgotten that central banks actually sell their cash to the banks.

In economic terms the "float" is the amount of cash in circulation. Traditional cash is a major source of float for central banks, as it is a non-interest bearing liability. When real cash is withdrawn from a bank, that money is no longer owned by the bank: it becomes a debt of the central bank to the bearer of the cash. But when money in bank current accounts is withdrawn from a bank by converting it into digital cash on a smart card, it is not really leaving the bank, and the bank can keep on playing freely with that money. The main economic effect of digital money will be to transfer the "float" from the central banks to the commercial banks who issue digital cash.[10]

In 1995 the U.K. float, was approximately £22.3 billion. If half the cash in circulation in the U.K. were to become digital cash, the Government's interest earning float would be reduced to around £11 billion, leading to a very significant loss of interest and an increase in the Government's borrowing requirements to maintain public services.

1.07   In anticipation of the deployment of digital cash by the banks, both the Bank of England and the Bank of Canada have had serious discussions with the banks who want to enter the digital cash arena in order to reach an agreement on a fair apportionment of this float. No agreement has as yet been reached.

There is also the "escheatment" issue. Currently, banks have to return to the central banks any monetary value that has been unclaimed for a long period of time (unused bank accounts, traveller's cheques, etc). All the major organisations who are proposing to issue digital cash have announced that their digital cash is exactly like cash: they will not refund the value left on lost cards. Moreover, there are already talks that some banks will offer an insurance for lost cards, an additional source of revenue.

Currently, when traditional cash is lost, it is to the benefit of the central banks since cash is a liability for them. Overall, we can say that it is to the benefit of the whole

---

[10] This issue does not just concern digital cash — it can also relate to propriatory tokens. In the early 1990s the Japanese Government forced NTT (Nippon Telephone and Telegraph) to deposit at the Japanese central bank half of the $700 million float that was "locked" on their phone cards.

society. When digital cash is lost, this is no longer the case because this float is not owned by the central banks, but by the commercial banks

It thus seems that commercial banks will, at least initially, benefit from escheatment. If governments decided to address this through the use of specific legislation to force them to give these sums back to the state, there could be serious problems with some systems. The Mondex system, for example, is designed in a manner to ensure that the digital cash is not traceable. Consequently the issuing bank would not have any information regarding how much Mondex value had been lost on a missing card.

CYBERLAUNDERING AND NET-SMURFING[11]

> Doug Drug Dealer is the CEO of an ongoing narcotics corporation who wishes to convert hard currency, the profits of his enterprise, into legitimate money. Doug employs Linda Launderer to hire couriers to deposit funds under different names in amounts between $7,500 and $8,500 at branches of every bank in certain cities (below the $10,000 cash transaction reporting limit). This is repeated twice a week for as long as required. Linda has in the meantime been withdrawing these same funds and depositing the money with Internet banks that accept e-cash. To be safe, she limits these transfers to $8,200. Now that the currency has been converted into digital e-cash, the illegally earned money has become virtually untraceable and Doug Drug Dealer has access to legitimate electronic cash.[12]

1.08

In moneylaundering jargon the couriers who deposit small amounts of illegal money are called "smurfs". Those engaged in this kind of activity in cyberspace are called "net-smurfs" or "cybersmurfs". The problem which regulatory authorities face in combating cyberlaundering is multifaceted:

- Present-day legislation to combat money laundering is based on what is termed "suspicious transaction reporting". A banker is under a duty to report a suspect transaction if he suspects that it is laundering illegally obtained money. This suspicion-based system breaks down when there is no banker involved in the transaction who is capable of becoming suspicious. Most cross-border transactions are conducted electronically, without anyone physically seeing them.[13]

- Many digital money cards issued by banks come in two forms: attributable; and non-attributable. Attributable cards are used to debit sums against a specified account. These are loaded onto a rechargeable card. Non-attributable cards cannot debit or credit bank accounts, but can accept transfers from other cards. Transfers

---

[11] The issue of moneylaundering and the technical discussion of its prevention is outside of the scope of this book. The authors would direct readers to the literature on this topic and would recommend as a starting point: U.S. Congress, Office of Technology Assessment, Information Technologies for Control of Money Laundering, OTA-ITC-630 (Washington, D.C.: U.S. Government Printing Office, September 1995).

[12] Mark Bortner "Cyberlaundering: Anonymous Digital Cash and Money Laundering".

[13] See further Bercu, "Towards Universal Surveillance in an Information Age Economy" (1994) 34 Jurimetrics J. 383; Gold M. and Levi M., Money Laundering in the U.K.: An Appraisal of Suspicion-Based Reporting London: Police Foundation, 1994.

are made by computer (with Internet access) and telephone, as well as by putting cards into a special wallet which moves sums from one card to the other. Where transactions involve a non-attributable card, the "record" shows "private". Peer to peer transfers are possible without requiring the parties to contact a third party. Hence, just like an actual cash transfer, the transaction is entirely anonymous. No data is held by banks on transfers.

● Money can be held on cards or PCs and transferred as long as both parties have non-attributable cards. One central concern is that cards with very high capacities could be used to move large sums across borders to a parallel banking system in such a way as to by-pass international wire transfer reporting requirements. Disintermediation, where money flows through non-traditional banking channels, is a growing problem for governments wishing to have control over their national economies. Electronic commerce is likely to increase the extent of the problem[14]

1.09   Not surprisingly, the problems with suspect transaction reporting are being technologically addressed through pattern matching other computer-based detection regimes. Developing effective technologies for reporting, or searching for relevant intelligence concerning electronic commerce transactions, however, is likely to impose significant capital and recurrent costs on those who have to install and operate the necessary systems. U.K. financial institutions, like their U.S. counterparts, have generally accepted money laundering reporting requirements as one of their general expenses of doing business. But in a world of falling margins and greater competition for financial services, it is going to be considerably harder to persuade bankers that they should bear the cost of what is, in effect, the investigation arm of a government anti-moneylaundering enforcement agency. There may be a good case for tax credits or bounty sharing with bankers to offset the expenses incurred in policing the digital money marketplace.

It is easy to see envisage how electronic commerce could be used to disguise activities:

> Charlie Crack is a member of a drug gang which markets crack cocaine to schoolchildren. His boss wants the money Charlie's gang gets for its sales to appear to be the profits from a legitimate business rather than drug dealing. The boss sets up a soft porn website selling ``tasteful'' shots of naked teen idols. Charlie is instructed not to accept money but to give bags of crack cocaine to children who show, using the records from their digital purses, that they have paid to download a proprietary image from the boss' website within the past 12 hours. The boss gets untraceable digital cash from a business which appears to be making clean money.

In the embryonic electronic market place there are currently no special controls regulating such cyberlaundering.

---

[14] For further discussion on this point see Paragraph 4.2.3 of "Security of Electronic Money" Report by the Committee on Payment and Settlement Systems and the Group of Computer Experts of the central banks of the Group of Ten countries Basle August 1996. This Report is a very useful primer on the underlying technical security issues affecting the use of Smart Cards.

HOW MUCH IS HYPE?

> If Europeans are looking to their governments and the European Union to make
> e-commerce as cosy as doing business in their own back yards, they will wait in vain.
> If they look to governments to create regulations that might hold back the competi-
> tive challenges that e-commerce could create, they might just as well seek highway
> speed limits to suit the horse and buggy.[15]

1.10

There is a general consensus that continental Europe is in the slow lane regarding growth in electronic commerce. This is mainly due to its telecommunications costs which are approximately five times higher than in the United States[16] and is compounded by fewer wired customers, higher hardware and software costs plus concerns about security, taxes and language problems.[17]

Business-to-business electronic commerce in Europe is expected to reach $11.8 billion by 2001[18] with big companies encouraging their business partners to follow them online, thereby increasing the demand for additional connections and bandwidth. European consumer Internet access spending will move at a much slower pace, climbing to an expected $4.6 billion in 2001. This should be contrasted with the global position: worldwide electronic commerce is currently estimated at about $10 billion and is expected to soar to $500 billion by 2002.[19]

In September 1998 Andersen Consulting analysed this difference and pointed to huge differences between U.S. and European attitudes towards electronic commerce.[20] The consultants reported that although 82 per cent of the 300 European executives interviewed recognise the strategic importance of electronic commerce, only 39 per cent are doing anything about it. Furthermore, only 19 per cent of European executives regard electronic commerce as a serious competitive threat to their business today.

1.11

This attitude should be contrasted with the United States where the electronic commerce marketplace — defined as the sale of goods via the Internet, proprietary online services and CD–ROM — was projected to have grown by 57.7 per cent to an estimated $28.2 billion during 1998.[21] Of this, $19 billion comprised business-to-business commerce.

Mass market electronic commerce relies upon a very large number of people having easy and daily access to the World Wide Web. However, claims of the current number of people who actually surf the Internet look suspicious. Surveys reporting that the number of Internet users in mid 1998 is somewhere between 50 million and 70 million people in the U.S. alone look over optimistic. One survey in June 1998[22] that had the number of people with the ability to access the Internet in the U.S. at more than 100 million looks just plain wrong.

---

[15] Louise Kehoe in the *Financial Times*, September 9, 1998.
[16] Source: Forrester Forum Europe, July 1998.
[17] Source: Interactive Media in Retail Group, July 1998.
[18] Source: Forrester Research Inc. " European New Media Strategies service", July 1998.
[19] Source: Andersen Consulting, **http://www.ac.com**.
[20] *ibid*.
[21] Source: "The Electronic Marketplace 2002: Strategies for Connecting Buyers and Sellers." Simba Information Inc., August 1998.
[22] Reported in *Newsbytes*, June 29, 1998.

Estimated Growth in U.S. Internet Uses[23]

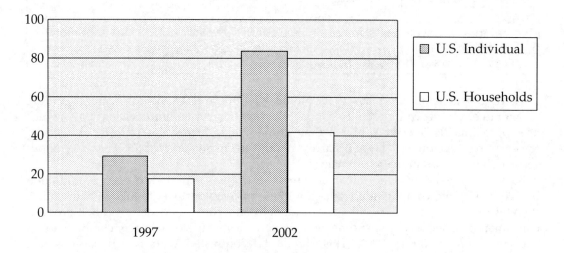

1.12   The authors tend to agree with a report from eMarketer[24] in July 1998 which estimated that the U.S. figure was about 37 million users in June 1998 about 18.5 per cent of the adult population. Some 52,000 new users go online in the U.S. every day. By the end of 1998, eMarketer estimates that the number of active users in the U.S. will reach 47 million or 23.5 per cent of the adult population.

On this same conservative basis and using year-end figures, individual Internet users in the U.S. are expected to increase 300 per cent from 28 million in 1997 to 85 million by 2002. In addition, U.S. Net households will number 44 million by 2002, up from the 18 million estimated to be online as of mid-year 1998.

The demographic profile of the typical net user is increasingly similar to that of the U.S. population — affluent and mature. The median age is now 38 years old, 59 per cent of the users are male, the median household income is $58,000 per year, 58 per cent of them are college graduates, 40 per cent of them are in professional managerial fields and 45 per cent of them are married.[25]

Two thirds of the current World Wide Web population reside in the United States and Canada, the latter having some four million users. There are now about 60 million Web users worldwide and about 90 per cent of them are English speaking. But the fastest growth in World Wide Web usage is now outside of the United States and eMarketer estimates that non.U.S. users will be outnumbering U.S. users by the end of the year 2000 with the main growth taking place in Europe, the Asia/Pacific Rim, South America and several underdeveloped world regions. The 1998 monetary crisis in the Asian Pacific region was not considered to affect the growth of Internet use in this key region.

---

[23] Source: eMarketer, July 1998.
[24] Internet: **http://www.emarketer.com**.
[25] Source: eMarketer, July 1998.

Estimated Growth in World Internet Users[26]

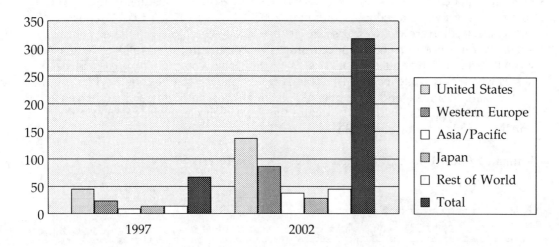

Will this growth in the use of the World Wide Web actually lead to growth in **1.13** electronic commerce? For various reasons we believe that it will. In particular, the purchase of branded goods of known characteristics is now cheaper and easier over the Web compared with its conventional retail purchasing.

Estimated Growth in U.S. Consumer Sales over the Internet[27]

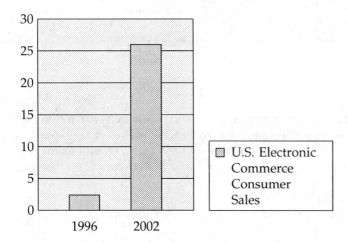

One 1998 report said that consumer-based e-commerce revenues totalled $1.8 billion in **1.14** 1996 but that this was likely to reach the $26 billion mark in 2002 because of improved

---

[26] Source: IDG.
[27] Source: eMarketer, July 1998.

technology, security, user-friendly websites and increased world-wide penetration of PCs and modems.[28] Another 1998 report concludes that consumer-based electronic commerce sales will exceed $42.2 billion in 2002.[29]

The spectacular growth will arise in business sales where the purchaser specifies the goods by reference to technical specifications or commodity descriptions. Near instant, virtually free information transmission is putting new competitive pressures on businesses which only trade locally. They can face devastating competition as rival suppliers from distant locations tender for business. If freight costs are only a small percentage of the cost of the goods (which is normally the case) then electronic commerce gives the purchaser a plethora of potential suppliers.

Estimated Growth in U.S. Business Sales over the Internet[30]

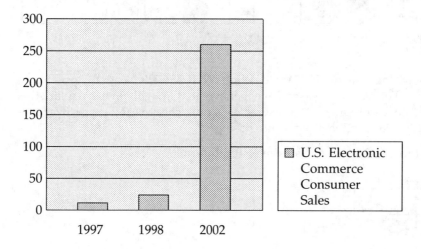

1.15   One study[31] concluded that business to business electronic commerce will account for the majority of Web-based revenues by 2002 and be worth $268 billion. By comparison, business-to-business e-commerce totalled $5.6 billion in 1997 and $16 billion in 1998. These growth figures are at the low end of expectations, and many reports are pointing to far greater levels of growth.[32]

Europe does appear to have grounds to worry. While there is legitimate concern regarding the need to establish a global scheme to deal with liability and regulatory

---

[28] *ibid.*
[29] Source: "The Electronic Marketplace 2002: Strategies for Connecting Buyers and Sellers." Simba Information Inc., August 1998.
[30] Source: eMarketer, July 1998.
[31] *ibid.*
[32] *e.g.* "The Electronic Marketplace 2002: Strategies for Connecting Buyers and Sellers." Simba Information Inc., August 1998.

issues involving digital signatures, cryptography and digital cash, there can be no doubt that world business is moving into cyberspace at an amazing pace regardless of the lack of legal certainty. Continental Europe has very little time to influence the regulation of electronic commerce and remains preoccupied with the Euro. The U.K., which (unlike Germany and Italy) has loyally waited on European Union developments in this sphere,[33] may now need to take unilateral action to protect its national interests and create a framework where U.K. business can safely participate in the American dominated arena.

SAM'S STORY

To close this introductory chapter we introduce Samantha Wesley, an assistant solicitor in a City firm in the Year 2004. Sam is an ordinary person, not especially computer literate but able to use computers in her ordinary daily life.   **1.16**

As usual Sam Wesley was already awake and washed as her radio alarm went off. It was raining and the radio confirmed that yesterday's rain sealed June 2004 as being the wettest English June on record. "Some things never change", muttered Sam as she bumped around the bedroom in the darkness trying not to disturb Tom. There was little chance of that — she could sleep through a thunderstorm. But the creaking floorboards moved the computer mouse on the work table which mistook them for start up requests and lit the screen up with the list of the day's reminders. Some were work related but most were pleasure. An urgent note flashed "Walking on Water", a reference to the new political musical which was opening at the Prince Alfred Theatre. Sam liked musicals but wanted to see the reviews of this one before committing herself. The temptation was too great. She sat down and clicked on the Electronic Telegraph icon, following the links to the review page.

"Is he waiving or drowning?" — John Diamond reviews "Walking on Water". [Short review follows]

Sam read the piece to the end and decided to book tickets. She clicked on the booking   **1.17**
link, the screen dissolved and she was at the Prince Alfred Bookings site. Two tickets at 90 Euros in the Front Stalls were available but the order form stated that the view was obstructed. Sam clicked on the "show me" icon and saw a picture of the stage as it would appear from her seat. It was clear that a huge pillar would block the view which in any event was strongly angled. "Not right for such a spectacular". But there were Dress Circle seats available at 105 Euros each and their views were unobstructed. She clicked to make a booking. The computer interrupted "Real or Pseudo Identity?" Was Sam prepared to give the theatre her real name? "Real" clicked Sam — she did not normally mind being known as a theatregoer and getting special offers from the Theatre Bookings website. But sometimes, when on a view for a client, Sam used a Pseudo

---

[33] To useful effect — See Chapter 5: "Payment Systems" where we show why the German digital signature legislation and its regulatory regime may be an unsuitable model for Electronic Commerce.

Identity. She had done so last week when checking out "Maestro" the play about the new Lord Mayor of London which was alleged to libel one of the firm's clients in a scene in a railway station.

The computer interrupted again "Collect Tickets or e-Tickets?" With a real identity, the theatregoer could collect the ticket from the theatre by showing his credit card or could ask for e-tickets which were fully transferable electronic vouchers which were downloaded onto a smart card like digital money and could be transferred from card to card. Only at the theatre when the anonymous smart card was waived before the sensor would the paper tickets be printed and the electronic vouchers voided on the card. The ticket agencies loved them and e-tickets to rock concerts were always high sellers on the Web auction sites. "e-tickets" clicked Sam. A moment later the workstation told her that there were two paid tickets for "Walking on Water" on the hard drive ready for transfer to her Smart Card.

1.18   Sam was turning to leave the workstation when a flashing icon caught her eye. It was the stock monitor flashing yellow with no sound, not critical but requiring attention. Sam clicked on the icon to open up her ESI stockwatch. Overnight in Tokyo, Kuji Chemical had announced research collaboration with Lanchester Molecular. Sam had a few shares in Lanchester Molecular in her portfolio and the computer was telling her that the company had been mentioned in news story within the last 12 hours. "I'll hold" she muttered to himself. But this caused her to look at her portfolio. Like most independent professionals Sam liked managing her own affairs. For three years she had been a Sponsored Member of CREST the U.K.'s registration and settlement system, developed by the Bank of England. This allowed her to benefit from all the advantages of electronic settlement of U.K. stocks and shares whilst continuing to keep her name on the company's registry thereby enabling her to receive all the shareholder rights direct from the company. But in recent months Sam had become interested in the revitalised Asian stock markets and had become a private customer of E*TRADE U.K. which allowed her to trade on the Singapore stock market. She reviewed the overnight trading — the U.S. trade figures had had little effect on trading in that part of the world although NASDAQ stocks were down. Looking at the figures changing from one market to the next Sam could almost see the tides of money ebbing and flowing around the world as night followed day.

There was no good reason to sell or buy and Sam, a student of Warren Buffett, always played the long game with her stock portfolio. It was time to get down to work.

And work meant problems. This morning was the second meeting with the receivers of Melvilles — it was hard to believe that the company had gone under despite the popularity of its goods. The Financial Times had called it "The First Roadkill on the Information Superhighway" and the litigation was predicted to go on for years.

Melvilles were an American department store with a good mail order division. They had gone onto the Web in a big way in the late 1990s mainly selling smart casual clothing under the slogan "The Passport to Pleasure". It had all gone wrong in a spectacular manner.

1.19   Melvilles mail order telephone sales operations had been in the Deep South of America taking advantage of low wages and cheap 1-800 services. It had seemed logical to build their Web sales operations on the same system. This was their first mistake. The local computer staff did not know of a world outside of Georgia. This mirrored the company: Harvey Melville Senior who had founded Melvilles in the 1940s never had gone outside of America and like most Americans did not have a passport. Melvilles assumed that doing business over the Web was going to be just like their telephone order business in the USA. It was not.

Melvilles problems had started in the Christmas of 1999 when it received a flood of orders from Germany all paid for by credit cards over the Web. It debited the cards and shipped the goods. A large proportion of the goods were rejected because the customer claimed either that he had not ordered the goods or that no agreement to purchase had been made under German law — because of a lack of paper signatures. The German credit card companies refunded all their customers and redebited Melvilles.

Why had the Germans rejected the goods? The answer lay in a message in a Usenet Group. Melvilles had been the target of a "hate campaign" aimed at the owner Senator Harvey Melville Junior. Senator Melville had been behind a strident campaign in the U.S. Congress which attacked unilateral German restrictions on the import of genetically modified soya beans from the United States. Bavarian farmers, steeped in thousand year old pure barley and water legislation on the quality of beer, believed that American was poisoning Europe for profit. The Usenet message, posted anonymously using a remailer, had outlined a no risk plan to hit Melvilles using pages of genuine credit card numbers and addresses. The highly computer literate German enviromentalists and patriots reacted almost instantly by placing thousands of orders for American shirts, pants and linen. Each order was carefully designed to be over $250 and therefore subject to the credit card companies' guarantees against misuse.

The timing was perfect. Melvilles serviced thousands of orders, 97 per cent of which were rejected. As the reports started coming back in the Year 2000 bug bit and there was massive data loss of internet records. Then the German Postal Authorities demanded extra storage payments from Melvilles, which was unable to meet them. It dumped the parcels on international charities and, as a result, Latvia ended up with the best dressed refugees in the world. Newsweek called the saga "The Revenge of the Soya" and many hackers claimed to have been the authors of the original anonymous Usenet message.

1.20

Melvilles struggled on for a few months more — a patriotic call to U.S. consumers to buy their goods fell on deaf ears — and then sought Chapter 11 protection. They had tried to sue the local law firm who had advised them on their contracts but the action collapsed when it turned out that they had never commissioned any new legal work when they created their website out of their mail order operation. The Web designers who created their site were "code fodder", kids newly out of college who worked on short contracts for peanuts. Melvilles' bankers, all local firms, were protected from the debacle by their agreements — it turned out that Melvilles had never sought explicit permission to take payments from credit cards over the Internet although the local bank managers knew that this was happening.

A final complication arose when Melvilles sent threatening letters to the thousands of credit card customers who had rejected the parcels. Several complaints were laid before the Berlin Data Protection Commissioner who had then instigated an enquiry into the security and auditability of Melvilles' data protection compliance.

But before she could turn to the Melville papers Sam spotted a new item in her business folder from "Starline DNA Testing". Curious, she clicked on the message icon:

''Do you really know who your relatives are? Are you really related to someone wealthy who died without knowing of your existence. Every year the IRS benefits from thousands of wealthy people dying without any known next of kin. Instead of the IRS getting rich you might be getting rich.

All it takes is a cotton bud wiped around your mouth and five dollars. Send us the cotton bud, a photograph, your personal details and the money and we will register your DNA on our database. Starline take similar swabs from all dead or dying citizens in all of the United States — our representatives are in every funeral parlour. Once we find a match we will notify you of your lost relative. For 45 per cent of your inheritance Starline provide you with the proof you require to enable you to regain what is yours.''

1.21   ''Junk mail'' thought Sam, ''nothing can get rid of it — only the messages get weirder.'' But as she deleted it she pondered was Starline really a front for an illegal human DNA classification project? ''Anything is still possible in America''.

The doorbell chimed and Sam went down to collect the mail. There was a recorded delivery item — a new smart card. This one was the ''CentralServices'' smart card — able to hold biometric data. ''Hold the package up with the bar code facing the camera'', said the Delivery man, taking his time stamped delivery photo. Sam posed, the camera flashed and she signed the touchpad with the stylus. ''You will be e-mailed the receipt within ten minutes. Reply to the message and sign it with your digital signature''.

Back inside, after drinking a cup of coffee, Sam unwrapped the package. The CentralServices smart card was a multifunction product. It was a credit card, a bank debit card, an electronic purse and a National Identity Card and Driving Licence.[34] It was also useless.

Or at least it was until it was authenticated. Sam read the instructions. 'Plug your card into the PC Card slot in your computer. Older machines may refer to this as the PCMCIA slot. Follow the instructions on screen as we connect you to the Internet for authentication''.

1.22   The card inserted Sam waited. The CentralServices logo appeared on the screen, a rotating image of the Euro coin which each time it spun displayed a different national version of its face. ''Trying to connect you'' said the prompt at the bottom of the screen.

In less than a minute the card got the computer to connect it to the issuer's switching centre. A picture stated to appear on screen — it was Sam at her front door holding up the package containing the card. ''If you can confirm that this is you please reply to this message using your digital signature. Sam digitally signed the photograph and returned it. Up came the message 'VoicePrint — Read the following sentence in your normal speaking voice' ''

Sam read ''It was the best of times, It was the worst of times''[35] The computer prompted 'Please confirm that you are not suffering from any temporary medical condition which is altering your voice''. Sam confirmed that she was not. Another

---

[34] Under an E.U. directive agreed to by the British Government some years ago all U.K. Driving Licenses from the year 2000 onwards will have to contain a photograph of the driver and will therefore act as *de facto* identity cards. We are anticipating that by 2004 there will be legislation allowing for a U.K. Driving Licence to be included within an approved Smart Card which will also serve the purpose of being an identity card for the citizen.

[35] Source: Charles Dickens — opening words of *A Tale of Two Cities*.

couple of phrases appeared to be read "Click your heels together three times",[36] "The secret of success is honesty and fair dealing. If you can fake those, you've got it made".[37]

The voiceprint verification ended with a tiny beep: "Your card with be validated for use in 10 seconds. If it is lost or stolen telephone the call centre immediately you discover the loss. Thank you for using CentralServices". Moments later the computer beeped again. Sam removed her activated smart card then changed her mind and plugged it back in. A few keystrokes later she had transferred her e-tickets to "Walking on Water" onto the new card ready for the show.

Having put the smart card into her purse Sam turned back to the computer to check her e-mail. There was an urgent message from her Cluster Manager, Fabrio Lopez. She clicked on the icon:

1.23

> "Sam, I need you to take over the Alsace copyright dispute today instead of continuing with the Melville matter. Jimmy tells me that you have got him up to speed on it and thinks he can cope. Alsace is a different matter. Discovery was a disaster — the client "forgot" about the automatic electronic journal on his network which the other side demanded. The Chancery Master has ordered it to be handed over by 4.30 p.m. tomorrow. Tonight I reviewed it and it appear to contradict almost everything we have been told in the witness statements. Thank God we didn't serve them early as I had been minded to do just before the Without Prejudice meeting!
>
> I need you, as a matter of urgency, to make an annotated version of the Witness Statements cross referenced to the Electronic Journal with queries on every entry where the one does not corroborate the other. Remember that Exchange of Witness Statements is due in eight days and we go for trial in the middle of next month.
>
> Here are the files. They are too big for you to work on at home. Toni has pencilled in a video conference with the client to discuss the statements on Friday starting at 6 a.m. (sorry about the hour but the client is in Islamabad).
>
> Regards, Fabrio"

Sam glanced at the size of the attachments. They were massive: far too big to print out. Yet that was not the problem. Electronic discovery meant that she should do the comparison work on screen. To do so lawfully she needed at least a twenty one inch monitor[38] rather than the fifteen inch one she had at home; electronic discovery always required a lot of screen comparisons and could easily lead to excessive eye strain. A 2002 Health and Safety Executive case[39] had ruled that an employer whose employees teleworked had to supply its staff with a safe system of working and this meant that the employee's home workstation had to comply with the minimum E.U. requirements. Failure to require an employee to use a large high definition monitor for electronic discovery applications was a clear breach of the employer's duty under Health and Safety requirements.

1.24

This was why Fabrio had said that they were too big for Sam to work on at home. The computer systems with twenty one inch screens were all at Cluster Support H.Q. in town.

---

[36] " . . . and you will be back in Kansas" (Source: Frank Baum *The Wizard of Oz*).
[37] Source: Groucho Marx.
[38] We are assuming that flat screen monitors remain very expensive in 2004.
[39] Please note — there is no such case, this is fiction written in late 1998.

Sam started putting on her business clothes ready for the commute. As she sprayed on her perfume she noticed that she was running low in "Reality".

"Reality" by Jean Paul Gaites was the "passionate expression of the next generation". It was the first totally synthetic perfume made not from traditional flower and animal extracts but in a biotechnology plant at a secret location.[40] The perfume was not available in supermarkets or chain stores but was only stocked in Europe in Business Class boutiques at selected airports and in one store on Faubourg St Honoré in Paris.

1.25   But Europe was not the world as the manufacturer has discovered. "Reality" could be bought for one tenth its normal European retail price on the Internet. There was nothing that Jean Paul Gaites could do to stop it save for restricting his sales only to Europe. He had sold a very large shipment of "Reality" to a distributor in India in the belief that India was like the European Union and allowed manufacturers to use European trade mark owners to stop the importation of identical goods sold outside of the European Union.[41] Indian law however was different and had a policy of 'exhaustion of rights" whereby a local trade mark owners rights were said to be "exhausted" if they were used against goods or services which had been lawfully put on the market by the manufacturer anywhere else in the world. The Indian dealer sold the shipment to SuperNorvge the Norwegian supermarket chain who promptly put it on sale on their website as well as in their stores. Like India, Norway also had international exhaustion of rights as part of its law. By being outside of "Fortress Europe" it was able to cut the best trade deals for its population. As it was also a member of European Free Trade Association (EFTA) there was no lawful way that that the European Union could stop or hinder exports from Norway. If a person bought goods from a Norwegian website it was like them travelling to Norway and buying the goods there.

Sam connected to the SuperNorvge site — an easy task since she had "bookmarked" the page in her browser. "Smart Shopping?" it asked. Sam clicked "Yes" and inserted her new CentralServices card. The list of SuperNorvge goods at discount prices screened endlessly across her display — designer jeans, trainers, exclusive makes of accessories and stockings. "May we update your personal record?" Sam had no worries regarding giving SuperNorvge access to the size-related personal information on her smart card — her body size and personal characteristics — since Norway had one of the toughest data protection regimes in the world. Today it was just "Reality" that concerned her and she ignored the prompt and clicked on "perfume". The site checked her smart card and prompted "Reality". She pulled the perfume bottle icon into the virtual shopping basket and clicked OK. "Your purchase, including express courier shipping, will cost you 97 Euros (including delivery, U.K. import duty and U.K. VAT). Delivery within four hours — Confirm?"

It was an easy decision to make.

---

[40] The advertising suggested that "Reality" was created by the Gods out of pure atoms of spring water and electricity. It was in fact made in part of a disused chemical plant on Merseyside.
[41] See Judgment C-355/96 *Silhouette International Schmied GmbH & Co. KG v. Hartlauer Handelsgesellschaft mbH* (July 16, 1998) **http://europa.eu.int/cj/en/cp/cp9849en.htm.**

— • 2 • —

THE ESTABLISHMENT OF A BUSINESS: WORKING ELECTRONIC COMMERCE

"On the Internet, it takes heart, smarts and luck to make a buck"[1]

INTRODUCTION

There are a number of requirements which need to be considered when establishing an electronic commerce business. One novel requirement concerns domain names which are a new species of intellectual property with their own complex regulatory framework. Another emerging area of legislation is spamming.[2] But there are other more conventional topics: the European Distance Selling Directive regulates the content of websites and gives consumers buying goods and services various rights. There are also many goods and services whose sales are specifically regulated. Some cannot be sold at all, others can only be sold on specific terms. We explore the need for websites to have disclaimers brought to visitors' attention. Web auctions are a particularly interesting phenomenon which have the potential for creating a global free market in standard products and services. But there currently are a number of problems which have to be resolved before they can grow out of their niche markets. Finally, as the importance of electronic commerce grows, so do the competition law issues which arise. All of these topics we address below.

2.01

DOMAIN NAMES

A domain name is a human comprehensible alternative to the string of numbers, *e.g.* 234.532.80.69 called an I.P. address (Internet protocol) address, which webservers use to identify each other on the Internet. The creation of memorable domain names as an alternative to numerical I.P. addresses has spawned a new industry and a trade in valuable domain names.

2.02

---

[1] Rick Lockridge of CNN "Even experts still puzzling out how-to's of Net business" (March 27, 1998).
[2] Technical terms such as this are defined in the Glossary.

When a company decides it wants to establish a website, the first issue it needs to address is the choice of its domain name. Ideally the company would like to have many highly memorable domain names which would all "map" onto the same string of numbers. But domain names are a scarce resource and disputes arise when more than one company tries to get the same name. Each domain name must be unique. This obviously causes an immediate conflict with the trade mark system.[3]

Registration is meant to be a simple procedure of applying to the appropriate national registry with a registration fee. In practice, for commercial companies, it is sensible to use a domain registration agent who will have established facilities to register domains in national registries all over the world. Domain registration agents all have websites where a potential customer can instantly check, free of charge, to see if a particular domain name is available. The best domain registration agents give detailed advice regarding national registration requirements and administrative problems. For example the French national registry will not allow anyone to have a ".fr" registration unless the applicant has offices in France and is registered for VAT in France.

In the U.K. the body in charge of domain names is Nominet; in the U.S. it is InterNIC under a contract from the National Standards Institute (NSI). Each national registry has different policies of domain name allocation, and most have adopted a dispute policy and rules specifying what can and cannot be registered.

Types of Domain Names

2.03   There are two main kinds of domains — generic domains and country domains. Generic domains are the most prized and are meant to indicate a global presence. The U.S. National Standards Institute (NSI) regulates their use under a fairly relaxed regime which is slightly biased towards U.S. interests. Although, in theory, all U.S. bodies should use their country domain rather than a global domain the NSI established a system whereby U.S. organisations treated the generic domains as though they were really the U.S. country domain. Thus American colleges[4] use the global stem ".edu"; the U.S. navy[5] uses the global stem ".mil" without any country indication and the U.S. Democratic Party[6] uses the stem ".org" again without any country indication. But the relaxed NSI registration rules have meant that the ".com" domain is open to anyone. Any company with global ambitions can apply for a generic registration — there are many U.K. and European companies whose domain names have the stem ".com".[7] For example, the web address of Field Fisher Waterhouse, the law firm of one of the authors, is: **www.ffwlaw.com**.

---

[3] Simply put the same trade mark can be used for a number of different types of goods. A U.K. trade mark (*e.g.* "Polo") can be registered to different companies for confectionery, clothing and motor cars. But only one company could have the domain **http://www.polo.co.uk/**.

[4] *e.g.* Harvard University is **http://www.harvard.edu/** (and not http://www.harvard.ac.us/).

[5] **http://www.navy.mil/**.

[6] **http://www.democrats.org/**.

[7] *e.g.* the BBC, which one might think of as being totally British, (with key domains of **http://www.bbc.co.uk/** **http://news.bbc.co.uk/** and **http://www.bbcresources.co.uk/**) today indicates its global ambitions with **http://www.beeb.com/** and **http://www.bbcworldwide.com/**.

Country domains are based upon the international two letter code (the ISO-3166 list). Within each country domain are sub-domains for different types of activity. For example "http://www.bookpages.co.uk" is an Internet bookstore in England. The ".co" is a sub-domain indicator showing that it is a commercial site within a country domain. The "uk" stem indicates that the domain is located in the U.K. and is regulated by the U.K. national body, Nominet.

The shortage of global domain names has led to a number of proposed new domains (.shop .web .arts .info .rec .firm .nom) to allow businesses and individuals to have unique but meaningful Web addresses. Originally these new domain names were scheduled to become active in February 1998, but the plans were upset by the release on January 30, 1998 of the U.S. Government's "Green Paper" — a proposal describing its views on how the Internet's Domain Name System should be run. In February 1998 the European Union and many other international groups publicised their response which castigated the U.S. Government for assuming authority over the Internet and disregarding many of the ideas set forth in a Memorandum of Understanding about the introduction of the new names. As a result in June 1998 the U.S. Government issued a "White Paper" suggesting that the entire process be re-examined by a group of 15 representative organisations. At the time of press, there is considerable debate over who will form this group and what action it will take.[8]

2.04

Trade Marks and Passing Off

A trade mark is any sign capable of distinguishing goods or services of one origin from those of others. A trade mark can be protected by registration. In the U.K. there are two routes to protection. A national registration can be obtained through the U.K. Patent Office under the Trade Marks Act 1994 or a mark can be registered as a Community trade mark under European Community Law.[9] If someone has registered a domain name incorporating a trade mark then the domain name holder could be in breach of the Trade Marks Act 1994. Section 10 of the Trade Marks Act 1994 states that:

2.05

> "A person infringes a registered trade mark if he uses in the course of a trade a sign which identical or similar to the registered trade mark in relation to identical or similar goods or services."

The tort of passing off is committed if a defendant wrongly represents in the course of trade that there is a connection between the defendant and the plaintiff. This is considered further in the next section in the important case of *Marks & Spencers v. One in a Million* in the context of "cybersquatting".[10]

---

[8] There is an information site at **http://www.gtld.com/** which contains the latest news and comment about the proposed new names.
[9] Council Regulation No 40/94 on Community Trade Mark which is administered by the Office for Harmonisation in the Internal Market.
[10] Court of Appeal, July 23, 1998.

Domain Name Disputes

2.06   The case of *Prince plc v. Prince Sportswear Group Inc.* is a good example of the type of domain name dispute which arises between companies.[11] The source of the dispute is a fundamental mismatch between trade mark rights and the domain name system.

In January 1997, Prince Sports Group, a manufacturer of tennis racquets, sent a "cease and desist" letter to Prince PLC, a U.K.-based information technology (I.T.) company. The letter complained about the I.T. company's registration and use of the domain name "prince.com." The letter claimed that the sports group had a number of PRINCE trademark registrations (including in the U.K.) and alleged that the I.T. company's use of the domain name amounted to trademark infringement and unfair competition under the Lanham Act. Prince Sports Group also complained to the NSI requesting that the domain name be put on hold, pending the resolution of the dispute.

Since 1995 Prince plc had operated a website under the domain name "prince.com" which it had been assigned under the then "first come first served" policy of the NSI. However, in September 1996, the NSI issued its Domain Name Resolution Policy (Revision 2)[12] which has indirectly enabled any U.S. federal trade mark holder or holder of a foreign trade mark to pre-empt the rights of pre-registered genuine domain name holders.

2.07   Under this revised policy, if a second company can show that it is the owner of a U.S. federal registered trade mark or a foreign registered trade mark pertaining to that name, the first party which has registered the domain name loses that registration. Such a loss of registration can be put on hold if the first party can also either prove that it has a U.S. federal trade mark registration or a foreign trade mark registration, or has commenced proceedings in a "court of competent jurisdiction" to protect that domain name.

When NSI wrote to Prince plc intimating that it was about to re-allocate the domain name, Prince plc could neither show it owned a trade mark, nor confirm that it had commenced proceedings in a U.S. court (which some might say was the right "court of competent jurisdiction"), and so were in danger of losing the domain name in favour of Prince Sportswear Group Inc. However the NSI advised Prince plc that it could commence proceedings against Prince Sports Group in any court of competent jurisdiction and further said that if Prince plc brought such a suit, NSI would not put the name on hold pending resolution of the action and would abide by any resulting court order.

Accordingly Prince plc filed suit in the High Court in London alleging that the statements made by Prince Sportswear Group Inc. (that Prince plc was "infringing and diluting its trade mark rights") constituted groundless threats under section 21 of the U.K. Trade Marks Act 1994. Neuberger J. granted Prince plc a declaration and injunction pursuant to section 21(2) of that Act. NSI accepted that the threats were groundless and Prince plc continues to have use of the "prince.com" domain name.[13]

2.08   The NSI's revised policy is a flawed attempt at dealing with the rights of trademark owners. It ignores the fact that the trademark registrations may not cover the specific services and goods in relation to which the domain name is being used. Trademark

---

[11] CH — 1997 — P No. 2355 (July 18, 1997).
[12] For details of this policy see **http://www.rs.internic.net/domain-info/internic-domain-6.html**.
[13] CH 1997 — P No. 2355 (July 18, 1997).

registrations should, in these cases, be irrelevant in resolving domain name disputes. Further, it takes no account of common law rights which a domain name registrant may have acquired — the unregistered trade mark or passing off rights.

However, the NSI revised policy is of some use in protecting legitimate traders from others passing off their websites as being associated with them. For example, it appears that a U.K. trade mark owner could invoke the NSI revised policy against a U.S. company which had acquired a ".com" registration and was passing off goods or services as being those of the U.K. company.[14]

Cybersquatting

The issue of cyber squatting was clarified and the practice of domain name piracy was effectively buried in the U.K. in the *One in a Million* decision.[15]   **2.09**

The case concerned the business of One in a Million Ltd, which had registered the plaintiffs' names and trade marks as Internet domain names, without their consent, and then sought to sell them. The plaintiffs (Marks & Spencer Plc, J. Sainsbury Plc, Virgin Enterprises Ltd, British Telecommunications Plc, Telecom Securicor Cellular Radio Ltd and Ladbrokes Plc) claimed that the defendant was passing-off and infringing their registered trade marks. They also claimed that the defendant's activities constituted threats of passing-off and infringement and that they were entitled to injunctive relief. The defendant accepted that the trade names Marks & Spencer, Sainsbury, Virgin, BT, Cellnet and Ladbroke are well known brand names with substantial goodwill attaching to them. It had registered ladbrokes.com; sainsbury.com; sainsburys.com; marksandspencer.com; marksandspencer.co.uk; cellnet.net; bt.org; virgin.org; britishtelecom.co.uk; britishtelecom.net and britishtelecom.com. The defendant claimed that it registered domain names with a view to making a profit either by selling them to the owners of the goodwill, using the blocking effect of the registration to obtain a good price, or, in some cases, selling them to collectors or to other persons who could have a legitimate reason for using them. It argued that this could not amount to passing off or a threat to pass off.

The Court of Appeal, dismissing the appeal of *One in a Million* and granting a   **2.10**
permanent injunction, held that the registration of a distinctive name such as "marksandspencer" made a false representation to persons who consulted the register that the registrant was connected or associated with the name registered. This constituted passing off. The Court further held that the registration was an erosion of the exclusive goodwill in the name which damaged or was likely to damage Marks & Spencer Plc. Aldous L.J. felt that domain names comprising the names Marks & Spencer were instruments of fraud because any realistic use of the name would result in passing-off. This justified injunctive relief. The other trade names were all household names

---

[14] There have been several cases in the United States on domain names most of which have settled. In *MTV Networks v. Curry*, a former employee of the rock music cable television service obtained the site name "mtv.com" and offered reports on the rock music industry at the Internet site. The case settled on undisclosed terms. (*MTV Networks v. Curry*, 867 F.Supp. 202 (SDNY 1994)). In *Kaplan Education Center Ltd v. Princeton Review Management Corp.* a test preparation service obtained a domain name that resembled that of a rival service and then placed disparaging material about its rival at the site. Despite Kaplan's demand for injunctive relief and damages (as well as attorneys' fees), the monetary claims were not established and the arbitration panel simply required PRI to release the name. (94 CV 1604 (S.D.N.Y. 1994)) .

[15] *Marks and Spencer plc and Others v. One in a Million Ltd*, Court of Appeal, July 23, 1998.

denoting the respondents. The Court decided that the defendant's motive was to use the respondents' goodwill, and to threaten to sell the domain name to another who might use it for passing-off in order to obtain money from the respondents. The value of the domain name lay in the threat that they would be used in a fraudulent way. The registrations were made with the purpose of appropriating the respondents' goodwill. They were instruments of fraud and injunctive relief was appropriate. Aldous L.J. stated that:

> "there was clear evidence of systematic registration by the appellants of well-known trade names as blocking registrations and a threat to sell them to others."

He went on:

> "the purpose of the so-called blocking registration was to extract money from the owners of the goodwill in the name chosen. Its ability to do so was in the main dependent upon the threat, expressed or implied, that the [defendants] would exploit the goodwill by either trading under the name or equipping another with the name so he could do so."

2.11   The decision of the Court seems to have been influenced in no small measure by the attitude of the defendant. In August 1997, it had threatened to involve the media if British Telecommunications took legal action against it over the domain name bt.org. It later offered to sell the name for £4,700 plus VAT. The name burgerking.co.uk was offered for sale to Burger King for £25,000 plus VAT in September 1996, the defendant pointing out that if Burger King did not buy it, it "would be available for sale to any other interested party". A similar threat was made implicitly to Intertan U.K. Ltd (Tandy) at about the same time. After the case BT issued a statement containing the following:

> "This judgment in proceedings in which BT has taken a leading role, represents a significant victory on behalf of businesses with valuable trade marks which have been the target of abusive activities by unprincipled domain name pirates and cybersquatters who seek to take speculative advantage of the goodwill established in well-known marks. It reinforces the view that the domain names clearly perform a trade mark function and that trade mark owners can legitimately expect to have their rights protected on the Internet. The message to those who want to register domain names and avoid conflict with trade marks is "don't imitate, differentiate!""

The defendant sought leave to appeal to the House of Lords but was refused.

This case, at the time of writing, is the highest considered U.K. case on domain names. Together with Prince, it indicates that it is important:

- when registering a domain name to undertake trade mark searches to avoid conflict with trade mark owners;

- when a potential conflict is discovered seek agreement with the trade mark owners to avoid potential passing off problems. If it can be established that there is no likelihood of passing off or trade mark infringement the domain name should be safe to use;

- Do not attempt to blackmail the trade mark owners (or, conversely, give in to intimidation by the trade mark owners when there is no likelihood of passing off or trade mark infringement — see *Prince*).

'First Come, First Served'

The 1997 decision of the Vice Chancellor, Sir Richard Scott, in *Pitman Training Limited et al v. Nominet U.K.*[16] illustrates the support of the law to the "first come, first served" policy of domain name registration and the importance of early registration.

    2.12

The case concerned the domain name www.pitman.co.uk and arose because both of the plaintiffs, Pitman Training Limited and PTC Oxford Limited (a franchisee of the first plaintiff), and the second defendant, Pearson Professional Limited, were entitled to use the name or style "Pitman" for their respective trading purposes. All these three parties could trace back their rights in the name to Sir Isaac Pitman in the nineteenth Century who founded not only a publishing business, but also a training business and an examination business.

In February 1996 Pearson Professional Limited sent a request to Nominet for registration of the domain name pitman.co.uk for use in its publishing business. The application was noted as received and confirmed on February 21, 1996. Thereafter, Pearson Professional Limited did not have a nominal I.P. address assigned to the domain name but left it as a registration in limbo while the company made plans for the development of the site. However, in April 1996, the first plaintiff, Pitman Training Limited, enquired as to whether the domain name pitman.co.uk was still available for allocation. Owing to an error, Pitman Training was told that the name was indeed still available, and it was duly registered to the company's business.

The first plaintiff started to use the domain name in July 1996. It was not until December that year that Pitman Publishing, a training division of Pearson Professional, which was then ready to go "live" with its e-mail service and website, found that its domain name had been re-allocated to Pitman Training without its knowledge or consent. The Vice Chancellor refused Pitman Training's claims to be allowed to continue using the name and ordered the immediate reassignment of pitman.co.uk to Pearson Professional.

    2.13

It should, however, be pointed out that the litigation would not have arisen had Pearson Publishing taken the prudent step of registering a temporary I.P. address with the domain name pitman.co.uk. A single page announcing that the domain name had already been assigned would have stopped Pitman Training from making an investment based on the error.

There is a fully automatic system for changing the I.P. addresses associated with particular domain names, and a switchover from a temporary I.P. to a new permanent I.P. where a site has been constructed normally takes between 12 to 48 hours. Consequently, although not legally necessary, it is sensible for any registration to be immediately supported by connecting the domain name to a temporary page publicising the domain name ownership.

---

[16] *The Pitman Training Ltd v. Nominet U.K.* [1998] Tr.L.R. 173.

THE DISTANCE SELLING DIRECTIVE

2.14   The Distance Selling Directive[17] was adopted by the European Parliament and Council in May 1997 and is due to be implemented by June 4, 2000. The Directive is designed to protect consumers against some of the risks involved in distance selling. It will make significant changes in the practice of those who use the Internet to sell goods and services to European consumers. By protecting consumers against some of the risks involved in buying goods at a distance it is intended to encourage and increase confidence in such methods of selling and also harmonise laws in all Member States so that all European consumers have equal access to goods and services in other Member States. Essentially, the Directive covers five main areas, the provision of information about the contract and its terms (Articles 4 and 5); the right of withdrawal (Article 6); the obligations as to performance by the supplier (Article 7); payment by card (Article 8) and inertia selling (Article 9).

What is a Distance Contract?

2.15   A *distance contract* is any contract concerning goods and services concluded between a supplier and a consumer under an organised distance sales or service provision scheme run by the supplier who, for the purposes of the contract, makes exclusive use of one or more means of distance communication up to and including the moment at which the contract is concluded.[18] The key to the applicability of the Directive is a contract where the supplier and the consumer do not come face to face prior to the conclusion of the contract (telephone sales, mail order or electronic commerce). Therefore, a transaction where the seller makes initial contact by using a distance communication but concludes the contract face to face is not covered by the Directive. The ambit of the Directive is therefore very wide. Annexure 1 of the Directive contains an indicative list of the means of communication for distance selling. It includes unaddressed printed matter, press advertising, telephone sales with or without human intervention, videotex (microcomputer and television screen) with keyboard or attached screen and electronic mail.

Who is a Consumer and who is a Supplier?

2.16   A *consumer* is any natural person who, in contracts covered by the Directive, is acting for purposes which are outside his/her trade, business or profession. This is a rather strange definition since it appears to exclude protection for sole traders. This means that a computer programmer who buys software over the Internet for incorporation into his/her products would not be a consumer. However, the implications from early documentation and debate behind the legislation is that a consumer is a non specialist dealing with an undertaking in a superior bargaining position. It is thought likely that this purposive construction of the definition would be adopted in any contested case, thereby protecting sole traders.

A *supplier* is defined as any natural or legal person who, in contracts covered by the Directive acts in his/her commercial or professional capacity.

---

[17] Directive 97/7/EC.
[18] Article 2(1).

Excluded Contracts

Certain types of contract are excluded from the ambit of the Directive; other types of contract are exempted from some of the provisions of the Directive. The excluded contracts are:

2.17

- Contracts relating to financial services — these are regarded as different from other contracts because they have specific legislation which is applicable and do not ordinarily gain protection of consumer protection legislation.

- Contracts concluded by means of automatic vending machines or automated commercial premises. These are excluded because they are unlikely to create the same sort of issues as purchasing goods using distant methods.

- Contracts concluded with telecommunication operators through the use of payphones. Again, this does not create the same sort of issues requiring consumer protection as other contracts.

- Contracts for the construction of sale of land are excluded as a special category.

- Contracts concluded at auction — the common practice whereby people bid by means of telephone — is considered separate from other types of contract.

The obligations relating to prior information, written confirmation, the right to withdraw and performance within 30 days do not apply to contracts for the supply of food beverages and other such consumable items and to contracts for the provision of accommodation, transport, catering or leisure services where a supplier agrees to provide the services on a specified date.[19] This is only logical as it would make no sense if a consumer could book an air ticket, take the flight and then exercise the right of refusal.

Successive Operations

Many consumers buy books and CDs from so-called book and music clubs. The Directive at recital 10 refers to these type of contract as comprising "successive operations" or "a series of separate operations over a period of time". Such transactions may be treated differently by Member States laws. The Directive is stated to require compliance at the time of the first of the series of successive operations even though there may be a number of separate contracts. This has been criticised by some commentators[20] as concentrating on the fact that consumers only need to be notified of contractual terms on initially joining the club but they still need the protection of the Directive for matters such as the right of refusal and the provisions of inertia selling after the initial period.

2.18

Prior Information Requirements

Article 4 of the Directive specifies that prior to the conclusion of any distance contract, (*i.e.* before the contract is entered into not before performance is concluded) the consumer shall be provided with the following information:

2.19

---

[19] There is an exception in the case of outdoor leisure events where the supplier can reserve the right not to apply Article 7(2) in specific circumstances.
[20] See the Article by Robert Bradgate at 1997.4 Web JCI.

- the identity of the supplier and, in the case of contracts requiring payment in advance, his/her address;

- the main characteristics of the goods or services;

- the price of the goods or services including all taxes;

- delivery costs, where appropriate;

- the arrangements for payment, delivery or performance;

- the existence of a right of withdrawal, except in certain cases specified in the Article where this right does not exist;

- the cost of using the means of distance communication, where it is calculated other than at the basic rate;

- the period for which the offer or the price remains valid; and

- where appropriate, the minimum duration of the contract in the case of contracts for the supply of products or services to be performed permanently or recurrently.

None of these requirements should cause a company selling via a website any difficulties. Nevertheless, until enacting legislation is introduced, it is not known whether a failure to provide this information will lead to a supplier not being able to enforce the contract and/or potential actions by the Director General of Fair Trading.

Provision of Information in a Comprehensible Manner

2.20   The Directive requires the consumer to be provided with the Article 4 information in a clear and comprehensible manner and in good time before the conclusion of any distance contract (meaning before the contract is made, not before performance of the contracts is concluded). In addition, the information must be provided in a way appropriate to the means of distance communication used with due regard to the principles of good faith in commercial contracts and the rules of protection of vulnerable people such as minors. The concept of providing information in good faith will be difficult to implement into U.K. law which does not recognise such general require- ments. The requirement of good faith essentially means that people supplying goods using electronic commerce should deal openly with their consumers supplying the required information in a comprehensive and legible form.

One contentious issue was the language in which the requisite information should be supplied. The European Commission took the view that if the consumer replied to an advertisement in an English-language newspaper, it was reasonable that the information be supplied in English. In discussions certain Member States took the position of requiring the use of the consumer's language. Since the language to be used for distance contracts is a matter left to Member States, one can envisage situations where the language used is not that of the host country of the recipient. It is likely that any such deliberate use of a language which is different from that the host country supplier would be in breach of good faith requirements.

Written confirmation of Information[21]

The Directive requires that in distance contracts for the sale of goods, the consumer must **2.21**
receive written confirmation of most of the Article 4. information in a durable medium
available and accessible by him/her. This recognises that using the world wide web and
electronic mail is ephemeral[22] due to the lack of permanence in the medium. In the case
of services, the requirement is to provide confirmation in good time during the
performance of the contract. There is a partial exemption for goods delivered by the
supplier to a third party (such as gifts). No confirmation is required for either goods or
services where the information has already been provided in writing with another
durable medium. The consultation paper of the Department of Trade and Industry[23]
indicates that the DTI considers electronic mail meets the definition of confirmation in a
durable medium.

Right of Withdrawal

The most significant impact of the Directive is contained in Article 6 of the Directive **2.22**
which creates a general right of withdrawal. This is a right which many consumers
already have in other transactions such as when buying goods from magazines where
the Mail Order Protection Scheme applies and in certain credit agreements regulated by
the Consumer Credit Act 1974.[24] Every consumer who is party to a distance contract has
at least seven working days (*i.e.* an actual period of between 10 and 12 ordinary days
most of the year and two weeks at Christmas) to withdraw from it at will without
having to give any reason. No penalty can be levied and a full refund is due to the
consumer such refunds must take place within 30 days. Only the direct costs of
returning the goods are payable. However, there are some significant exemptions to
these rules. The "cooling-off" period will not apply to gaming/lottery services and
travel services. Nor will it apply to unsealed audio or video recordings, records or
computer software and CD–ROMs. Furthermore, it will not apply for newspapers,
periodicals and magazines and certain other situations referred to in Article 6(3).

   From the wording it would therefore appear that it will apply in the case of books that
are not periodicals or magazines. Book shops that offer books over the Internet appear to
be caught — it would be open to a consumer to order a few novels for Christmas,
receive them, read them, decide that he/she did not like them and successfully demand
his/her money back early in the New Year.

Performance

Unless the parties have agreed otherwise the supplier must execute a customer's orders **2.23**
within 30 days from the day following that on which the consumer forwarded his/her
order to the supplier.[25] Accordingly, it is open for a supplier to agree a longer than 30

---

[21] Article 5.
[22] Recital 13.
[23] June 1998 Consultation Paper — *Distance Selling* — implementation of E.U. Directive 97/7 on the Protection of Consumers in respect of Distance Contracts.
[24] See the Consumer Protection (Cancellation of Contracts Concluded Away from Business Premises) Regulations 1987.
[25] Article 7(1).

day period with a consumer but this could lead to challenges under the Unfair Contract Terms Act 1977 and in particular the Unfair Terms and Consumer Contracts Regulations 1994.[26]

Where a supplier is unable to perform the contract because the goods or services are not available the supplier must inform the consumer of this situation and refund any sums received within 30 days.

Member States are permitted to enact the Directive in such a way that the supplier may provide the consumer with goods or services of equivalent quality or price provided that the consumer is informed of this possibility prior to the conclusion of the contract. It is further provided that the consumer must be informed of this possibility in a clear and comprehensible manner. The cost of returning the goods following the exercise of the right of withdrawal are to be borne by the supplier and the consumer must be informed of this. In any event any contractual clauses which purport to permit a supplier to provide goods or services of the same quality and price but of a different description to those ordered will potentially be challengable by a consumer under the Unfair Contract Terms Act 1977 and the Unfair Terms and Consumer Contract Regulations 1994.

Payment by Card

2.24   The success of electronic commerce depends on consumers having the confidence that when they make payment prior to delivery or performance of goods or services that they will be protected. There is also concern regarding fraudulent use of credit & debit cards. On the fraudulent use of credit & debit cards Article 8 provides that a consumer may request cancellation of a payment where fraudulent use is made of his/her payment card and that in the event of such fraudulent use the consumer is to be re-credited with the sums paid.

But there remain problems with goods purchased from abroad using credit or debit cards. In respect of credit cards section 75 of the Consumer Credit Act 1974 provides that, for transactions in excess of £100, if a credit card holder (a *debtor*) has "any claim against the supplier in respect of a misrepresentation or breach of contract he shall have a like claim against the creditor". On the face of it a U.K. consumer should be able to bring a claim against his U.K. card issuer if goods supplied by an overseas supplier are not of satisfactory quality. Although there are a few tenuous arguments which suggest that a U.K. card issuer could avoid liability[27] the better view is that section 75 covers overseas credit card transactions.[28]

The same cannot however be said to apply to debit cards where the consumer uses a debit card and receives unsatisfactory goods. In these circumstances the consumer will have no claim against his card issuer. Within the European Union he/she currently has to pursue an action against the supplier in the country where the contract was made —

---

[26] See para. 3.87.

[27] See the discussion in para. 2–076 of *Encyclopedia of Consumer Credit Law* by A. G. Guest and M. G. Lloyd.

[28] See the Director General of Fair Trading 's review of section 75 in *Connected Lender Liability* (March 1994) pp. 26–28 and Report No. OFT 132 Connected lender liability — a second report by the Director General of Fair Trading on section 75 of the Consumer Credit Act 1974 (May 1995) where the Director General stated that his view was (and remains) that overseas transactions are covered by the law as it stands.

effectively litigating abroad. But after the Directive has been brought into force the customer will be able to sue the foreign supplier locally in respect of contracts made in the European Union. Thus an English consumer will be able to bring a complaint against a German supplier in an English court with English law being applicable. The judgment of the court will be fully enforceable against the German supplier. And national consumer protection organisations will work together to ensure compliance with the highest consumer standards.

Inertia Selling

The Directive requires Member States to take measures necessary to prohibit the supply of goods and services to a consumer without their being ordered by the consumer beforehand and where such supplier involves a demand for payment. In the U.K. the Unsolicited Goods and Services Act 1971 has effectually out-lawed some inertia selling. The Unsolicited Goods and Services Act 1971 makes it an offence to demand payment for unsolicited goods. Since the Directive applies to both goods and services U.K. law will need to be amended to extend the protection of this Act to services.

2.25

Binding Nature

Article 12(1) of the Distance Selling Directive expressly states that the consumer may not contract out or waive rights conferred by the Directive. The second leg of Article 12, which is addressed to Member States, requires them to implement legislation which will invalidate any attempts to deprive consumers of their rights under the Directive through a non-EU Member State choice of law.

2.26

Burden of Proof

In the case of a dispute the burden of proof concerning information, confirmation, time limits and consumer consent will be on the supplier rather than the consumer.

2.27

Conclusion of the Distance Selling Directive

The Directive is the first consumer orientation legislation which is primarily focused on electronic commerce. Distance selling is subject to little specific statutory regulation in the U.K. although there is an element of self regulation by codes of practice and trade associations. However, the Directive fails to address certain crucial legal issues such as:

2.28

- which legal system should be applied to transactions?
- how should transactions be authenticated?
- how can electronic privacy and data protection be ensured?

On the question for which legal system applies, this appears to fall within the Rome Convention of the Applicable Law and the Brussels Convention on Jurisdiction and Enforcement of Judgments.[29] The law of the consumer's home state would normally be

---

[29] See Chapter 4.

applicable (Rome Convention, Article 5.3.4) and the courts of his/her place of residence would normally have jurisdiction. In practice, because of the dispute resolution provisions, this is not likely to be a real problem. The Directive (Article 11(2)) provides for mutual recognition of consumer bodies who could bring legal actions or administrative complaints if such actions or complains were allowed under the Member State's law. Taking the explicit role of Member States and consumer bodies in protecting consumers' rights arising out of distance selling agreements, a company will be faced with a losing battle if it attempts to engage in sharp practice with choice of law clauses and purported waiver of consumer rights.

The question of how a transaction should be authenticated is best answered by a practical approach. It is wise to use the best mature technology and always be able to "unwind" transactions.[30] Business is creating professional standards which are likely to be acceptable paradigms of authentication.[31] But these are still being developed. Until there is consensus it is prudent to only use secure servers for all direct selling activities over the Web, with proper firewalls and well-documented procedures that are fully auditable. Suppliers should also ensure that individual transactions with particular customers can be unwound within the necessary time frame, as customers who pay by credit card will have to have their accounts recredited within a reasonable time. Although the Directive makes no mention of any time to recredit, it is likely that a period of 30 days or less will be imposed as a benchmark by reference to Article (6)(2).

MANAGING THE SITE

Commenting on the site

2.29 A fact which seems obvious but which is often forgotten, is that companies inviting people to send electronic mail must ensure that they read it and respond to it in a timely manner. They must also handle the personal information supplied by the potential customer in a lawful way.

The customer may be asking a question, commenting on some part of the site, warning you of a danger or complaining about your product. A good way of responding is to design the website so that every electronic mail receives a standard automatic response. An example of this is shown below.

> This is an automatic response — thank you or your message. All e-mails to us are reviewed. However, this process takes time and, owing to the volume of e-mail received, we do not undertake to respond personally to your message.

Having made the statement all e-mails are reviewed, it is important to follow through. This should be one of the responsibilities of the Webmaster — the company official in

---

[30] On technical reasons concerning the use of SET for authentication see the section in Chapter 5 on *Secure Electronic Transactions and the Microsoft Patent*.
[31] See the section in Chapter 6 on *Principles of Good Practice — the BSI and DISC codes*.

charge of the site.[32] He/she will be able to sift and sort out the messages, forwarding those which are important to the appropriate people in the company and responding in a suitable manner to those which deserve a personal reply.

The customer will often supply the company with personal information — his/her name, age, interests etc. Companies need have a policy regarding dealing with this data; the safest policy being to discard it after review. Personal data should not be gathered from this source without a suitable warning being given — only when the customer has registered his/her interest through filling in an electronic form with appropriate warnings should the data become a company asset.

Registering for automatic notification

One very useful modern feature of a number of sites is automatic notification of changes. Customers give their names and electronic mail addresses; whenever the specified section of the site changes, an electronic mail is sent directly to them, telling them that the site has changed.

2.30

This service is often free for both the company and the customer — it is paid for by advertising. The notification message contains an advertisement for some product or service selected by the notifier. The notification message also always contains a message telling the customer how to stop receiving further notifications of changes.

Use of notifiers with unsolicited advertisements is not considered to be improper — the Legal Advisory Board of the European Commission uses one of these services on its pages. However, problems could arise if the notifier accepted advertisements for goods and services which were not of a kind considered suitable for the target market. For example, strict controls exist in Sweden regarding advertising and children; a toy company could therefore encounter problems regarding unsolicited advertising to children if it used a notifier service that targeted them.

With notifiers, the personal data, the link between the name and the e-mail, is not normally supplied to the company but is retained by the notifier. Care should therefore be taken in selection of notifier to ensure that the organisation is handling personal data in a legal and decent manner. Dangers arise if, through inadequate computer security, the mailing list used by the supplier is passed to a spammer.

Registering interest by filling in an online form

Under Data Protection laws, every time a customer completes an online form, important issues and duties arise regarding the acquisition of data.[33] The first issue concerns the manner in which the information may be acquired and the nature of the information being sought. Other issues include important duties regarding management and the re-use and storage of data. This section looks only at the initial issues of acquisition of data and its nature.

2.31

---

[32] Additionally a new type of software termed an automated Message Centre is a key feature of many major commercial systems. The Message Centre downloads the incoming mail from customers, stores it in a database, and then sends back an acknowledgement with a tracking number. Mail is sorted into "pools", depending on its subject or other criteria. Individual employees of the company then retrieve mail and respond to it. Their answer goes back to the Message Centre, which then tracks the response for future reference (e.g. ISO 9002) before forwarding it to the customer with the appropriate tracking number intact.

[33] See Chapter 7.

Acquisition of data

2.32   Principle 1 of the Data Protection Act 1998 says: "The information to be contained in personal data shall be obtained, and personal data shall be processed, fairly and lawfully". The term "lawfully" is easy to determine; stealing a customer list is clearly wrong. But the term "fairly" raises subjective issues. In determining whether information has been obtained or acquired fairly, Schedule 1, Part 2 of the Act provides that regard shall be had to the method by which it was obtained, including in particular whether any person from whom it was obtained was deceived or misled a to the purpose or purposes for which it is to be held, used or disclosed.

It would therefore be unfair to encourage customers to complete a form under the representation that they are entering a competition to win a prize if the personal data so obtained were to be used for a mailing list, unless this fact was made known to the customers at the time and they had the opportunity to tick a box saying that they did not want to be included on the mailing list.

SPAMMING

2.33   Spam is the term given to unsolicited e-mail on the Internet which is often sent by electronic commerce business trying to sell goods and services. Spam is a characterised by users sending extremely large (often 50 million plus) numbers of e-mails which can block Internet Service Providers (ISP) services[34] making it impossible to carry normal traffic to and from their customers. ISPs have found that the bogus use of addresses on their systems has caused them to be blacklisted so that their honest customers are unable to exchange mail with parts of the outside world.

This problem of "spamming" has led Washington State to enact the world's first legislation designed to prevent it.[35] The Washington law makes it illegal to use a dummy or forged return address and to put false or misleading information in the subject line. Lawbreakers may be subject to pay the recipient $500 and the Internet Service Provider $1,000 for each offence. It has been reported that a Seattle man has collected $200 from a company who sent him spam mail under this law.[36]

Trespass

2.34   To date there have been no U.K. reported cases on spamming. In the U.S. there has been over 20 reported cases.[37] These have involved some of the largest U.S. based ISPs (AOL, CompuServe and Prodigy) instituting proceedings against spammers such as Cyber Promotions.[38] It was held that the transmission of electronic message to CompuServe's server without CompuServe's permission was a trespass to CompuServe's property as

---

[34] A report by Novell in April 1998 found that spam cost U.K. businesses up to £5 billion in lost time.
[35] The U.S. State of Nevada also now has such laws and California is considering their introduction.
[36] See in **http://www.sjmercurty.com** (San Jose Mercury News) for September 1998.
[37] These are listed and some transcripts are available at **http://www.fmls.edu/cyber/cases/spam.htm1**.
[38] Case No. C2–96–1070 United States District Court for the Southern District of Ohio. Final consent order and other judgments are available at **http://tigerden.com/junkmail/cases/index.html**.

the volume of spam was burdensome to CompuServe's server to be sufficient to constitute a trespass even though no actual physical damage was suffered.

In the U.K. it is also likely that a Court would find spamming to be trespass. The Torts (Interference with Goods) Act 1977 created a tort of wrongful interference with goods. Section 1 of the 1977 Act provides that wrongful interference means:

> "(a) conversion of goods (also called trover);
> (b) trespass to goods;
> (c) negligence so far as it results in damage to goods or to an interest in goods;
> (d) any other tort so far as it results in damage to goods or to an interests in goods".

"Goods" are defined in section 14 of the 1977 Act as "all chattels personal other than things in action or money". This provided stated meanings to the common law of torts.[39]

The question which the U.K. Courts may one day have to determine is whether the act of spamming causes a sufficient impact with someone's property for there to be a tort. So long as the spamming is of sufficient significance to cause some damage to the ISPs server then an action for trespass could be made out. Dumping very large quantities of mail on a relay server can (and usually does) saturate the server's capabilities and/or connectivity. If — as usually happens with spam — a large proportion of the addresses are undeliverable, and the alleged originator's address is also undeliverable (for obvious reasons) the server keeps trying to return the undeliverable mail.[40] **2.35**

However it may be that the Courts in the U.K. will not get to consider this issue as MSN and other ISPs have announced that they have introduced anti-spamming email software in their services and introduced I.P. filtering. These technologies (termed "spamicide") appear to be reasonably effective.

The Computer Misuse Act 1990

The Computer Misuse 1990 Act was enacted to deal with hackers and those who sent and planted computer viruses. Since spamming was not known about when the 1990 Act was implemented it certainly was not the intention of Parliament for it to cover such activities. Under section 3 of the 1990 Act: **2.36**

> "A person is guilty of an offence if . . . he does any act which causes an unauthorised modification of the contents of any computer; and at the time when he does the act he had the requisite intent and the requisite knowledge".

Section 3(2) sets out the requisite intent required under section 3(1). This states that the intent is:

> "An intent to cause a modification of the contents of any computer and by so doing:
>
> (a) to impair the operation of any computer;
> (b) to prevent or hinder access to any program or data held in any computer; or

---

[39] See para. 3.05 of Chapter 3 for further discussion on meaning of goods.
[40] A number of network administrators have told one of the authors that they have had to take their mail servers down for several days after being used as an (unauthorised) spam relay point.

(c) to impair the operation of any such program or the reliability of any such data."

A prosecution under this Act will only be viable if the specific type of intent in section 3(2) can be shown. However since the originator of the spam will have had to disguise his/her originating address the legitimacy of his/her activities will already be questionable and it would not be too difficult for a jury to conclude that the person had sufficient intent for the criminal offence under section 3(2) to be made out.[41]

Trade Mark Issues of Spamming

2.37   Spamming may also raise trade mark concerns when unsuspecting users receive spam mail which is sent using electronic mail addresses consisting of domain names and trade marks owned by other entities. This misleads the recipients into believing that the owner of the trade mark sent or endorses the electronic mail, thereby causing confusion and potentially damaging the trade mark owner's reputation. In the U.S. case of *Hotmail Corp v. Van$ Money Pie Inc.*, Hotmail (the Microsoft owned electronic mail provider and owner of the Hotmail trade mark and domain name) was granted an injunction against the defendants who sent spam electronic mail messages advertising pornographic material with return Hotmail electronic mail addresses.[42]

DISCLAIMERS

2.38   A website, whether it is for information purposes only or as part of an electronic commerce business to buy and sell goods, can create legal liability for the electronic commerce business in each country from which someone accesses the site. Disclaimers (or health warnings) should be included in all websites to try and limit the legal liability of the electronic commerce business or publisher.

The extent to which liability can be excluded or restricted can vary from country to country. It is not possible to draft a disclaimer which will work in every country a website can be accessed. Apart from the obvious language problems, different countries permit different exclusions. Under U.K. law it is not possible, for example, to exclude liability for death or personal injury caused by negligence[43] or for defamation.[44]
Accordingly, a disclaimer may minimise the risk of legal liability but whether a court would uphold an attempt to exclude liability will depend on the circumstances.

---

[41] The section 3 offence does not cover "reckless" damage or modification and this limitation was said to be a safeguard to ensure that people would not be prosecuted for merely inadvertent acts. However use of a false address could be said to indicate that the spammer knew that his activities would or were likely to cause damage. See *Akdeniz Y.* [1996] 3 Web JCLI "Section 3 of the Computer Misuse Act 1990: an Antidote for Computer Viruses!" **http://webjcli.ncl.ac.uk/1996/issue3/akdeniz3.html** and Battcock, R. (1995) *The Computer Misuse Act 1990: 5 years on* (includes a complete list of cases prosecuted under Computer Misuse Act 1990 up to July 1995) at **http://www.strath.ac.uk/Departments/Law/student/PERSONAL/R—BATTCOCK/.**
[42] [1998] W.L. 388389, 47 U.S.P.Q. 2d 1020 (N.A. Cal., April 16, 1998) (No. C–98 JW PVT ENE, C98—20064 JW).
[43] Unfair Contract Terms Act 1977.
[44] But note that wider Section 1 of the Defamation Act 1996, there is a codification and expansion of the defence of innocent dissemination making it available to printers, and broadcasters in respect of unrecorded statements by persons for whose acts the broadcaster is not responsible. Section 1 should inform U.K. Internet Service providers about defamation liability.

The governing law of a disclaimer is normally the one in which the page is accessed by a viewer. It may not work, but it is prudent to provide that the viewer accepts the law which governs the disclaimer is English law if the website owner is a U.K. business.

It is important that a disclaimer is brought to the attention of a viewer. They should not be included on a separate legal page which a view can optionally visit, possibilities for locating a disclaimer include: **2.39**

- on the web page directly which contains the product or services information;

- on the entry page which requires a visitor to acknowledge before gaining entry to the rest of the website;

- a prominent link entitled "Product Disclaimer" which should be placed at various places on the site;

For example, the following is an example of a disclaimer of liability:

> With respect to the information available on this sit (ABC Limited) expressly excludes any representation or warranty (express or implied) to the fullest extent possible. (ABC Limited) makes no representations about the materials in this site or any sites linked to this site. You agree to accept the application of English law to govern matters between (ABC Limited) and yourself.

AUCTIONS

There has been a dramatic increase in growth in online auctions both aimed and consumers and business. Not surprisingly, there is no specific legislation dealing with online auctions but this trend does raise interesting legal questions. An auction is merely a particular manner of contracting and rules relating to when an offer is accepted and when it is revoked are considered in Chapter 3 and apply equally to auctions. **2.40**

What makes on-line auctions interesting is the question of the method of acceptance by the auctioneer. Section 57(2) of the Sale of Goods Act 1979 states that "a sale by auction is completed on the fall of the auctioneer's hammer or in any other customary manner." With online auctions there is the practical problem that there is no auctioneer's hammer. In practice, this problem seems to be resolved by setting a closing time on the website by which all bids must be placed. The highest bid at the time the auction closes is bound to contract unless the reserved price has not been reached.

Section 12(2) of the Unfair Contracts Terms Act 1977 states "in the sale by auction the buyer is not in any circumstances to be regarded as dealing as a consumer". Therefore, people engaging in online auctions may not receive the wider protection of consumer legislation and any exclusions of liability may not be subject to the reasonableness test. However, this does not place a consumer in any different position to ordinary auctions. The Distance Selling Directive specifically excludes auctions from the ambit of the Directive.

It is particularly important with online auctions that terms and conditions for sale are brought to any potential bidder's attention. In addition, there are some statutory formalities which apply to auction sales and which by analogy will apply to online **2.41** auctions. Thus, section 57(3) of the Sale of Goods Act 1979 requires the auctioneer to display their full name and residence and copies of the Auctions (Bidding Agreements) Act 1927 and 1969 in a conspicuous part of the auction room and keep them there during the time the auction is being held. Online auctioneers entering into contracts governed by English law, will need to ensure that the website has appropriate links to copies of these Acts.

Although no auction licence is required to conduct an auction, some London boroughs have introduced Codes of Practice and licence conditions relating to auctions conducted in their locality. Conducting an online may therefore be a way of by-passing such controls.

However Internet auctions remain prone to what is delicately termed "accidental fraud". Participants often fail to pay for goods or fail to deliver goods on time not because they have a fraudulent intent but because they forget, go on holiday or are not really expecting to make a purchase and then find themselves obligated. To deal with these problems a new type of intermediary is appearing. These companies, for a fee, provide assurance that goods are delivered and paid for with a money back guarantee. If something goes wrong, the company takes the loss.

REGULATED ACTIVITIES

2.42   Electronic commerce is about doing business electronically and many goods and services which may be sold or traded on-line have specific laws, rules and regulations which either restrict or regulate those goods and services. Any person proposing to sell on-line a particular goods or services should check the relevant rules which regulate that particular goods or service. It is outside the ambit of this book to give a detailed consideration to specific rules which in particular industries the following sections provide only summaries of the relevant legal environment for just a few of the main products which are commonly sold on-line.

Gambling

2.43   Gambling is predicted to be one of the real growth areas of electronic commerce. It has been estimated that £6 billion will be gambled on-line by 2002 as bookmakers take advantage of the Internet's huge audience reach and cost savings.[45]

In the U.S., in particular, there are concerns about the legality of gambling on-line, with only some U.S. states permitting gambling, and there are further concerns about the proliferation of illegal on-line gambling. In 1997 Senator Kyl introduced a bill, to be called the Internet Gambling Prohibition Act of 1997, to amend the Federal criminal code to prohibit and set penalties for gambling via the Internet and for engaging in the business of gambling on the Internet. The bill, known as the "Kyl Bill", is at the time of this book going to press in committee. In March 1998, the authorities in Manhattan charged 14 American owners and managers of six off-shore companies with illegally using interstate telephone lines in relation to on-line betting, even though the defendants

---

[45] Datamonitor.

claimed to have been granted licences in the places where their offshore companies were based, namely the Caribbean and Central America.

In contrast to the U.S.'s prohibitive stance, some states are taking are more enlightened approach. For example, InterLotto is licensed in Lichtenstein to run an Internet lotto. In New Zealand and Australia, Internet gambling licences are available to individuals who satisfy stringent requirements, the theory being that disreputable organisations will not get involved.

In November 1997, the First International Symposium on Internet Gambling Law and Management met in Washington D.C. The legal issues considered included: different cultures' attitudes to gambling; the fact that some jurisdictions, particularly in the Pacific and Caribbean, are actively promoting on-line gambling in their territories because of the taxation revenue; and whether an international treaty was necessary.

2.44

In Great Britain, there have so far not been any legislative attempts specifically to regulate or prohibit Internet gambling, so it is necessary to look at legislation drafted before the invention of the Internet. Gambling is governed by a complex regulatory regime, with different regulations applying depending on whether the gambling involves betting, gaming or lotteries. The relevant Acts are the Betting, Gaming and Lotteries Act 1963, the Gaming Act 1968, the Lotteries and Amusement Act 1976 and the Betting and Gaming Duties Act 1981.

The gambling related offences under these Acts include the following:

2.45

- It is unlawful in Great Britain to promote or be concerned in a foreign lottery.[46]

- It is unlawful in Great Britain to promote or be concerned in a lottery in Great Britain unless it is part of the National Lottery or falls into one of the other limited exceptions.[47]

- It is not permitted to sell lottery tickets using a machine, which may preclude the sale of lottery tickets via the Internet. However, if a person is involved in the sale, then it may not be prohibited.

- It is an offence to use premises (other than an approved racecourse or licensed track) for the purposes of betting with persons resorting to them unless the premises are duly licensed.[48]

In relation to Internet betting, the following question arises: does a website constitute "premises" and therefore need to be licensed? The Courts have defined premises to include any place or vessel. It is not necessary to prove that people have "resorted to" the premises unless the only evidence of the betting is that a transaction took place, in which case physical resorting must be proved. The Courts have also held that there is no need to prove physical entrance to the premises, it is enough to show a "close physical connection" between the person and the premises.[49] It is arguable that a connection to a website hosting an Internet casino, for example, would fall within the definition, in which case the website should be licensed.

---

[46] Lotteries and Amusements Act 1976, section 2(1).
[47] Lotteries and Amusements Act 1976, section 1.
[48] Betting Gaming and Lotteries Act 1963, sections 1(1) and 9(1).
[49] *R. v. Brown*, 1995.

- Under the Gaming Act 1968, it would not be permissible to set up an on-line casino or bingo club because the club would require a licence, the licence can only be granted to a members' club, and the members must be present when the gaming takes place.

- Betting may not take place in the streets or other public places.[50] Public places are not defined in the relevant Act, but it is certainly arguable that the Internet constitutes a public place.

- It is an offence to advertise a gaming establishment in public.[51]

In addition, there are various regulations which apply to anyone carrying on general betting businesses in Great Britain. These include obligations to keep such books, records and accounts as the Commissioners of Customs & Excise may direct. Electronic records may not be sufficient for these purposes.

Financial Services On The Internet

2.46   The regulators of financial services providers have recently started to address how the use of new communicating media should be controlled.

In the U.K., at a general level, the statutory provisions and indeed the detailed rules are the same for advertising or selling financial products via the Internet as for using traditional means such as mailings, meetings or telephone calls.

Advertisements issued in the U.K.

2.47   Investment advertisements must be issued or approved by a U.K. authorised person and have certain required contents and risk warnings. The Financial Services Act currently provides that an advertisement is issued in the U.K. if it is directed at or "made available" in the U.K. other than in a newspaper, journal, magazine or other periodical publication published outside the U.K. or in a sound or television broadcast transmitted principally for reception outside the U.K.

Due to their global reach, websites are, necessarily, made available in the U.K. Consequently any website page which may lead investors to invest in an investment identified on the page needs to be considered as an investment advertisement issued in the U.K. (This contrasts with the position in the U.S., where regulation only applies to websites which are targeted at U.S. persons, assessed under minimum contact tests.)

In considering whether an enforcement action should be taken if there is a breach of the advertising requirements, the Financial Services Authority has issued formal Guidance (2/98) stating it will take into account the following:

2.48   (a) whether the website is located on a server outside the U.K.;

(b) the extent to which the underlying investment or investment service to which the advertisement relates is available to U.K. investors who respond to the advertisement (including whether it is available through other media into U.K. investors);

(c) the extent to which positive steps have been taken to ensure that the U.K. investors do not obtain the service as a result of the Internet route;

---

[50] Betting Gaming and Lotteries Act 1963, section 8.
[51] Section 5(1) of the Gaming Act 1968.

(d) the extent to which the advertisement was directed at persons in the U.K., in relation to which it will consider:

- disclaimers and warnings that the services are only available in certain countries and may not be available in particular countries where they were not legally available;
- whether such disclaimers and warnings could be viewed by visitors to the site in the same browser format as the rest of the site;
- whether the contents of the site are written in a manner which makes it clear that it is not aimed at U.K. investors (*e.g.* Is it in English? Are financial projections in sterling?);
- whether those responsible for the site and/or sponsors or advisers appear to have notified the existence of the site to a U.K. search engine or to the U.K. section of a search engine or to any other U.K. orientated compendium of worldwide websites or listing of investment opportunities;
- whether those responsible for the content of the site appear to establish any e-mail, news groups bulletin board or chapter and facility associated with the site and that associated facility appears to have been used actively to promote the investment in the U.K., *e.g.* sending out unsolicited e-mails or posting material to a news group or chat room or through any other unsolicited approach;
- whether those responsible for the contents of the website and/or the sponsors or advisers appeared to have advertised the site in the U.K. in a printed publication or by broadcasting (although advertisements contained within a TV or satellite or sound broadcast which is principally for reception outside the U.K. would be less relevant here).

(e) the extent to which positive steps have been taken to limit access to the site.

Investment business

Investment business activities, such as investment advice, dealing in investments or arranging deals in investments, can only be carried on by an authorised person who is subject to detailed rules as to how to conduct such business. **2.49**

The U.K. regulation of investment business prevents global business accessing the U.K. market without:

(a) the activities being conducted through the overseas persons exemptions; these require compliance with cold calling and advertisement restrictions. Generally this means no cold calling and fitting within investment advertisement exemptions (which usually mean directing advertisements to a limited category of certain recipients and so necessitating limited access to the websites concerned), or

(b) ensuring no investment business activities are involved, so there is an investment advertisement but it contains no investment advice and no transactions can be carried out on the Internet itself, or

(c) involving an authorised person to fulfil the investment business activities which are involved.

Again the FSA will refer to the criteria set out above in relation to investment advertisements when deciding whether or not to take any enforcement action for breach of the investment business requirements.

The wider picture

2.50   The E.U. has started to address similar issues and there is a prospect, in the medium term, of E.U. Member States introducing a common basic framework of regulation. The draft Distance Selling Directive for financial services acknowledges the need to set new principles which will cover the constant development of new distance selling methods including those not yet in widespread use. However, E.U. directives set out minimum common standards and so difficulties with various detailed sets of regulation, even in different European countries, may continue.

More generally, we are a long way from seeing any agreement on jurisdictional scope and a more co-ordinated global approach to the details of financial services regulation of the Internet.

Pornography

2.51   Much of the sophisticated technology which has made the Internet so powerful has been pioneered by the world of adult entertainment. Sales of pornographic magazines are falling because cyberporn is such a big e-commerce market. It is ironic, then, that these developments have led to so much debate over the dangers of the Internet. It has led to worldwide discussion on how to regulate the on-line porn industry. This in turn has led to extra concerns for Internet Service Providers (ISP) worried about their liability for obscene or indecent material transmitted via their services, whether hosting Usenet newsgroups or simply providing Internet access.

In the U.K., a lot of the law relating to pornography is contained in the Obscene Publications Act 1959 (as amended by the Criminal Justice and Public Order Act 1994). Under this Act, it is a criminal offence for any person either (1) whether for gain or not, *to publish* an obscene article; or (2) *to have* an obscene article for publication or gain.[52]

Material is obscene if its effect, or the effect of part of it, is such as to tend to deprave and corrupt persons likely to read, see or hear it.[53] A pornographic article or photograph displayed on the Internet would be accessible to such a large number of people, including children, that it is more likely to be categorised as obscene than a pornographic photograph in a magazine with limited circulation and access because it is kept on a top shelf in a newsagent.

2.52   Publication of obscene material includes the display, showing or circulation of the material and, since the Criminal Justice and Public Order Act 1994, this includes the transmission of electronically stored data. An Internet Service Provider is at risk of being liable for the offence of publication if it, for example, hosts a Website displaying obscene material.

ISPs are also concerned about unknowingly committing an offence of possession. The possession offence involves ownership, possession or control of an obscene article, for publication or gain. It is possible that an ISP acting as a host, charging a subscription fee, giving access to the material is committing the offence. Simply providing access may not constitute the possession offence.

Other criminal offences include the following:

---

[52] Obscene Publications Act 1959, section 2(4).
[53] *ibid.*

- Under the Telecommunications Act 1984 it is an offence to send, by means of a public telecommunications system, a message (or other matter) which is grossly offensive or of an indecent, obscene or menacing character.[54] This includes the transmission of data via a telecommunications system such as the Internet.

- The Broadcasting Act 1990 contains offences of publication and possession in relation to programme services, which could cover live or recorded material available on-line.

- The Protection of Children Act 1978, as amended by the Criminal Justice and Public Order Act 1994 makes it an offence to take, make, permit to be taken, distribute, show, possess intending to distribute or show, or publish any indecent photograph or "pseudo photograph" of a child. Photograph includes data stored on a computer disk or by other electronic means which is capable of being converted into a photograph/image.

- Under the Criminal Justice Act 1988 it is an offence to possess an indecent photograph of a child.

- The Indecent Displays (Control) Act 1981 makes it an offence publicly to display indecent matter in a place. This is particularly relevant to cyber cafes and libraries providing Internet access. However, it is not an offence if the place charges a fee for access to the material and is barred to people under 18 years of age. The Act could apply to Internet Service Providers.

- It is an offence to incite or conspire to commit certain sexual offences abroad.[55] This legislation is directed at sex tourism and applies to Internet e-mails sent or received in England and Wales.

There are some defences available to Internet Service Providers. If the ISP has not examined the obscene article and has had no reasonable cause to suspect that it was obscene material, it will not be guilty of the offence.[56]   **2.53**

Of particular interest to Internet Service Providers, is the defence set out in the Broadcasting Act 1990. A person or company would not be liable for the offence of publishing or possessing obscene material if it did not know and had no reason to suspect that the programme or material would include material making it liable to be convicted of an offence. A service provider hosting a Usenet newsgroup involving suspicious sounding names would probably not be able to take advantage of this defence as it would probably know, or should have suspected, that the material was obscene.

On-line service providers are also concerned about the implications of the recent conviction of the director of CompuServe in Germany who was sentenced to two years in prison and a fine (suspended) for the distribution of child pornography through newsgroups. The Internet community was shocked by this result, partly because the

---

[54] Telecommunications Act 1984, section 43(1).
[55] Sexual Offenes (Conspiracy and Incitement) Act 1996.
[56] Obscene Publications Act 1959, section 2(5).

director and company had taken steps to block the newsgroups it was told about and then discovered as a result of its own investigations. In addition, German legislation provided defences broadly similar to the U.K. defences described above (no knowledge or reason to suspect material was obscene), which many thought would protect the director. Commentators take the view that the case was wrongly decided and the case is currently under appeal.

The on-line community is taking steps to self-regulate. Organisations such as the Internet Watch Foundation and the Internet Service Providers Association have been set up to self-regulate areas including cyber porn.

Travel

2.54   Airlines and businesses in the travel sector have proved to be amongst the earliest success stories of electronic commerce. Airlines have regarded Internet sales and E-tickets as means of reducing distribution costs and saving money in terms of ticketing paperwork and staffing. However, the travel industry is heavily regulated. The Package Travel, Package Holidays and Package Tour Regulations 1992 (the "Package Travel Regulations") apply to those who organise and sell "packages" (as defined) or those to whom packages are sold, in other words tour operators and travel agents. The Package Tour Regulations will apply to material placed on the worldwide web. The extent of application depends upon whether, before booking, a customer obtains additional information from other sources or if a customer can book directly from the Internet without obtaining any other information. In addition, the Civil Aviation (Air Travel Organiser's Licensing) Regulations 1995 may also apply. In most respects material on the world wide web for sale of travel and holidays is regulated in the same way to brochure material.

2.55   The Package Travel Regulations only apply to "packages" sold or offered for sale in the U.K. A package is defined as a pre-arranged combination of at least two of three components, namely transport, accommodation, and other tourist services not ancillary to transport or accommodation and accounting for a significant proportion of the package. Regulation 4 provides that a tour operator or travel agent is liable to compensate a consumer for any loss suffered as a result of misleading information contained in any descriptive matter concerning a package, the price of a package or other conditions applying to the contract. Hence, any inaccuracy in any descriptive material on the Internet which concerns a package does create the risk of a civil claim for damages, whether for a tour operator or travel agent

Consumer is defined in the Package Travel Regulations as the person who "takes or agrees to take the package . . .". Hence, before Regulation 4 has any application a booking will have to have been made. The consumer will need to demonstrate not only loss but that that loss arose as a result of misleading information in the Internet material.

Regulation 5 is concerned with brochures and imposes various requirements about the contents of brochures. While, at first blush, this might seem wholly inapplicable, ABTA and various Trading Standards Officers have publicly stated that they regard any material from which a package can be booked as constituting a brochure for the purposes of Regulation 5.

2.56   Regulation 7 provides that, before a contract is made, a customer must be given information about passport and visa requirements applicable to British citizens, about health formalities required for the journey and the stay and the financial protection arrangements entered into by the tour operator providing the package. Hence, material on the world wide web will need to contain this information, unless it can be guaranteed that, before a contract is made, customers will be given this information from another source.

Where material on the Internet does not contain the information required by Regulation 5 and/or Regulation 7 but that information is contained in a brochure tour operators are advised to refer specifically to such a brochure, and to include a statement that the details which are contained on the Internet are not full details but merely introductory ones.

Regulation 9 provides that, before the contract is made, the consumer must be given the terms of the contract "in writing or such other form as is comprehensible and accessible".

The effect of Regulation 9 is that the information detailed above would either have to be contained in the material on the Internet or, if not, given to the customer before the issue of a confirmation invoice. If the terms are not given to consumers before the contract is made, they will not be incorporated in the contract. Particularly where there are terms limiting liability and taking advantage of compensation limits in International Conventions, it would be somewhat unfortunate, to say the least, to lose that protection.

COMPETITION LAW

Introduction

As discussed elsewhere, general principles of law have and will prove themselves well able to adapt to the new environment of electronic commerce. The same can be said for competition law whose application to electronic commerce and new electronic media is already being seen in anti-trust scrutiny of mergers and joint ventures between companies in converging telecoms and media industries; the review and replacement of the U.S. Government's contract with NSI; the major E.U. push for de-regulation in the telecommunication field; and challenges brought by competition authorities in the U.S. and the E.U. against alleged abuses by Microsoft. **2.57**

What is clear is that even though the new environment presents new challenges, the same general principles of competition law will apply to conduct affecting electronic commerce as to any other type of commercial activity.

E.C. Competition law

The main pillars of E.C. competition law are found in Articles 85 and 86 of the Treaty of Rome, in the E.C. Merger Regulation[57] and in the regulations made under the Treaty of Rome. **2.58**

Article 85 — 81

Article 85 provides as follows: **2.59**

---

[57] Council Regulations 4064/89 and 1310/97.

"1. The following shall be prohibited as incompatible with the common market: all agreements between undertakings, decisions by associations of undertakings and concerted practices which may affect trade between Member States and which have as their object or effect the prevention, restriction or distortion of competition within the common market, and in particular those which:
  (a) directly or indirectly fix purchase or selling prices or any other trading conditions;
  (b) limit or control production, markets, technical development, or investment;
  (c) share markets or sources of supply;
  (d) apply dissimilar conditions to equivalent transactions with other trading parties, thereby placing them at a competitive disadvantage;
  (e) make the conclusion of contracts subject to acceptance by the other parties of supplementary obligations which, by their nature or according to commercial usage, have no connection with the subject of such contracts.

2. Any agreements or decisions prohibited pursuant to this Article shall be automatically void.

3. The provisions of paragraph 1 may, however, be declared inapplicable in the case of:
  — any agreement or category of agreements between undertakings;
  — any decision or category of decisions by associations of undertakings;
  — any concerted practice or category of concerted practices;

which contributes to improving the production or distribution of goods or to promoting technical or economic progress, while allowing consumers a fair share of the resulting benefit, and which does not;

  (a) impose on the undertakings concerned restrictions which are not indispensable to the attainment of these objectives;
  (b) afford such undertakings the possibility of eliminating competition in respect of a substantial part of the products in question."

In brief, the main elements are as follows:

2.60
- *'agreements . . . decisions . . . concerted practices'*
  There is no requirement for a formal written agreement for Article 85 to apply. An agreement may be oral, informal or a "gentleman's agreement". An agreement may also be inferred from the conduct of the parties and this would include e-mails or agreements made electronically. 'Concerted practices' denotes co-ordinated conduct which may fall short of a concluded agreement; practical co-operation replaces the risks of competition.[58]

- *'undertakings'*
  To fall within Article 85, an agreement must be between undertakings. This term is defined very broadly and includes all natural and legal persons carrying on a commercial or economic activity. Whether or not a profit is realised, is irrelevant.[59] Although, in the absence of dominance, Article 85 would not catch

---

[58] See *ICI v. Commission* [1972] E.C.R. 619.
[59] See *Van Landewyck v. Commission* [1980] E.C.R. 3125.

unilateral conduct by one undertaking, the Commission may readily infer agreements (such as a network of smaller agreements) in order to capture an anti-competitive activity.

- *'restriction of competition'*   **2.61**
Article 85 prohibits agreements whose object or effect is to prevent, restrict or distort competition. It does not matter whether it is the object of the agreement to restrict competition or is merely the effect.

Article 85(1) sets out a non-exclusive list of examples of the types of restrictions which might be caught. A practical example which can be given is in relation to comparison-shopping on the Internet. Junglee and Netbot are both Internet comparison-shopping companies. Consumers visiting their websites are offered a service to find the best price for a product. Junglee has recently been acquired by Amazon.com, which sells books and CDs. If it chooses not to permit Junglee to provide price comparisons with other booksellers then whilst this might be restrictive of competition in a broad sense, it would not be caught by Article 85(1) because agreements between parents and subsidiaries are not caught.

Netbot has also been acquired, by Excite. Netbot may now not comparison-shop for books and CDs: consumers being allowed to search only one bookseller — Amazon. If this was a result of a market-sharing agreement or other restrictive agreement between Excite and Amazon, then this could be caught by Article 85(1) if the other criteria of Article 85 were satisfied (in terms of market foreclosure and effect on trade between Member States, which are considered below).

- *'effect on trade between Member States'*
In order for an agreement to be caught by Article 85 there must be an effect on trade between Member States. The pattern of trade must be influenced, directly or indirectly, actually or potentially. Where an agreement encompasses the whole territory of a Member State then it will be considered to have an intra-community effect. In the case of electronic commerce its universal scope means that this requirement should easily be satisfied.

Appreciability

In determining whether an agreement is caught by Article 85, the effect on trade   **2.62**
between Member States must be appreciable. Agreements of minor importance are ignored. The Commission has issued a statement of its policy, the Notice on Agreements of Minor Importance. Under the Notice, the Commission states that as a matter of policy (*i.e.* it may change and is not binding on national courts) it does not consider that an agreement will have an appreciable effect on competition if the parties combined market share is less than 5 per cent (for horizontal agreements) or 10 per cent (for vertical agreements).[60]

New approach to vertical restraints

Following extensive consultation by the Commission on proposals to reform the current   **2.63**
vertical restraints policy, the Commission has confirmed that it will adopt a single "very

---

[60] Commission Notice of January 30, 1997 (97/C29/03).

wide block exemption" to replace the existing categories of block exemptions. The framework of the proposed new block exemption will exempt from the scope of Article 85 all restraints which are not "black listed", unless the undertakings concerned exceed certain market share thresholds. Key features of the new block exemption regulation will be the following:

- Unlike previous block exemptions, it will now include both intermediate and final products, and also includes both goods and services. There will therefore no longer be any doubt as to its application to the software industry.

- The benefit of the block exemption will be limited by market share thresholds. It is not yet decided whether there will be a single or dual market share thresholds. If there is to be a single-threshold system, the benefit of the umbrella block exemption would be withdrawn completely when the market shares exceed 25–35 per cent. In the event of a dual-threshold system being adopted, the main market share threshold would be 20 per cent, above which there would be scope for exempting certain vertical restraints up to a higher level of about 40 per cent. The dual-threshold system thus provides for a graduated series of exemptions.

- Agreements falling within the safe harbour would be presumed to be legal. Those falling outside the safe harbour would not be presumed to be illegal but might require individual examination. The Commission would have the burden of proof to establish that the agreement was in breach of Article 85(1).

- National courts and national competition authorities will be given the power to determine when to withdraw the application of the block exemption, and also to determine whether or not the agreement benefited from the block exemption in the first place.

- The following will be considered to be hardcore restrictions that always fall outside the scope of the block exemption:

  - fixed resale prices or minimum resale prices

  - maximum resale prices

  - restrictions on active or passive resales (other than the case of exclusive distribution)

  - restrictions on members of a selective distribution system from selling to unauthorised distributors

  - restriction of cross-supplies between distributors at the same or different levels of distribution in an exclusive or selective distribution system

  - a prohibition on the supplier of an intermediate good not to sell the same good as a repair or a replacement good to the independent aftermarket

  - the combination, at the same level of distribution, of selective distribution and exclusive customer allocation.

The Commission Notice specifically states that agreements where the buyer of software sells on this software to the final consumer without obtaining any copyright over the software are considered to be agreements for the supply of goods for resale for the purposes of the block exemption.

Article 86   —8ᒪ

Unlike Article 85, which is concerned with anti-competitive agreements, Article 86 prohibits the abuse of a dominant position in a particular market. Article 86 provides:

2.64

"Any abuse by one or more undertakings of a dominant position within the common market or in a substantial part of it shall be prohibited as incompatible with the common market in so far as it may affect trade between Member States.
Such abuse may, in particular, consist in:

    (a) directly or indirectly imposing unfair purchase or selling prices or other unfair trading conditions;
    (b) limiting production, markets or technical development to the prejudice of consumers;
    (c) applying dissimilar conditions to equivalent transactions with other trading parties, thereby placing them at a competitive disadvantage;
    (d) making the conclusion of contracts subject to acceptance by the other parties of supplementary obligations which, by their nature or according to commercial usage, have no connection with the subject of such contracts."

In determining a party's position on a market it is necessary to define the relevant product and geographic market within which a party operates. In addition, the whole concept of electronic commerce raises questions as to the jurisdictional application of the competition rules (at national as well as E.C. level).

Geographic market

The very nature of the Internet is its global reach. A restrictive agreement between electronic commerce businesses can have universal effects. The Commission will have jurisdiction to investigate and enforce competition rules where effects are felt within the E.C., even though the parties may not have any physical connection with the E.C.[61]

2.65

Traditional constraints on the scope of a particular geographic market, such as transportation costs, are irrelevant in the context of electronic commerce. As a result, other factors may come into play in narrowing the scope of the market, such as language or even territorial restrictions on the face of the webpage soliciting interest. For example, an electronic commerce site offered only in Greek or Danish may lead to a market being defined by reference to Greece or Denmark.

Product market

Jurisprudence from the European Court of Justice requires a product market to be defined by reference to the products' characteristics which mean they are "particularly apt to satisfy an inelastic need and are only to a limited extent interchangeable with other products."[62] To the extent electronic commerce is only another vehicle by which

2.66

---

[61] See *the Wood Pulp case* [1985] E.C.R. 5193.
[62] See *Europemballage & Continental Can v. Commission* [1973] E.C.R. 215.

merchants sell their products, products sold over the Internet may not be defined as a separate product market. On the other hand, the Commission has been known to define product markets very narrowly, such as for spare parts.[63]

Dominance

2.67 In order to be caught by Article 86, a party must be in a position of dominance. Dominance has been defined as the ability to an appreciable extent to act independently of customers, suppliers and competitors. Many factors will be taken into account, including: market shares (including relative to other competitors); access to sources of supply and capital; technical knowledge of the undertaking and its competitors; barriers to entry; and the exclusionary effect of any distribution network.

The most important initial indicator is market share. A market share of 40 per cent has been held to constitute dominance and 85 per cent is conclusive evidence of dominance.[64]

Abuse

2.68 Article 86 gives a number of examples of abuse. Abuse may consist of exploitation of customers, exclusion of potential competitors, discrimination without objective justification and may occur on a market on which the dominant undertaking is not dominant. The most significant case in relation to such abuse is the current battle between Microsoft and the U.S. anti-trust authorities concerning Netscape, and the bundling by Microsoft of its Internet browser with its operating system (currently Microsoft Windows 98). Whether this is simply the addition of a new application or illegal tying by a dominant supplier remains to be determined by the courts.

U.K. Competition Act 1998

2.69 Receiving the Royal Assent in November 1998, the Competition Act substantially redraws the landscape in the U.K. for competition regulation. The new law has the following key features:

- The new law is a prohibition-based system modeled on Articles 85 and 86 of the E.C. Treaty of Rome and prohibits anti-competitive agreements and the abuse of a dominant position.

- Current domestic competition legislation — the Restrictive Trade Practices Act, the Resale Prices Act and most of the Competition Act — will be repealed.

- Individual, block and parallel exemptions may be granted.

- Fines of up to 10 per cent of U.K. turnover may be imposed for breaches.

- Sanctions may be imposed on corporate officers personally.

- Protection will be given to agreements already exempted under E.U. law.

- The Director General of Fair Trading will have extensive powers of investigation and enforcement.

---

[63] See *Hugin v. Commission* [1979] E.C.R. 1869.
[64] See *United Brands* [1978] E.C.R. 207; *Hoffman La Roche* [1979] E.C.R. 461.

- The Office of Fair Trading will be primarily responsible for enforcing competition law.

- Sector regulators, including in particular Oftel, will have concurrent powers of enforcement with the OFT.

The Chapter I Prohibition

Section 2(1) of the Act prohibits agreements which may affect trade within the U.K. and which may prevent, restrict or distort competition. The wording of the prohibition is substantively the same as the wording in Article 85(1) (which is set out above).   **2.70**

The Chapter I Prohibition sets out a non-exhaustive list of prohibitive practices, similar to Article 85:

- Fixing, purchasing or selling prices or other trading conditions.

- Limiting or controlling production, markets, technical development or investment.

- Sharing markets or sources of supply.

- Applying dissimilar provisions to equivalent transactions with other trading parties.

- Making the conclusion of contracts subject to acceptance of supplementary obligations which have no connection with the subject matter of such contracts.

Offending provisions are automatically void and unenforceable. The effect of this could be to render an agreement unenforceable, any amounts due irrecoverable and any intellectual property rights licensed unenforceable.

Section 60 of the Act requires that, as far as possible, the U.K. authorities and courts interpret the prohibition of anti-competitive agreements in a manner which is not inconsistent with the principles laid down by the Treaty of Rome and the European Court in respect of E.C. competition law, with decisions of the ECJ and of the Commission, and also to have regard to any statements made by the Commission.

The Government's intention is that the Chapter I prohibition apply to horizontal agreements (*i.e.* between undertakings operating in the same level of production and distribution) and that, in general, the majority of vertical agreements (*i.e.* between undertakings operating in different levels of the production distribution chain) should be excluded on the basis that such agreements do not raise competition concerns. It is intended that specific provisions be introduced to exclude vertical agreements from the scope of the Chapter I Prohibition (other than in the cases of price-fixing agreements and reciprocal agreements between competitors).

Exemptions

The Director General of Fair Trading has power to grant individual exemptions. An   **2.71**
individual exemption may be granted retroactively and subject to conditions and obligations. Any exemption granted must be for a fixed term although this may be extended. In order to gain an individual exemption, the agreement must satisfy certain criteria which are the same as those set out in Article 85 (3) of the Treaty of Rome (as set out above).

The Director General is empowered under section 6 to recommend to the Secretary of State that certain classes of agreement which satisfy the exemption criteria should be exempted by way of a block exemption. An agreement which satisfies the criteria of any block exemption (either one specifically made under the U.K. Competition Act or under regulations of the European Commission) will be automatically exempt from the Chapter I Prohibition and there would then be no need to notify the agreement to the Director General for an individual exemption. As noted above in the discussion concerning Article 85, the environment for block exemptions under E.C. competition law is being revised through the introduction of an over-arching block exemption.

The Chapter II Prohibition

2.72   The prohibition on the abuse of a dominant position (introduced by section 18(2) as the "Chapter II Prohibition") is the most radical change to U.K. competition law. The prohibition is based very closely on Article 86 of the E.C. Treaty (which is set out above). Although certain types of conduct will be excluded by the legislation, no exemption can be granted from the prohibition. In addition, there will be a procedure under which clearance can be obtained from the Director General. Breach of the prohibition may result in the imposition of fines. The Director General will also be able to impose "cease and desist" orders.

The key elements of the Chapter II Prohibition are:

- any conduct amounting to an abuse
- of a dominant position in a market
- within any part of the U.K.
- by one or more undertakings
- which may effect trade within the U.K. or any part of it

De minimis

2.73   Guidance Notes will be issued by the OFT and from the draft of the Guidance Notes the following points can be made:

- The Chapter I Prohibition applies to agreements which have an "appreciable" or significant effect on competition. The OFT takes the view that agreements will have no appreciable effect on competition if the parties' market share does not exceed 10 per cent.
- Regardless of the market share held by the parties an agreement will be considered to be caught by the Chapter I Prohibition if it is made between competitors and directly or indirectly fixes prices or shares markets.
- Other factors will also be relevant such as entry conditions or the characteristics of buyers and the structure of the buyers' side of the market.
- There is intended to be an annual turnover threshold below which the Director General will not impose penalties for breaches of the Chapter I Prohibition.
- In relation to the Chapter II Prohibition a firm with a market share below 20–25 per cent will generally not be regarded as dominant.

- Conduct of minor significance is excluded from the scope of the Chapter II Prohibition and it is intended that an annual turnover threshold be set for determining what amounts to conduct of minor significance.

Investigation and Enforcement

The Director General will have primary responsibility for investigation and enforcement of the competition laws. His/her powers are intended to be comparable to those of the European Commission and he/she will have the following powers:

2.74

- To enter and search premises — unannounced where necessary.

- To examine and copy documents.

- To require "on the spot" explanations of documents found.

- To impose interim measures pending completion of the investigation.

Failing to cooperate with the Director General will be a criminal offence. If the Director General finds that there has been an infringement of either the Chapter I or Chapter II Prohibitions, he/she may give directions to bring the infringement to an end and this include the termination or modification of an agreement or conduct.

Conclusion on Competition Law

The introduction into domestic U.K. law of competition rules substantively the same as Articles 85 and 86 of the E.C. Treaty of Rome means that, given the global nature of electronic commerce, conduct which might not meet the appreciability test for purposes of E.C. law might well meet the test within the domestic U.K. market. Since the Competition Act imports E.C. jurisprudence to assist in interpreting the Chapter I and Chapter II Prohibitions, Commission decisions and notices regarding some of the cases discussed earlier in this section will be relevant in determining, for example, whether particular conduct might be abusive or constitute restrictions of competition.

2.75

— • 3 • —

ON-LINE CONTRACTS

> "In some areas, government agreements may prove necessary to facilitate electronic commerce and protect consumers. In these cases, governments should establish a predictable and simple legal environment based on a decentralised, contractual model of law rather than one based on top-down regulation."[1]

In the past, most on-line or electronic contracts were conducted in the context of Electronic Data Interchange (EDI). EDI systems, for example, linked suppliers with retailers and assembly plants with parts manufacturers in order to reduce inventory, automate reordering procedures and eliminate paper work. These systems were imposed on continuing relationships and thus pre-agreed 'interchange agreements' or 'trading partner agreements' could be made. The agreements, many of which were available in 'model' form, were overriding contracts that specified everything pertaining to the future relationship: on-line contract formation; attribution of risk; operation procedures; security; even technical aspects such as the standard format of the data fields. Since interchange agreements were extremely detailed and explicit, very little litigation occurred in the area, making the structure they imposed a legal success. **3.01**

In sharp contrast, electronic commerce and the new on-line contracts of cyberspace do not necessarily involve parties in a continuing relationship. Rather, electronic commerce typically deals with real time, one-off transactions between parties who have never met. Thus, on-line contracts no longer have the luxury of a pre-agreed umbrella agreement that settles disputes; instead, parties must rely on their standard terms and conditions and the courts' interpretation of the law.

Electronic commerce businesses and consumers alike have clamoured for legislation to deal with the lack of internet specific laws. Many wonder whether English law can cope with transactions in the fast developing and virtual world of cyberspace. As this chapter shows, in most cases the English legal system does indeed possess the flexibility and laws to deal with this new commercial medium. Electronic commerce is not lawless and on-line contracts fit very nicely into the English law framework. **3.02**

---

[1] U.S. President William J. Clinton and Vice President Albert Gore, Jr., "A Framework for Global Electronic Commerce," March 18, 1998, Washington, D.C. **http://www.iitf.nist.gov/elecomm/ecomm.htm.**

This chapter deals with on-line contracts, from their inception to their completion. It is divided up into five sections. Paragraph 3.03 gives an introductory view of contracts and discusses the various subjects with which on-line contracts will likely deal. Paragraph 3.10 examines pre-contractual considerations, such as advertisements and 'knowing the customer.' Paragraph 3.28 deals with on-line contract formation and applies to the on-line environment the four contractual requirements: offer; acceptance; consideration and intent to create legal relations. Paragraph 3.58 addresses writing and signatures, conventions left over from the paper world, and how they will figure in the realm of electronic commerce. Paragraph 3.68 analyses standard terms and conditions; what they should include and how on-line vendors should display them.

CONTRACTS AND TYPES OF CONTRACTS

3.03   A contract is an agreement which will be enforced by the law. In general, English law allows contracts to be formed in any available manner — orally, by telephone, by written document or by fax. It even allows a contract to be formed on the basis of the conduct of the parties. Accordingly, people are not debarred from forming legally binding contracts by e-mail and the world wide web. The virtual or 'digital' nature of the agreement theoretically presents no impediment to its recognition under English law.

Some jurisdictions and model laws, concerned about the legal recognition of electronic contracts, have offered specific legislation affirming their validity. For example, the Model Law on Electronic Commerce of the United Nations Commission on International Trade Law (UNCITRAL) states:

> "In the context of contract formation, unless otherwise agreed by the parties, an offer and the acceptance of an offer may be expressed by means of data messages. Where a data message is used in the formation of a contract, that contract shall not be denied validity or enforceability on the sole ground that a data message was used for that purpose or stored by electronic, optical or similar means, including electronic mail."[2]

3.04   A 'data message' is defined as "information generated, sent, received." Singapore enacted a similar clause in its Electronic Transactions Act in July 1998. So far, the U.K. has not passed such specific legislation (although it has been promised by the Government), but there is no reason to believe that contracts made on-line will be treated any differently by the courts than those made by conventional methods simply because the contract has been made on-line.

On-line contracts and sales typically fall under three categories: goods, services, and digitised services. These three distinctions are important to on-line businesses when considering laws on consumer protection, implied terms and liability because many statutes define their scope based on whether a purchase is a good or a service.

---

[2] UNCITRAL Model Law on Electronic Commerce (1996), Article 11(1).

Goods

Under the Sale of Goods Act 1979 (as amended by the Sale and Supply of Goods Act 1994), goods are defined as "all personal chattels other than things in action or money."[3] This includes consumer products such as toys, clothing, and books. Electronic sales of goods will usually involve ordering over the Internet (either through e-mail or a website) and a shipment of the goods by post or courier to the purchaser. Traditionally, a transfer of tangible property is required for a sale of goods but, as paragraph 3.07 below considers, this convention may change to accommodate the sale of digital information.   **3.05**

Thus a sale of goods over the Internet is governed by the Sale of Goods Act 1979. Among other things (pre-contractual representations, etc.), the Act requires that:

> "Where the seller sells goods in the course of a business, there is an implied term that the goods supplied under the contract are of satisfactory quality."[4]

To determine satisfactory quality, a court considers whether the particular item was reasonably fit for its intended purpose, its price, defects, and other relevant attributes.

Services

Over the years, the courts have sought to distinguish between goods and services. It is not always immediately apparent. The general overriding conclusion is that a service is where "the substance of the contract . . . is that skill and labour have to be exercised,"[5] or where the contract between supplier and consumer is unique in each case.[6] For example, purchasing a copy of standard software at a store is a sale of goods; a contract with a firm to write bespoke software is a sale of services.   **3.06**

Services, which include on-line banking, financial services, and gambling, are governed under the Supply of Goods and Services Act 1982, which imposes significantly less stringent standards on the merchant. Instead of requiring satisfactory quality, the contractor need only perform the service with reasonable care and skill to the degree "expected of a professional man of ordinary competence and experience."[7] In other words, the law focuses more on the ability of the performer, not necessarily the end result of his/her actions.

Digitised services

The Internet offers the opportunity to do what Negroponte calls "being digital."[8] Certain products, such as software, video, books, music, and even newspapers and magazines, no longer have to be physically delivered in hard copy format to the purchaser.   **3.07**

---

[3] Sale of Goods Act 1979 (as amended 1994), s.61(1) and Supply of Goods and Service Act 1982, s.18. The same definition is used in Section 14 of the Torts (Interference with Goods) Act 1977.
[4] Sale of Goods Act 1979 (as amended), s.14.
[5] As in the case of an artist painting a person's portrait. *Robinson v. Graves* [1935] 1 K.B. 579 at 587.
[6] As (in the United States) the case of contact lenses. *Barbee·v. Rogers* 425 SW2d 342 (1968).
[7] *Chitty on Contracts* 13–024.
[8] Nicholas Negroponte, *Being Digital*, New York, A.A. Knopf, 1995.

Suppliers can instead send the products in digital form over the Internet providing both time and cost savings.

However, a new question arises concerning digitised services: are they goods or services? As previously mentioned, electronic commerce businesses will find this distinction important because it determines the terms implied into the contract (see paragraph 3.78) and therefore the standard of quality that their products will have to satisfy.

U.K. courts have been far from definitive on whether digitised services and digital information constitute 'goods.' For example, in the Scottish case of *Beta Computers (Europe) Ltd v. Adobe Systems (Europe) Ltd,*[9] the court essentially regarded a contract for standard, non-customised software as *sui generis* (*i.e.* the only one of its kind):

> "It was not an order for the supply of disks as such. On the other hand, it was not an order for the supply of information as such. The subject of the contract was a complex product comprising the medium and the manifestation within it or on it of the intellectual property of the author."[10]

3.08   In contrast, the leading Court of Appeal case of *St Albans City and District Council v. International Computers Ltd,*[11] the highest judicial consideration so far in the U.K. of whether software is goods adhered to a traditional good-service distinction, Sir Iain Glidewell decided that while a computer program on a disk clearly falls within the definition of a 'good,' a computer program *per se* did not:

> "In both the Sale of Goods Act 1979, s 61, and the Supply of Goods and Services Act 1982, s 18, the definition of goods includes 'all personal chattels other than things in action and money.' Clearly, a disk is within this definition. Equally clearly, a program, of itself, is not."[12]

The judgment in *St Albans*, however, runs into difficulty when applied to digitised services. If *St Albans* were not confined to its particular facts, it could lead to an illogical situation where identical digital products fell under different regimes merely because they were sold using a different medium. Computer programs sold to the licensee on a floppy disk would be goods, whereas programs transmitted directly via the Internet or over the telecommunications system would constitute a service. Similarly, a video bought at the store on a VHS tape would be a good but video-on-demand would not.

3.09   These illogical distinctions are likely to mean that the English courts will view digitised services as a dematerialised form of goods. In *Advent Systems Limited v. Unisys Corporation,*[13] the U.S. Court of Appeal for the third Circuit felt that there were strong policy arguments for classifying mass market software as goods:

---

[9] *Beta Computers (Europe) Ltd v. Adobe Systems (Europe) Ltd* 1996 S.L.T. 604.
[10] *ibid.* at 608 (cited in Lloyd 415).
[11] *St Albans City and District Council v. International Computers Ltd* [1996] 4 All E.R. 481. First instance at [1995] F.S.R. 686.
[12] *St Albans v. ICL* [1996] 4 All E.R. at 493. However, though a computer program is not a good (and therefore is not subject to the statutory implied term as to satisfactory quality), Glidewell L.J. ruled *doita dicta* that the quality term is still implied under common law.
[13] *Advent Systems Limited v. Unisys Corporation* (1991) 925 F.2d 670, U.S. CA, Third Circle, LEXIS 2396.

"Computer programs are the product of an intellectual process, but once implanted in a medium are widely distributed to computer owners. An analogy can be drawn to a compact disc recording of an orchestral rendition. The music is produced by the artistry of musicians and in itself is not a "good," but when transferred to a laser-readable disc becomes a readily merchantable commodity. Similarly, when a professor delivers a lecture, it is not a good, but, when transcribed as a book, it becomes a good."[14]

Although the court in *Advent* refers specifically to intellectual property placed in a tangible form (book, disk, etc.), there is no reason why intellectual properties available in digitally-packaged form cannot be considered as merchantable commodities. Placing the software, music, or information into digital form is conceptually equivalent to placing it into a book, compact disc, or other tangible medium. Further emphasising the point, digital data have attributes which most closely resemble tangible goods; they are 'moved,' 'distributed,' 'stored,' etc. An alternative view is that they are certainly not services because they do not create a unique contractual relationship, nor do they depend on the exercise of skill or labour, and therefore should be considered as goods.

Back in the nineteenth century, a court once symbolically viewed the telegraph as a virtual pen of "copper wire a thousand miles long."[15] Using a similar mental leap, courts in the future are likely to view digitised services as a virtual version of 'goods' in order to maintain a consistent legal framework.

PRE-CONTRACT CONSIDERATIONS

Before transacting a sale and forming a contract with a customer, electronic commerce merchants have to create a presence on the Internet through a website, newsgroup advertisement, electronic mail list, etc. The culture of cyberspace encourages an attitude of 'anything goes,' with the principal maxim being *caveat emptor* (let the buyer beware). However, electronic commerce is just like any other form of commercial activity and is bound by the same regulations and legal principles regarding pre-contractual behaviour. In addition, electronic commerce businesses may need to verify the identity of their customers, since they may not wish (or may not be legally allowed) to transact with all people from all jurisdictions. Failure to observe these considerations can have a major impact on the performance and enforceability of the subsequent contract.

3.10

Advertisement

Advertising and other means of promoting goods and services are subject to many regulations which vary significantly among different jurisdictions. For example, Germany has strict rules against comparative advertising in contrast to both the U.K. and the U.S.[16] Some advertising is further regulated by industry-specific rules (*e.g.* tobacco,

3.11

---

[14] *ibid.* at 675.
[15] *Howley v. Whipple (U.S.)* 48 N.H. 487 (1869).
[16] Unfair Competition Act (Germany), section 1. Cited in Dennis Campbell, ed., *Law of International On-Line Business*, London, Sweet and Maxwell, 1998.

bookmaking and gambling) and where it is aimed at a particular audience (such as children). A detailed examination of global advertising laws is beyond the scope of this book, although a more detailed analysis of U.K. advertising law can be found in Chapter 8. Nevertheless, the pre-contractual claims and representations made in advertising can have a significant impact on the resulting contract. And this section addresses those concerns.

Unilateral v. Bilateral contracts

3.12 Generally, contracts are bilateral, meaning that both parties are bound; there is "the exchange of a promise for a promise."[17] For example, when a person orders merchandise from a website, a bilateral contract is formed because the merchant promises to send the goods in exchange and the customer promises to pay.

However, on-line advertisements can create unilateral contracts, where only one party (*i.e.* the advertiser) is bound.[18] In a unilateral contract, an announcement offers money or some other reward for the performance of an action, and this announcement is considered to be a standing offer. The accepting party does not need to notify the advertiser; he/she only needs to do the required act. The well-known case of *Carlill v. Carbolic Smoke Ball Co. Ltd* concerned unilateral contracts. The defendant offered £100 to any person who contracted influenza after using its smoke balls as directed. The plaintiff did exactly as suggested, caught influenza, and sued for the £100; the court enforced the contract. Unilateral contracts are not only dangerous because a careless advertisement can create legal obligations, but also because they can be enforced by multiple parties. As Bowens L.J. suggested in *Carlill*, "It is an offer made to all the world."[19] If five people had used the smoke balls and contracted influenza, Carbolic would have been liable for £500; if ten, £1000.

On-line advertisements therefore need to be carefully drafted to ensure that customers (and the courts) interpret them as advertisements, not unilateral contracts; otherwise a company with a website offering £500 to anyone finding a bug in its program may find itself liable for more money than originally anticipated. Merchants can use disclaimers to emphasise that the 'webvertisement' is only an advertisement or an invitation to treat, not an offer or unilateral contract.

Express Terms

3.13 Historically, one principal problem faced by the courts in this area was whether a representation (often verbal) made prior to contract creation constituted an express term, even though it was not detailed in the written contract. At first, this possibility appears unlikely, since according to the parol evidence rule,

> "if there is a contract which has been reduced to writing, verbal evidence is not allowed to be given so as to add to or subtract from, or in any manner to vary or qualify the written contract."[20]

---

[17] *Chitty on Contracts*, 1-022.
[18] *Restatement of Contracts* (1932) section 12. *Restatement of Contracts* (2d, 1981) section 45 renames unilateral contracts as "option contracts." *Chitty on Contracts*, 1–022.
[19] *Carlill v. Carbolic Smoke Ball Co. Ltd.* [1892] 2 Q.B. 484; affd [1893] 1 Q.B. 256.
[20] *Goss v. Lord Nugent* (1833) 5 B. & Ad. 58 at 64, cited in *Chitty* 12–081.

This restriction is not limited to oral evidence; it also includes drafts, preliminary agreements, and other prior representations.[21] As a result, the weight and finality given to written contracts seems exceptionally high. If one assumes that computer documents constitute writing (paragraph 3.60), on-line contracts should theoretically be subject to only the specified terms.

However, the ambit of the parol evidence rule is extremely restricted; it applies only in instances where the court finds that the contract lies solely in the document. Thus, a court may find that part of the contract was verbal or in a previous statement, or, in the case of on-line contracts, in another e-mail or on a different web page. As the court ruled in *J. Evans & Son (Portsmouth) Ltd v. Andrea Merzario Ltd*, "the court is entitled to look at and should look at all the evidence from start to finish in order to see what the bargain was that was struck between the parties."[22] As a result, on-line statements made by e-mail or on web pages prior to contract formation may be interpreted as express contractual terms, despite their absence from the 'actual' contract written or otherwise. In addition, in the interests of fairness or justice, the courts might also use the Misrepresentation Act 1967 (paragraph 3.14) or the concept of collateral contract (paragraph 3.15) to hold an on-line merchant liable or contractually bound to a prior representation.

The lesson to be learned is that, if an on-line customer enters into a contract due to some representation made by the electronic commerce business, the courts have many ways of holding the electronic commerce business responsible. The representation can possibly be an express contractual term even (though not explicitly stated in the same location) part of a collateral contract, or a misrepresentation under the Misrepresentation Act 1967.

Misrepresentations

Pre-contractual statements or conduct, though they may not form actual contractual **3.14** terms, do nonetheless affect a contractee's decision-making process. Hence, both common law and the Misrepresentation Act 1967 hold suppliers accountable for any untrue statements of fact which induce the customer to enter into a contract. A victim of misrepresentation may affirm the contract or seek a remedy in the courts and obtain damages and/or rescission of the contract depending on whether the misrepresentation was made fraudulently, negligently, or innocently.[23]

Electronic commerce does not raise any new issues in this area. The Misrepresentation Act and the common law apply to on-line contracts just as to conventional ones and will impose liability for untrue statements of fact made on websites, by e-mail or elsewhere in cyberspace.

---

[21] *Chitty* 12–081.

[22] *J. Evans & Son (Portsmouth) Ltd v. Andrea Merzario Ltd* [1976] 1 W.L.R. 1078 at 1083.

[23] For specifics on misrepresentation law, the reader is referred to a standard text on contracts, such as *Chitty*.

Collateral Contracts

> A millionaire goes to a website and reads the technical specification of an satellite navigation system. She commissions the construction of a yacht and in her contract with the boat builder specifies that the yacht should use the particular satellite navigation system. The system is faulty and in consequence the yacht hits a submerged rock and sinks.

3.15 A collateral contract is one which is independent of, but subordinate to, an agreement affecting the same subject matter. If a representation induces a person to form a contract with a third party, the court may hold that there was a collateral contract with the representation. For example, in *Shanklin Pier Ltd v. Detel Products Ltd,*[24] the plaintiff relied on representations made by the defendant, a paint manufacturer, regarding the suitability of its paint, to form a contract with a third party, a painting contractor. (The contract stipulated the use of the defendant's paint.) When the plaintiff discovered that the paint was inappropriate, it successfully sued the defendant for damages under a collateral contract.

Product statements on a website can constitute the grounds for a collateral contract (possibly formed unbeknownst to the site owner). In the above scenario the millionaire may have a claim against the manufacturers of the satellite navigation system under a collateral contract. Thus, even if a business uses a website for purely promotional purposes and does not anticipate creating contracts on-line, it still must take care not to make misrepresentations.

Verifying Identity: Knowing the customer

3.16 On-line merchants do not want to sell goods or services to everyone on the Internet. For example, trade embargoes may block sales to particular countries, (*e.g.* Iraq, Libya, Cuba); local laws may prohibit the sale of certain goods or content (*e.g.* tobacco, pornography, etc.) to minors. Further, how does an electronic commerce organisation know that the on-line person has the authority to buy or transact? Children purchasing goods without permission or the means to pay and hackers manipulating financial accounts are major concerns for the electronic commerce business.

The faceless, impersonal nature of cyberspace makes it difficult for businesses to "know their customers." Although technical developments (*e.g.* digital signatures, smart cards, etc.) may provide effective solutions in the future, for now on-line businesses will have to resort to indirect methods for verifying identity and blocking web access from unwanted jurisdictions.

Countries or States

3.17 There are a number of reasons why businesses will often want to limit the countries or jurisdictions with which they want to transact.

Export/import restrictions. Many products, such as encryption software and other dual-use technology, are subject to export restrictions (often for national security reasons)

---

[24] *Shanklin Pier Ltd v. Detel Products Ltd* [1951] 2 K.B. 854.

under laws such as the Dual Goods and Related Use (Export Control) Regulations 1995.[25] Failure to monitor the location of the transacting party, particularly for digitised services such as downloadable encryption software, could result in an on-line supplier being in breach of these statutes. On the flip side, many jurisdictions have import restrictions. For example, the United States Department of Agriculture rigorously regulates the importation of fruits and vegetables. Suppliers may wish to exclude these products as well.

Commercial embarrassment. In the media spotlight, the public quickly discovers the people and the countries with which a merchant does business. Even if not subject to government regulations, some businesses may choose to avoid dealing with particular countries, for public relations reasons.

Consumer Protection Legislation. As paragraph 3.81 details, many jurisdictions have consumer protection laws that imply mandatory terms into consumer contracts. Some of these terms may be surprisingly unfavourable to foreign merchants. On-line businesses wishing to avoid draconian legislation or foreign lawsuits may wish to refuse purchasers from some jurisdictions.

Illegal or regulated activity. Some on-line content or activities, such as financial services, gambling, or pornography, may be legal in some areas and illegal (or subject to heavy regulation) in others. To the relief of on-line businesses, many jurisdictions will not enforce their regulations and laws on Internet sites unless there is evidence of directed activity. The policy of the Financial Services Authority in the U.K. regarding financial services advertisements reflects this position.

3.18

However, even without purposely directed activity toward a particular jurisdiction, some long-arm statutes (often found in the United States) may seek to bring a website owner into the foreign court anyway. For example, in *Minnesota v. Granite Gate Resorts*,[26] a number of Minnesota residents accessed a Nevada website advertising a forthcoming international Internet gambling site. Consequently, a Minnesota court claimed personal jurisdiction, stating that the defendants had "purposefully availed themselves of the privilege of conducting commercial activities in [Minnesota]."[27] It should be noted that *Granite Gate* involved merely advertising, not even actual gambling activities.

A similar scenario regarding pornography occurred in *U.S. v. Thomas*.[28] A Federal court in Tennessee claimed jurisdiction, applied local obscenity standards, and convicted a website owner based in California. The 'passive' nature of a website provides no defence. As was held in *Playboy Enterprises Inc. v. Chuckleberry Publishing*[29]:

"[An Internet site can be viewed as] an "advertisement" by which [the foreign site] distributes its pictorial images throughout the United States. That the local user "pulls" these

[25] Dual Goods and Related Use (Export Control) Regulations 1995, Statutory Instrument No. 1191.
[26] *Minnesota v. Granite Gate Resorts* 568 N.W.2d 715.
[27] ibid.
[28] *United States v. Thomas* (1996) Nos. 94–6648/6649 FED App. 0032P (6th Cir.).
[29] *Playboy Enterprises Inc. v. Chuckleberry Publishing Inc.*, 939 F.Supp. 1044 (S.D.N.Y. 1996). See Chapter 4.

images from [the foreign] computer . . . as opposed to [the site] "sending" them to this country, is irrelevant. By inviting United States users to download these images, [the foreign site] is causing and contributing to their distribution within the United States."

3.19   Thus, there are a host of reasons why on-line merchants should regulate access to their sites and exclude users from unwanted jurisdictions. The consequences of carelessness in this area are not only potential embarrassment or difficult-to-enforce contracts, but possible civil liability and/or criminal sanctions (*e.g. U.S. v. Thomas*). Merchants of physical goods have less concern, since they can check the delivery address and act accordingly. However, merchants of digitised services face a tougher challenge, since the location and identity of the customer is not as apparent. Although near-perfect technical solutions (such as digital signatures, etc.) are not yet readily available, there are still a number of methods available to prevent unwanted site visitors and to minimise legal liability.

Web server checks. Every computer on-line has an Internet (I.P.) address (either permanently or temporarily assigned). Although this address does not necessarily indicate the customer's country of origin and can be masked,[30] a web server can perform this simple check as a preliminary verification.

Alternatively, servers can utilise 'cookies'[31] to get a general geographical location by detecting the time zone offset used by the customer. If the server only wants to do business within the U.K., it could reject customers with time zone offsets other than 0 (Greenwich Meridian) and +1 (British Summer Time).

These server checks are not foolproof but can provide a fair degree of protection against the risk and, furthermore, the fact that server checks were used would be taken into account by any court when determining whether the server was intending to sell its digitised services in the relevant jurisdiction.

3.20   *Site disclaimers.* Site disclaimers can exclude 'unfriendly' jurisdictions through statements such as "This website is intended only for people inside the United Kingdom." These disclaimers discourage unwanted customers and can reduce the risk of legal liability by explicitly defining the intended audience. However, disclaimers must be consistent with the site owner's actions. In *Granite Gate*, despite the use of site disclaimers urging users to "consult with local authorities regarding restrictions," the court held that the defendants' subsequent actions were a "clear effort to reach and seek potential profit from Minnesota consumers."[32]

On-line contract construction. On-line advertisements need to be carefully constructed so that they are only invitations to treat, not offers. This gives the on-line business the option to accept or refuse dealings with particular customers after obtaining their specific details (location, age, etc.) without raising the spectre of a breach of contract.

---

[30] IP addresses can be masked through a technique called 'weaving,' where a user connects to the web site via a number of other computers, creating layers which hide his original location.
[31] Cookies are pieces of information sent from the customers computer (web browser) to the web server for convenience. For example, cookies may contain the user's name, e-mail address, etc. See Chapter 2.
[32] *Minnesota v. Granite Gate Resorts* 568 N.W.2d 715.

Impostors

To prevent fraud, some on-line services, particularly banks and financial services, need **3.21** to verify the identity of a person before allowing him/her to make withdrawals or move funds. Authenticating a specific person presents a different problem from checking location, however, because the customer will often have already had a prior relationship with the on-line service provider. Therefore, the customer will likely possess a password, PIN (personal identification number), digital signature key, or some other form of identification.

Most of these on-going service contracts will specifically outline security procedures and attribute responsibility based on predetermined principles. Even without explicit terms, the courts are likely to find that if a password or PIN is used, the recipient (in this case, the on-line service provider) is entitled to rely on it unless notified of a problem. Responsibility for securing the authentication information lies completely with the owner of the key. The court in *Standard Bank London Ltd v. The Bank of Tokyo Ltd*[33] reached this conclusion regarding 'tested telexes' (telexes authenticated by a secret code):

> "The recipient would be able to rely on a tested telex unless it was on notice that the telex was not what it purported to be. Where a clear representation was made in the ordinary course of business, normally the recipient would be fixed with notice of dishonesty, or of facts that should put it on inquiry as to dishonesty, or if it had been wilfully blind."[34]

The problem authentication poses to the creation of a continuing on-line relationship **3.22** (*e.g.* before a person establishes an on-line bank account) is quite similar to one already faced in the physical world. Traditionally, businesses such as banks rely on applications, letters of reference and other similar documents to vouch for a new customer's identity. On-line merchants will have to resort to analogous methods. Digital signatures and a framework of 'trusted third parties' may make this process easier in the future, and are discussed in Chapter 5.

Authentication of a person is usually based upon:

(1) Something they know (*e.g.* password or PIN)
(2) Something they have (*e.g.* magnetic card or smart card)
(3) Something they are (*e.g.* voiceprint, fingerprint etc.)

Current mass domestic market authentication technology is based upon passwords and PINs. Retailers and bank automatic teller machines use cards with magnetic stripes for authentication. Voice and fingerprint identification remain confined to specialist high security areas.

Difficulties arise when a supplier reduces authentication security to enable it to address a wider market. Catastrophic consequences can follow if the supplier reduces security by too great an amount as its contracts will require corroboration for their validity to be accepted in court. The determination of appropriate authentication security requires specialist professional risk assessment to take account of specific facts and circumstances.

---

[33] *Standard Bank London Ltd v. The Bank of Tokyo Ltd* [1996] 1 CTLR T-17.
[34] *ibid.*

Minors

3.23   In cyberspace, companies will have great difficulty discerning whether the customer is forty-eight years old or merely eight. Minors (anyone under the age of 18) thus present two interesting problems to on-line merchants. First, the sale of certain goods and content to minors, such as tobacco, alcohol, and pornography is unlawful. Without adequate measures to ensure that customers are adults, website owners may again find themselves liable to civil or criminal sanctions. Second, under English law, contracts made by minors for things other than necessities (food, clothing, shelter, etc.) are voidable.[35] In addition, although these contracts are unenforceable against the minor, they are enforceable against the merchant.[36] The situation leaves on-line companies in a precarious position which they have good reason to avoid. They must fulfil their contractual obligation, but have little recourse if the child defaults on payment.[37]

3.24   *Sale of illegal goods to minors.*   One remedy available to companies wishing to avoid dealing with minors on-line is the Content Advisor found on most web browsers. The software is based on ratings created by the Recreational Software Advisory Council (RSAC) to limit the degree of sex, violence, and language accessible to children. To avoid legal action for distributing to minors, providers of digitised services can acquire a rating that will restrict access accordingly. On-line sellers of goods could use a similar tactic to ensure that only adult customers made purchases. Unfortunately, the RSAC software only currently has four categories: language, nudity, sex, and violence. RSAC would need to amend this list to make it relevant to electronic commerce activities such as gambling, the purchase of tobacco etc. On the basis that a parent who wanted his/her children protected from language, nudity, sex, and violence would also wish to protect them from gambling and tobacco products, it might be reasonable for a supplier to wrongly classify its site as containing nudity and sex just to get the RSAC system to impose its current restrictions. Nevertheless, on-line providers must still rely on parents to take preventative actions regarding their children. The RSAC content advisor only works if parents enable it and change the relevant settings.

Purchases by minors and their capacity for entering into binding contracts.

> "The law on this topic is based on two principles. The first, and more important, is that the law must protect the minor against his inexperience which may enable an adult to take unfair advantage of him or induce him to enter into a contract which, though in itself fair, is simply improvident (*e.g.* if the minor for a fair price buys something he cannot afford). This principle is the basis of the general rule that a minor is not bound by his contracts. The second principle is that the law should not cause unnecessary hardship to adults who deal fairly with minors. Under this principle certain contracts with minors are valid; others are voidable in the sense that they bind the minor unless he repudiates; and a minor may be under some liability in tort and in restitution."[38]

---

[35] *Merchantile Union Guarantee Co. v. Ball* [1937] 3 All E.R. 1.

[36] Minors' Contract Act 1987, s.2. Originally, all aspects of contracts made by minors' were governed under the Infants Relief Act 1874, but the Minors' Contract 1987 repealed it, reverting most of the relevant rules back to common law.

[37] Under a breach, merchants can only recover the actual goods delivered to the minor, if the minor is still in possession of them. Minors' Contract Act 1987, s.3.

[38] *Treital: Law of Contract* (9th ed.) p. 494.

Over the past few years various U.K. companies have found themselves with unenforce- **3.25**
able contracts made with children. Telephone companies have installed telephone lines
for children without their parents' knowledge and have then been faced with unenforceable telephone bills.

Minors in the U.K. are frequently issued with debit cards by banks and building
societies. These are not credit cards but permit a minor to buy goods and services
provided there are sufficient funds in the account. It is possible for a minor to go to a
website and use his/her own debit card to make a purchase. The goods shall have been
paid for before they are received. In practical terms this is of great significance since any
dispute between the minor and the vendor will be an attempt by the minor for
repayment of money and not an attempt by the vendor to get money out of a minor. To
recover a wrongful payment the minor, as plaintiff, would have all the problems of
litigating and, in particular, proving that the goods were not necessities. Consequently,
in practical terms it is fairly safe to sell goods and services to minors using their own
debit cards.

It is difficult to contemplate circumstances where the electronic business might be at
genuine risk through accepting debit cards from minors for goods which it delivered to
the minor on its normal terms of business. There might be an outside risk that a
merchant whose business was selling goods which were not necessities (*e.g.* music CDs)
could find itself at the receiving end of an action brought for repayment to a minor of
monies paid for the goods. Furthermore, if a minor purchased goods from a merchant
based in another jurisdiction the risk of litigation becomes almost insignificant.

The position is slightly different if the minor, having paid for the goods, changes his/ **3.26**
her mind before the goods have been delivered. If the minor makes the vendor aware
that he/she is a minor and wishes to withdraw from the transaction, the vendor would
not be entitled to rely upon its normal terms of business regarding cancellations. The
minor would be entitled to a full refund. Good business practice would require that the
bank or building society who issued the minor with the debit card would find some
means to charge back the transaction upon notice by the minor of the circumstances.

The position, however, is different when the contract is made by a child using a
parent's credit or debit card without permission. In these circumstances the transaction
should be treated as if the card had been stolen. Once the parent is made aware of the
transactions having taken place he/she has an opportunity either to ratify the transactions (in which case the contract will be with the parent), or deny the validity of the
transaction. If the parent denies the validity of the transaction the credit card company
may have an action against the parent in negligence for failure to keep the credit card
details confidential. On the basis of modern practice, though, this is unlikely to be
pursued. All the information being sought to validate a "cardholder not present"
transaction is present on the face of the card. It is unlikely that a court would deem this
information to be confidential.

A more practical barrier to denying the validity of the transaction would be the
associated problem of reporting the minor's crime to the authorities. Most parents would
balk at having their children prosecuted for theft and the socially acceptable solution is
to accept the validity of the minor's transactions and thereby save the minor from the
implications arising from a prosecution for theft. But sometimes this is not possible.

Employees

3.27   Companies have devised elaborate procedures to ensure that there are checks and balances on the actions of employees.[39] For example, in order to make large purchases, an employee might require the 'signing-off' of a superior. These paper-based methods are often slow and bureaucratic. One of the promises of electronic commerce is to remove much of this inefficiency.[40] However, e-mail and web purchasing also allow greater opportunities to circumvent conventional procedures and controls if the business has not been re-engineered to reflect the new risks. Should employers be econcerned about employees making unauthorised contracts? Are these on-line contracts enforceable?

English law provides that if an employee has the apparent authority to conclude a contract, the employer will normally be bound, regardless of whether the employee had the actual authority to do so or not.[41] Other jurisdictions, such as the United States, have similar doctrines.[42] Thus, as long as an on-line business is reasonable in assessing the authority of the purchaser/contractor, it will form fully enforceable contracts.

To prevent problems of unauthorised action by employees, employers need to establish clear policies delineating what employees can do with their e-mail accounts and Internet connections. Staff should also be educated and trained regarding the risks. In addition, since apparent authority is established through symbols of authority, such as business cards and letterhead, corporate policies should regulate representations such as the 'signature tags' at the bottom of e-mails. It may also be wise for senior management to publish and circulate to all likely vendors a document setting out the true extent of the contractual authority granted to employees.

CONTRACT CREATION

3.28   Under English law, the formation of a contract requires four elements: offer; acceptance; consideration; and an intention to create legal relations. For example, on-line contract formation could proceed in the following manner:

> The consumer offers three Euros (the offer price) to a music website to listen to a new track to be included on a forthcoming Elton John CD. The website accepts the offer and begins to download a high quality digital recording. In this situation, the parties exchange something of value (consideration), namely the three Euros from the consumer to the website owner and the supply to the consumer of the digital recording of the music, and they intend on forming a binding agreement. Thus all the requirements for a binding contract are present.

---

[39] This practice is also reflected in auditing where a company can find the reliability of its business records being questioned if there is an inadequate separation of responsibilities. See Chapter 5 "Evidence, Security, Watermarking and ECMS".

[40] Within companies, "groupware" technologies such as Lotus Notes allow the construction of an electronic equivalent of these paper-based procedures with electronic "chits" being signed off for approval or payment.

[41] *Chitty on Contracts*, 31–038.

[42] *3 Am. Jur. 2d Agency* Section 71 (1986); *Restatement (Second) of Agency*, Section 8A (1958).

An understanding of the contract formation process is critical to on-line businesses; a contract that fails to satisfy any of the requirements may be unenforceable. On the other hand, the courts might construe certain actions by consumers or electronic commerce merchants as constituting the required elements, even though there was no desire to make an offer or acceptance at the time.

The exposition on the elements of contract below will enable businesses to be more mindful of their actions on-line. It will also indicate the methods for constructing websites to safeguard the commercial and legal interests of electronic commerce businesses.

Offer

When a person makes an offer, he/she is expressing a desire to enter into a contract (based on specified terms and conditions) on the understanding that if the other party accepts it, the agreement will be legally binding. Offers can be made using virtually any form of communication — by post, fax, telex, telephone, and now by electronic mail and the world wide web.

3.29

English law states that if a reasonable person would interpret a particular action or communication as an offer (a readiness to bind oneself), it is an offer whether the party intended it or not.[43] Thus, the appearance of an offer is more important than actual intent. This doctrine represents a significant danger to electronic commerce businesses. Careless on-line statements or poorly constructed websites can constitute making unintentional offers to the world that result in unwanted binding legal contracts once consumers accept.

Invitation to treat

To protect themselves from making unintentional offers, on-line merchants need to observe the fine distinction between an offer and an invitation to treat. Invitations to treat are advertisements that promote the sale of products, but are not offers in themselves (nor unilateral contracts). For example, English law holds that shop displays and price-lists are invitations to treat. For example, in *Pharmaceutical Society of Great Britain v. Boots Cash Chemists (Southern) Ltd*,[44] the court held that:

3.30

> "It is a well-established principle that the mere exposure of goods for sale by a shopkeeper indicates to the public that he is willing to treat but does not amount to an offer to sell. . . . The customer is informed that he may himself pick up an article and bring it to the shopkeeper with a view to buying it, and if, but only if, the shopkeeper then expresses his willingness to sell, the contract for sale is completed."[45]

Similarly in *Fisher v. Bell*, the court said:

> "It is clear that, according to the ordinary law of contract, the display of an article with a price on it in a shop window is merely an invitation to treat. It is in no sense an offer for sale the acceptance of which constitutes a contract."[46]

---

[43] *Chitty on Contracts*, 2–002.
[44] *Pharmaceutical Society of Great Britain v. Boots Cash Chemists (Southern) Ltd* [1951] 2 Q.B. 795.
[45] *ibid.* at 801.
[46] *Fisher v. Bell* [1961] 1 Q.B. 394 at 399.

When a customer approaches the store counter with a product it is only an offer to buy, not acceptance of an offer made by the store. The store then has the option of accepting the offer and complete the contract, or refusing it.

A similar principle is likely to apply to electronic mail price lists and websites. Websites are the electronic analogue of shop windows and catalogues, advertising the descriptions of products and their prices. Electronic mail price lists similarly are analogous to circulars in conventional commerce. These analogies, however, are still conjecture, since no case law has yet verified websites as invitations to treat. Furthermore, pre-written order forms with the on-line merchants' standard terms and conditions could be construed (albeit unlikely) as offers, since they are designed and written by the supplier. In order to minimise the risk of an unfavourable court decision, websites and electronic mail solicitations should have disclaimers explicitly defining them to be invitations to treat, and not offers. These disclaimers will ensure that electronic commerce businesses have the ability to select their customers and manage their supply of goods.

Select of customers

3.31 As mentioned in paragraph 3.16, for many reasons, electronic commerce businesses merchants may not wish to deal with all customers from all jurisdictions. By retaining the power to accept or refuse, businesses can refuse undesirable customers and jurisdictions without fearing breach of contract. Additionally, if the vendor intends to accept orders from only U.K.-based customers, a notice on the website stating that "The contents of this website are for U.K. customers only" is advisable.[47]

Manage supply

One of the primary reasons why the courts introduced the invitation to treat principle was to protect traditional businesses from supply shortages or limited supplies. As the court decided in *Grainger & Son v. Gough:*

> "The transmission of a price-list does not amount to an offer to supply an unlimited quantity of the wine described at the price named, so that as soon as an order is given there is a binding contract to supply that quantity. If it were so, the merchant might find himself involved in any number of contractual obligations to supply wine of a particular description which he would be quite unable to carry out, his stock of wine of that description being necessarily limited."[48]

The same argument applies to electronic commerce. On-line merchants cannot necessarily accurately assess the number of replies they will receive in response to a solicitation. If the website or electronic mail price list were considered as an offer, the merchant would potentially have innumerable contracts with people throughout the world, all of whom could sue for breach if it did not deliver the advertised product.

---

[47] See Chapter 2.
[48] *Grainger & Son v Gough* [1896] A.C. 325 at 334.

Errors or garbled offers

Electronic mail can frequently become garbled due to transmission problems such as **3.32** incompatible formats, changes in languages or keyboard sets, or even firewalls[49] removing attachments.[50] The offeror will probably not be held liable for the error if the recipient had reason to suspect a transmission problem. However, in certain circumstances (*e.g.* if the error is undetectable), the offeror could be held liable for inaccuracies if the offeree subsequently accepts the offer and forms a contract. Ensuring that electronic mail solicitations are invitations to treat and requiring the customer to make the offer reduces this risk.

Acceptance

After the offer has been made, the offeree accepts it and thus creates a contract. In **3.33** cyberspace, acceptance is a contentious issue because the offeror and the offeree are distanced in time and space. Where is the contract actually formed? How is it formed? In what ways can acceptance be communicated? This section addresses these questions and others related to the creation of an on-line contract.

As explained in the previous section, depending on how the courts interpret a website or other on-line advertisement (as either an invitation to treat or an offer), the customer response could be viewed as either an acceptance or an offer (respectively). This section assumes that the website is an invitation to treat, that the customer response is an offer and thus it is the electronic commerce vendor who accepts and forms the contract.

Attribution of computer acts to a person

One of the advantages of electronic commerce is the automation of tasks which **3.34** previously required human involvement. Computers can receive orders on-line and, in some electronic data interchange systems (EDI), even keep track of inventory and automatically place orders when supplies run low. This raises an important issue: can a computer accept an offer and create a contract? For example, if a person wishes to buy a book and makes an offer to an on-line bookseller, can the merchant's web server accept the offer and create the contract?

English law and most other legal systems, have a tradition of attributing the actions of a machine to the person who instruct it to execute a particular routine.[51] In *Thornton v. Shoe Lane Parking*,[52] the court ruled that a customer contracted with a car park machine

---

[49] Firewalls are dedicated computers which guard the entrance to a network (usually belonging on a particular company or organization). Their job is often to block any potentially malicious files (such as e-mails and their attachments) and to prevent intrusions by hackers.
[50] "Attachments" are formatted documents that are appended to e-mail messages. A good example of a formatted document is a word processing file that contains information regarding the text layout (font, font size, justification, bold text etc). Currently informal studies have estimated that approximately 50 per cent of attachments to e-mail messages between organisations are lost or corrupted in their transmission. This loss or destruction arises owing to incompatibilities between different e-mail systems.
[51] For an early fictional account of how the law deals with computers acting on their own see *Haddock v. The Generous Bank Limited, Computer 1578/32/W1, The Magical Electronic Contrivances Limited and the Central Electricity Board*; one of Sir A. P. Herbert's "Misleading Cases" (Penguin 1963).
[52] *Thornton v. Shoe Land Parking Ltd* [1971] 1 All E.R. 686.

(representing the owner) when he fed in his money and received a claim ticket. As Denning L.J. suggested:

> "[The customer] was committed at the very moment when he put his money into the machine. The contract was concluded at that time. It can be translated into offer and acceptance in this way: the offer is made when the proprietor of the machine holds it out as being ready to receive the money. The acceptance takes place when the customer puts his money into the slot."[53]

3.35   In the United States case of *State Farm Mutual Auto. Ins. Co. v. Brockhurst*,[54] the court ruled that since the computer only operated as programmed by the insurance company, it was bound by the contract formed (in this case, an insurance renewal). Based on these two precedents, the English courts would probably decide that a web server, as an agent of the on-line business, can both make offers and accept offers in order to create contracts. Web-automated contracts therefore need to be carefully constructed to prevent the creation of unwanted contracts. Otherwise, as long as the customer reasonably believes that the computer accepted the offer, the contract will be fully binding, regardless of what bugs the server might have or what the on-line terms might state (*e.g.* price, quantity, product, etc.). In addition, not only must merchants ensure that the prices, terms and conditions are accurate, they must also be wary of 'free-text' boxes that would enable the customer to change the terms of the agreement. For example, if the sale is for £500 and the customer can type into the free-text box, "I agree to the price of £50," the supplier might be held to the lower price.

Although the standard terms could state that the contract is a contract of adhesion (in which the conditions of the contract are fixed) those terms prohibiting amendments may not be enforced by the courts.[55] Thus, to minimise risk, a properly constructed website should not allow the customer to change or input additional terms into the contract. The customer is only presented with fixed prices and conditions, and can only click a button to send the offer.

Similar arguments apply for electronic mail if an on-line business wants to provide a prewritten contract for the customer to send as an offer. Without some technical means of ensuring message integrity, the customer could easily change the standard terms and conditions to benefit himself/herself instead of the merchant. Use of technical solutions such as hash functions or digital signatures can prevent this problem.

Valid methods of acceptance
3.36   Acceptance is the unconditional agreement to the presented offer. It cannot be a message merely notifying the offeror that the offer has been received; nor can it involve a change of terms, as this amounts to a counteroffer (paragraph 3.49). Unless explicitly specified in the offer, acceptances can generally be made via any communication method that is

---

[53] *ibid.* at 689.
[54] *State Farm Mutual Auto. Ins. Co. v. Brockhurst* 453 F.2d 533 (10th Cir. 1972).
[55] *N.B.:* In the normal context, however, a contract of adhesion is usually a take it or leave it *offer* by the supplier to be accepted by the customer. In this on-line scenario, the supplier is trying to impose terms on the customer's offer, further complicating matters.

'reasonable' in the circumstances. Speed and reliability of the method are taken into consideration in determining whether it is reasonable. For example, using the post to accept a time-sensitive offer originally made by electronic mail may be unreasonable. Generally, accepting an offer by the same means by which it was originally communicated (or by a faster and more reliable method) should be sufficient,[56] unless the terms of the offer explicitly insist on a single method.

Contracts can even be accepted by a 'click-wrap'. A click-wrap is where the contract is presented in a window on-line, and the customer is asked to click an 'Offer' or 'I accept' button. Although English courts have not yet deal and with click-wrap agreements, a United States District Court held them to be enforceable in America.[57] An English court would probably similarly recognise click-wrap contracts.

The on-line merchant can implicitly accept a customer's offer through some form of action. For example, in *Brogden v. Metropolitan Railway*,[58] where the parties had acted in accordance with an unsigned draft agreement for the delivery of consignments of coal, it was held that there was a contract on the basis of the draft. That interference was drawn from the performance in accordance with the terms of the draft agreement.[59] Similarly, in *Weatherby v. Banham*,[60] the court ruled that the unsolicited sending of goods was an offer made by the supplier that was accepted if the recipient used them.[61] In cyberspace, the supplier can accept by sending the ordered goods, by transmitting the data.

Generally, acceptance cannot be assumed from silence.[62] However, for on-line contracts, since a prudent supplier will rigidly specify all the terms in the offer, silence may be construed as acceptance because one might reasonably assume that the supplier will accept its own terms. As always, the best method of removing this risk is for a supplier to specify in the contract how it will communicate an acceptance.

Contract creation

The instant of acceptance is the instant of contract creation. When and where a contract is created can be critical if a dispute ever arises. The exact time of acceptance is important if there are competing acceptances (*e.g.* a unique object is sold to the first person to agree to the terms) or if the offer is revoked at some point. The location of acceptance plays a role in the law, jurisdiction and implied terms which will apply to the contract.

Historically, the instant of contract creation was less important because parties tended to be in the same country, and most contracts were formed in-person. As businesses began to utilise post, phone, fax, and telex for transactions, the courts developed new rules. Even so, contracts were still generally confined within one country. However, global electronic commerce makes choice of law (paragraph 4.18) and jurisdiction

3.37

3.38

---

[56] *Tinn v. Hoffman & Co* (1873) 29 L.T. 271 cited in Cheshire 51.
[57] *Hotmail Corporation v. Van Money Pie Inc., et al.*, C98-20064 (N.D. Cal., April 20, 1998).
[58] Brogden (1877, 2 A.C. 666).
[59] *G. Percy Trentham Ltd v. Archital Luxfer Ltd and Others* [1993] 1 Lloyd's Rep. 25.
[60] *Weatherby v. Banham* (1832) 5 C. & P. 228.
[61] Under the Unsolicited Goods and Services Act 1971, such 'inertia selling' is now prohibited in the U.K. In other words, the law views the merchant as having offered a gift to the consumer, and thus the consumer does not have to pay for the goods if he uses them.
[62] Felthouse v. Brindley (1862) 11 C.B.N.S. 869.

(paragraph 4.02) significant concerns. Thus, the moment of on-line contract creation takes on a new, greater level of importance.

The English courts developed two rules, the postal rule and the receipt rule, to determine the moment of acceptance for contracts formed by post and telex. An examination of these two rules, which attempt to most fairly distribute risk, might suggest how the courts will deal with electronic mail and web contracts.

3.39   *Postal Rule:*   According to Lindley J. in *Byrne v. Van Tienhoven,*

> "It may be taken as now settled that, where an offer is made and accepted by letters sent through the post, the contract is completed the moment the letter accepting the offer is posted, even though it never reaches its destination."[63]

The postal rule, first established in *Adams v. Lindsell,*[64] seemingly places an unfair burden on the offeror, because the offeror is contractually bound to a contract before being notified. The reason for the principle is the attempt to distribute risk to those most able to control it. The offeror alone selects the method for communicating an acceptance. If the offeror wishes to use the post then the risks should fall to it. Also, once the acceptance is posted, the offeree loses control over the risks of miscommunication or non-delivery. Thus, the law minimises the risk for the offeree by default, but the offeror is well-positioned to change it.

3.40   *Receipt Rule:*   The courts have used the receipt rule for instances in which the two parties have continuous communications. For example, if the two parties are communicating over the phone or in-person, the offeror must hear the acceptance, and only then is the contract created.

The receipt rule further applies to modern methods like telex. As Parker L.J. stated in *Entores Ltd v. Miles Far East Co.*[65] concerning acceptance using telex:

> "Where, however, the parties are in each other's presence or, though separated in space, communication between them is in effect instantaneous, there is no need for any such rule of convenience [postal rule]. To hold otherwise would leave no room for the operation of the general rule that notification of the acceptance must be received. An acceptor could say: 'I spoke the words of acceptance in your presence, albeit softly, and it matters not that you did not hear me'; or 'I telephoned to you and accepted, and it matters not that the telephone went dead and you did not get my message."[66]

3.41   The House of Lords later confirmed this ruling in *Brinkibon v. Stahag Stahl und Stahlwarenhandelsgesellschaft mbH*[67] which involved a telex acceptance. Essentially, the principle is that if both parties are in continuous communication during the acceptance, the burden of notification falls on the accepting party (offeree), who has immediate

---

[63] *Byrne v. Van Tienhoven* (1880) 5 C.P.D. 344 at 348, cited in *Cheshire* 54.
[64] *Adams v. Lindsell* (1818) 1 B. & Ald. 681.
[65] *Entores Ltd v. Miles Far East Co.* [1955] 2 Q.B. 327.
[66] *ibid.* at 336.
[67] *Brinkibon v. Stahag Stahl und Stahlwarenhandelsgesellschaft mbH* [1983] 2 A.C. 34.

feedback. Even in the case of telex or fax, where both parties are not necessarily personally involved, the devices communicate with each other and there is feedback. The offeree is thus in the best position to discover a transmission fault and can re-send the message as needed.

One should note, however, that with respect to the time of contract formation, the time at which the telex, fax, or electronic mail (see below) is expected to be read may be more important than the actual time of receipt. According to *Schelde Delta Shipping BV v. Astarte Shipping Ltd (The Pamela)*,[68] if an acceptance is sent outside of normal business hours, receipt is not effective until the opening of business the next day (or, in the case of *Schelde*, on the Monday morning after the weekend).

Rules for on-line acceptances.   In light of the postal rule and the receipt rule, where **3.42** will electronic mail and web contracts be formed? As previously mentioned, this question is important, because the place of creation affects many factors critical to dispute resolution such as implied terms, choice of law, and jurisdiction. No case law has decided this question yet, but looking at the attributes of both forms of communications may reveal what the courts might decide if such a dispute should arise as it inevitably will.

(1) Electronic Mail

As the electronic analogy of post electronic mail seems most suited for the postal rule. Electronic mail is not instantaneous and the sender does not normally receive any immediate or continuous feedback concerning the delivery of the message. Once the offeree clicks the 'send' button, control of the messages is lost. The electronic mail is sent off into the Internet and routed around by various computers until it reaches its destination. The same issues of uncertainty for sending messages through the post apply to e-mail as well. Whether electronic mail acceptances are effective at the time of sending or at the time of receipt, one party will be uncertain as to whether contract creation has occurred. Thus, the courts might as well choose the rule that gives the earliest time of acceptance.

If electronic mail acceptances fall under the postal rule, on-line contracts would form at the instant the offeree sent the message. Consequently, unless there was a contractual term to the contrary, the residence or place of business of contract formation would be the location of the offeree, not at the offeree's mail server and certainly not at location of the offeror. If a merchant structures the contract negotiation process so that the solicitation is an invitation to treat and the customer makes the offer (as previously assumed), then the sequence works perfectly. When the merchant sends the electronic mail acceptance, the contract is formed within the merchant's jurisdiction (indeed, exactly where the merchant is located).

Nonetheless, reasons also exist for arguing that electronic mail acceptances be subject **3.43** to the receipt rule. The courts originally formed the postal rule on the basis that the post was reasonably fast and very reliable.[69] Electronic mail, however, is not as reliable as the

---

[68] *Schelde Delta Shipping B.V. v. Astarte Shipping Ltd (The Pamela)* [1995] 2 Lloyd's Rep. 249.
[69] After all, back in the nineteenth century, the Royal Mail delivered letters several times a day in London.

post. In cyberspace, electronic mails can get lost,[70] become garbled, and are often rejected by corporate firewalls.[71] In addition, unlike the postal service but similar to the telex in *Entores*, the sender (offeree) of an electronic mail message is likely to know if a message does not arrive at its destination. If there is a transmission fault or a non-existent address the electronic mail will often be "bounced back" to the sender with an error message indicating that it was not received by the intended person. Unlike the post, electronic mail is usually fast enough (returned within a few hours) for the sender to take remedial action if an error should occur.

Nevertheless, just because an electronic mail message arrives at its destination does not necessarily mean that the electronic mail is coherent or complete. Normally, there should be enough information in an incoherent electronic mail to enable the receiver (offeror) to ask the sender to re-send the message. However, severe incompatibilities or problems can result in both parties never understanding each other. (Here is a genuine difference between electronic mail and postal mail; letters in the post do not get accidentally rewritten by the postal authorities at each end.) Given these reasons, particularly the reduced reliability and increased risk of non-delivery, does a postal rule for e-mail place an undue burden on the offeror? Perhaps the receipt rule is in order.[72]

3.44   If electronic mail does fall under the receipt rule, then, the contract would form at the offeror's location. However, a receipt rule for electronic mail raises a number of other thorny issues. For example, where does receipt actually occur? Is receipt when the acceptance arrives at the offeror's mail server, when it is downloaded it onto the computer, or when the offeror reads it? The location of the mail server often differs from the offeror's computer and depending, on the frequency that a person checks and reads electronic mail, the respective times can also significantly vary. Whether a person has a continuous Internet connection or a 'dial-up' connection may also affect the time and location of receipt.

In determing the precise time of receipt, the courts will most likely use the aforementioned doctrine in *Schelde Delta Shipping B.V. v. Astarte Shipping Ltd (The Pamela)*,[73] based on the expected time of receipt. Accordingly, receipt will usually occur when the offeror downloads the message, since one would expect a user to read the message after downloading it from the server. Whether or not the offeror actually reads the acceptance will probably be immaterial. If the offeror refuses to read the electronic mail acceptance, the offeror will probably still be held liable. Additionally, the offeror is expected to download his messages with reasonable frequency. If the offeror seldom checks electronic mail (or is, about to go on holiday) there is probably a duty of care to inform the offeree, otherwise the acceptance will probably be effective after a reasonable time.

---

[70] Under the postal rule, if the e-mail acceptance is lost in the post, the contract is still binding. *Household Fire Insurance Co. Ltd v. Grant* (1879) 4 Ex.D. 216.

[71] Firewalls are dedicated computers which guard the entrance to a network (usually belonging on a particular company or organisation). Their job is often to block any potentially malicious files (such as e-mails and their attachments) and to prevent intrusions by hackers. *Note:* E-mails without attachments, that is to say simple ASCII messages are far less likely to get lost or corrupted than e-mail messages containing attachments.

[72] The receipt here must logically mean that the offeror has been able to read the message, not simply that the offeror's computer has received the message. The receipt should be intelligible to the offeror.

[73] *Schelde Delta Shipping B.V. v. Astarte Shipping Ltd (The Pamela)* [1995] 2 Lloyd's Rep. 249.

An alternative perspective[74] on acceptance might hold that receipt occurs when it **3.45**
arrives at a computer under the offeror's control. To hold the sender (offeree)
responsible for the electronic mail after that point would be unfair since the offeror
would then be in the better position to manage risks. Thus, if the offeror uses an Internet
service provider (ISP), acceptance will be effective only after the electronic mail is
downloaded off the server onto the computer. In accordance with recent court decisions,
this interpretation views ISPs as public telecommunication operators.[75] While the
electronic mail is on the ISP mail server, it is still technically 'in transit' and the
responsibility of the sender. However, if the offeror operates his/her own mail server
then acceptance would be effected when the electronic mail arrives there, transit being
complete.

Irrespective of exactly where and when receipt is actually effective, the receipt rule for
electronic mail contract formation unfortunately does not work with the contract
negotiation structure previously advocated for on-line merchants. If the supplier wishes
to retain the option of acceptance/refusal (the price lists being merely invitations to
treat), the customer must necessarily be the offeror. However, under the receipt rule, this
arrangement necessitates that the contract forms in the customer's jurisdiction, where
the customer receives the merchant's acceptance. On-line merchants thus face the
unwelcome prospect of forming and enforcing contracts in scattered jurisdictions
throughout the world.

Selecting and applying one of the existing acceptance rules to e-mail acceptances will
continue to pose problems because e-mail has attributes found both in posting messages
and in more instantaneous forms of communication. If and when disputes arise on this
subject, the courts will certainly have to make a difficult choice. In the meanwhile, there
is a possible solution for on-line businesses, discussed in paragraph 3.47 below, to
reduce the risks and uncertantities.

(2) Website contracts

Unlike electronic mail contracts, which fall somewhere in between the postal rule and **3.46**
the receipt rule and thus cause confusion, determining an acceptance rule for contracts
made over the world wide web is more straightforward. The world wide web exhibits
the features of a method of instantaneous communication (interactive and in real-time),
the sender has almost immediate feedback, and errors or faults are readily apparent. As
a result the receipt rule will probably apply to web contracts.

However, just as in the case of electronic mail, use of the receipt rule hinders the
creation of contracts within the on-line merchant's own jurisdiction. Again, if the
electronic commerce business retains the right to accept, the acceptance is not effective
until it reaches the customer, thus creating the contract in the customer's jurisdiction.
Paragraph 3.47 suggests a possible solution to this problem.

Specifying the means of acceptance. The receipt rule gives electronic commerce **3.47**
businesses a choice between two means of acceptance. Due to the sequence of exchanges
necessary to form a contract, merchants can only use one or the other of the two
following scenarios:

---

[74] Trystan C.G. Tether, Bird & Bird, "Contracting on the Internet," IBC Conference, January 28, 1998.
[75] *Zeran v. America Online* [1997] No. 97–1523 FED App. 1523P (4th Cir.). **Electronic Citation**.

- **Scenario A:** Merchants make it clear that their electronic mail solicitations and website catalogues or displays are only invitations to treat. The customer makes the offer (under standard terms and conditions written by the merchant) so that the merchant can accept or refuse the contract at its discretion, protecting its interests (as discussed in paragraph 3.30). However, under the receipt rule, the merchant's acceptance is not effective until the offeror (customer) receives it. Thus, the contract is created in the customer's (possibly foreign) jurisdiction. If a dispute later arises, the merchant may need to sue the customer in a foreign court. (See paragraph 4.01 on choice of law and jurisdiction issues).

- **Scenario B:** Although they may still disclaim their preliminary electronic mails and websites as invitations to treat, at some point, the merchants have to make the offers. The customer accepts the offer, and under the receipt rule, the contract forms when the merchant receives the acceptance. This scenario thus ensures that the contract is formed in the merchant's jurisdiction. However, once accepted by the customer, the merchant can no longer refuse the contract because it would be a breach. If supply of the particular product becomes scarce, the on-line merchant would be still liable, unless it can escape through some other means such as frustration using the legal doctrines of or impossibility.

3.48 Fortunately, on-line merchants may not have to make this difficult choice. Under English law, the receipt or postal rules only apply if the offer does not specify an explicit method of acceptance. Therefore, in most cases, the offeror can override the default rule and prescribe the method of acceptance.[76] Consequently, merchants might be able to act in accordance with Scenario A, but would additionally specify in the standard terms and conditions that acceptance is effective once sent (postal rule). This arrangement would succeed in retaining the on-line merchant's right to accept or refuse while ensuring that the contract is formed in the merchant's jurisdiction. Additionally, the standard contract should also have choice of law and jurisdiction clauses which are favourable to the supplier.

Whether or not the courts will decide that such favourable terms for the on-line electronic commerce business are unfair (and thus invalid) is unknown. In addition, many jurisdictions have mandatory consumer protection laws that will invalidate this construction in the case of consumer contracts. However, since on-line businesses essentially have nothing to lose, amending the standard terms and conditions to include these clauses may be worth considering.

Revocation and Counteroffer

3.49 Naturally, not all offers are eventually accepted. The offeree might reject the offer, or propose a counteroffer. The offer may lapse after a specified time or event, or it may be revoked by the offeror. For the most part, under the prescribed method of contracting, on-line businesses will be in the position of the offeree (with the right to accept) and will not need to worry about revocation or counter offering. However, in some cases, businesses may find themselves making the offer and thus should keep the relevant legal rules in mind.

---

[76] *Chitty on Contracts*, 2–042.

Lapse and Revocation. Terms usually included in an offer determine the time during which the offer is effective. As a result, an offer may lapse after a period of time or after some specified event. If the period of validity is not specified, the courts will imply that the offer lapses after a reasonable period. Determination of this reasonable period depends on factors such as the contract's subject matter and the method of communication used by the parties.[77]

In addition to the automatic lapsing of an offer, the offeror may revoke it at any time up until the moment of acceptance, irrespective of any terms that specify the period in which the offer is valid.[78] However, a revocation must be received (*i.e.* the receipt rule) before it is effective, as was expressed in *Byrne v. Van Tienhoven*.[79] This rule was traditionally used to resolve disputes where a revocation was posted before, but not received before, an acceptance was sent. Nonetheless, such a situation is unlikely to arise in electronic commerce, even if electronic mails fell under the postal rule.

3.50

On the Internet, the offeror can revoke an offer using electronic mail, but whether it can be revoked by placing a notice on a website is doubtful. Since the revocation notice needs to be actually received by the offeree, a web display will probably not suffice. This implication represents another reason why on-line merchants should be wary of creating unilateral contracts (paragraph 3.12).

Counteroffer and the Battle of the Forms. According to *Hyde v. Wrench*,[80] making a counteroffer necessarily means the rejection of the original offer.[81] If an offeree's counteroffer is subsequently rejected, it cannot then unilaterally resurrect and accept the original offer. The original offer is dead, and the original offeror is at liberty to restate the offer or not. Additionally, since an acceptance must be an unequivocal assent to all terms, if the 'acceptance' contains additional or modified terms, it is technically a counteroffer and no contract is formed.

3.51

In the course of normal contract negotiations, on-line businesses will, of course, seek to impose their own standard terms and conditions to protect their interests.[82] Although this situation will seldom occur in standardised web contracts, where the offeree has no opportunity to amend or change, it can certainly occur during electronic mail negotiations. For example, Party A sends its offer on its electronic mail template containing its standard terms and conditions. Party B, wishing to contract with A, sends the acceptance on its own standard electronic mail template with different (and probably conflicting) terms and conditions. Essentially, the two parties agree on all major points, such as product, quantity, price, etc., but the standard terms differ on ancillary issues, such as warranties jurisdiction or choice of law. This situation is known as the 'battle of the forms.'

As explained above, strictly speaking, no contract is formed. Neither party has unequivocally accepted the other's offer, but rather a series of counteroffers have been electronic mailed back and forth. In *Butler Machine Tool Co. v. Ex-Cell-O Co.*,[83] Lawton L.J.

3.52

---

[77] *Ramsgate Victoria Hotel Co. v Montefiore* (1866) L.R. 1 Exch. 109.
[78] *Routledge v. Grant* (1828) 4 Bing. 653, *Dickinson v. Dodds* (1874) 2 Ch.D. 463, and *Chitty on Contracts* 2–059.
[79] *Byrne v. VanTienhoven* (1880) 5 CPD 44.
[80] *Hyde v. Wrench* (1840) 3 Beav. 334. See also *Chitty on Contracts*, 2–063.
[81] *Trollope & Colls Ltd v. Atomic Power Constructions Ltd* [1962] 3 All E.R. 1035.
[82] Indeed, the reader will notice that construction of these standard terms and conditions is a substantial focus in this chapter.
[83] *Butler Machine Tool Co. v Ex-Cell-O Co.* [1979] 1 All E.R. 965.

favoured this 'no-contract' viewpoint. However, since a 'battle of the forms' occurs often in the commercial world, this view would invalidate many contracts. Lord Denning M.R. offered a slightly different perspective in *Butler:*

> "In many of these cases our traditional analysis of offer, counter-offer, rejection, acceptance and so forth is out-of date . . . The better way is to look at all the documents passing between the parties and glean from them, or from the conduct of the parties, whether they have reached agreement on all material points, even though there may be differences between the forms and conditions printed on the back of them . . . The terms and conditions of both parties are to be construed together. If they can be reconciled so as to give a harmonious result, all well and good. If differences are reconcilable, so that they are mutually contradictory, then the conflicting terms may have to be scrapped and replaced by a reasonable implication."[84]

Under Lord Denning M.R.'s interpretation, a contract is created, but neither party should benefit from the discrepancy in standard terms. The court must find mutual ground or else create some mutual benefit.[85]

3.53   Another perspective on the 'battle of the forms,' is found in the Uniform Laws on International Sales Act 1967, which is applicable only to international sale of goods and is only found in limited form in English law. However, it does offer an plausible alternative view. Article 7 of Schedule 2 states:

> "A reply to an offer which purports to be an acceptance but which contains additional or different terms which do no materially alter the terms of the offer shall constitute an acceptance unless the offeror promptly objects to the discrepancy; if he does not so object, the terms of the contract shall be the terms of the offer with the modifications contained in the acceptance."[86]

Under this interpretation, on-line merchants face a possible danger. If the offeree sends back an acceptance with new terms and conditions, and the offeror is silent, the offeror may become bound by the new terms unless a response is sent.

3.54   A similar danger derives from the actual facts in *Butler Machine Tool v. Ex-Cell-O Co.,* where the original offeror (the seller, Butler) received an 'acceptance' with new terms and conditions and then proceeded to send back the acknowledgement slip. As the court ruled:

> " . . . an acceptance of that counter-offer [the 'acceptance' with new terms and conditions] . . . is shown by the acknowledgement which the sellers signed and returned to the buyers."[87]

By sending the acknowledgement, the seller implicitly accepted the buyer's conditions. In this case, the implied assent is arguably stronger than in the case of silence (above).

---

[84] *ibid.* at 968d.
[85] According to Cheshire 168fn, "Lord Denning's views here are reminiscent of his views in *Gibson v. Manchester City Council* [1978] 2 All E.R. 583, [1978] 1 W.L.R. 520, which were emphatically disapproved of by the House of Lords [1979] 1 All E.R. 972, [1979] 1 W.L.R. 294. . . . Of course, the *Gibson* case did not involve a battle of the forms."
[86] Uniform Laws on International Sales Act 1967, Sch. 2, art. 7.
[87] *Butler Machine Tool Co. v Ex-Cell-O Co.* [1979] 1 All E.R. 965 at 968a.

Disputes involving 'battle of the forms' are complex. Consequently, on-line businesses should protect themselves by prudently refraining from any action that might implicitly indicate acceptance of the other party's terms and conditions. They should not return any forms provided by the other party, and should probably not even send electronic mails acknowledging receipt of an 'acceptance.' Failing to observe this caution may result in being inadvertently bound to unfavourable terms.

Consideration

Consideration is the element which typically transforms a mere promise into a legally binding contract. Consideration is often defined as the exchange of something of value, but can include a detriment to the promisee or a benefit to the promisor. In requiring consideration, common law represents contract as a sort of bargain where the promisee must pay or give something to the promisor in return for the goods, services, or other benefit it receives.

    3.55

English courts interpret the consideration requirement, and often will even 'invent consideration,' regarding something as consideration even broadly though the promisor did not necessarily want it.[88] Consequently, the requirement of consideration is usually easy to satisfy.

For normal commercial transactions, consideration poses no threat to on-line contracts and electronic commerce. The goods, services, or digitised services provided by the on-line merchant and the payment given by the customer fully satisfy the requirement for consideration.

The only possibly novel situation is with so-called 'web-wrap' or 'click-wrap' agreements, where a website requires a customer to agree to certain terms and conditions before delivering a digitised service. Many of these 'click-wrap' agreements protect free websites, shareware or freeware (software that is distributed on a trial or free basis respectively). Usually, the website requires a customer to agree to certain terms and conditions, which exclude liability or prohibit commercial use, before allowing the customer to download the digitised service. One concern is whether a click-wrap agreement has any consideration. Whether free software or access to a website represents a benefit and thereby consideration is probably likely, but unknown.

Intention to create legal relations

The final element of contract formation, the intent to create legal relations, is also easily satisfied under most circumstances. Indeed, in a commercial transaction with an explicit contract, intention is automatically presumed. The onus of proving otherwise "is on the party who asserts that no legal effect is intended, and the onus is a heavy one".[89] Disputes regarding this requirement typically only arise when some part of a letter or offer specifically mentions that no legal consequences will arise from it.[90]

    3.56

One should note that the intention to create legal relations discussed here does not relate to errors in judgment or belief. The former asks only whether the parties were

---

[88] *Chitty on Contracts*, 3–008.
[89] *Edwards v. Skyways Ltd* [1964] 1 W.L.R. 349, at 355. Cited in *Chitty on Contracts*, 2–106.
[90] *Rose and Frank v. Crompton* [1923] 2 K.B. 261; reversed [1925] A.C. 445.

interested in involving the courts in their agreement, as opposed to making an informal, friendly promise.[91] The latter, on the other hand, is dealt with by the doctrine of mistake which is applicable when one or both parties makes an error in judgment.

3.57 In the context of electronic commerce, which typically involves commercial contracts, intent will normally automatically exist. However, there is one possible exception, where an unclear or perhaps deceptive website dupes a consumer into making an unwanted contract. For example, an on-line merchant offering a digitised service may construct a makeshift website which gives no purchasing information and merely displays the product and a "Save" or "Download Now" button. An unsuspecting customer will probably assume that the service is free and has no intention of creating a contract when he/she clicks the button. In the event of a dispute, the courts would most likely not allow the on-line merchant to demand payment for the digitised services delivered on the basis of an absence of intention to create legal relations.

To avoid this possibility, on-line businesses should ensure that websites explicitly state the prices and terms of their digitised services. The customer should go through a sequence of web pages detailing the transaction terms and conditions, culminating in a 'last chance' screen where the customer either submits the offer or cancels it without legal ramifications. Establishing this purchasing framework will prevent misunderstandings and will lead to on-line contracts with greater enforceability.

WRITING AND SIGNATURE REQUIREMENTS

> The general rule of English law is that contracts can be made quite informally: no writing or other form is necessary.[92]

3.58 Probably the most common legal myth held by the general public is that contracts under English law must be in writing and have a signature. Indeed, most contracts, such as purchasing goods from a retailer, involve no written documentation at all. In most cases English law does not require writing or signatures;[93] these requirements only manifest themselves in specific statutes. Today, only a few types of contracts are specifically required by statute to be signed and in writing. For example, under Section 2 of the Law of Property (Miscellaneous Provisions) Act 1989,

> "A contract for the sale or other disposition of an interest in land can only be made in writing and only by incorporating all the terms which the parties have expressly agreed in one document or, where contracts are exchanged, in each."[94]

Additionally,

---

[91] As Cheshire and Fifoot 114 suggests, "Agreements are made every day, in domestic and in social life, where the parties do not intend to invoke the assistance of the courts should the engagement not be honoured. To offer a friend a meal is not to invite litigation."

[92] *Chitty on Contracts*, 4–001.

[93] The only exception is that prior to 1960, corporations were required to contract under seal. However, even this requirement was abolished under the Corporate Bodies' Contract Act 1960.

[94] Law of Property (Miscellaneous Provisions) Act 1989, s.2(1).

"The document incorporating the terms or, where contracts are exchange, one of the documents incorporating them (but not necessarily the same one) must be signed by or on behalf of each party to the contract."[95]

Other instances which require writing and signatures include leases for over three years,[96] consumer credit,[97] certain forms of insurance, deeds, wills, and the transfer of shares. Failure to abide by the requirements may render the contract inadmissible as evidence, unenforceable, or completely void.

3.59

As these examples make clear, there are only a few instances of when a signed, written contract is required by in writing. Most electronic commerce contracts will not be affected. Nevertheless, having signed and explicitly written contracts is generally helpful, since it increases certainty, provides evidence, and prevents the creation of hasty or careless contracts.

However, other jurisdictions may have far more stringent contract requirements. In the context of global electronic commerce, on-line businesses may need to comply with foreign requirements to ensure enforceability of their contracts. For example, in the United States, writing and a signature is currently required for, among other things, contracts for the sale of goods over $500 and contracts lasting over a year.

The Requirement of Writing

Under the Interpretation Act 1978, writing is defined as "typing, printing, lithography, photography and other modes of representing or reproducing words in a visible form."[98] Unfortunately, this definition does not answer the question of whether a digital contract satisfies the requirement of writing. For example, if a contract is displayed on a computer screen, it is indeed in visible form, but it is neither tangible nor permanent. Without any relevant case law for guidance it is difficult to predict how the courts will decide this issue.

3.60

However, in recent times, Parliament and the courts have generally appeared amenable towards expanding the definition of writing to include digital documents. The Civil Evidence Act 1995 removed previous requirements that documents had to be 'original' (in written form) in order to be admissible.[99] The Copyright, Designs and Patents Act 1988 defines writing as including:

"any form of notation or code, whether by hand or otherwise and regardless of the method by which, or medium in or on which, it is recorded."[1]

Finally, the court in *Derby & Co. Ltd v. Weldon* held that computer databases (files) are valid documents for discovery:

---

[95] *ibid.*, s.2(3).
[96] Law of Property Act 1925, s.52.
[97] Consumer Credit Act 1974.
[98] Interpretation Act 1978, Sch. 1.
[99] Civil Evidence Act 1995, s.8. Evidentiary requirements are discussed in chapter 6.
[1] Copyright, Designs, and Patents Act 1988, s.178.

"The database, so far as it contains information capable of being retrieved and converted into readable form, is a document within the meaning of R.S.C. Ord. 24 of which discovery must be given . . ."[2]

3.61 These trends suggest that courts will probably deem on-line and other digital contracts as 'writing'. Other common law jurisdictions such as the United States have similarly attempted to extend writing to include digital forms. The Uniform Commercial Code defines writing as "printing, typewriting, or any other intentional reduction to tangible form."[3] This tradition goes back to the nineteenth century when a U.S. court in reference to the telegraph suggested that:

"[i]t makes no difference whether that operator writes the offer or the acceptance . . . with a steel pen an inch long attached to an ordinary penholder, or whether his pen be a copper wire a thousand miles long."[4]

Similarly, other technologies such as telexes and faxes[5] were held to be writing in the U.S., culminating in this instructive opinion given in *Clyburn v. Allstate:*

"In today's "paperless" society of computer generated information, the court is not prepared, in the absence of some legislative provision or otherwise, to find that a computer floppy diskette would not constitute a "writing" within the meaning of [the Statute]."[6]

Signature Requirement

3.62 A signature is normally assumed to involve the writing of some name or identifying mark on a document. However, just as the courts have extended the definition of writing beyond and including on paper, so too have they broadened the concept of signature. The English law definition of signature is best summed up by the decision in *Goodman v. J. Eban Ltd*,[7] where the court validated the use of a rubber stamp as a signature:

"Where an Act of Parliament requires that any particular document be 'signed' by a person, then, *prima facie*, the requirement of the Act is satisfied if the person himself places on the document an engraved representation of his signature by means of a rubber stamp . . . The essential requirement of signing is the affixing in some way, whether by writing with a pen or pencil or by otherwise impressing upon the document, one's name or 'signature' so as personally to authenticate the document."[8]

Consistent with this interpretation, the more recent case of *Re a Debtor (No. 2021 of 1995)* held that a faxed copy of a signature satisfied a relevant statutory signature requirement.

---

[2] *Derby & Co. Ltd v. Weldon (No. 9)* [1991] 1 W.L.R. 652 at 654.
[3] Uniform Commercial Code s.1–201(46).
[4] *Howley v. Whipple* 48 N.H. 487 (1869).
[5] *Bazak International Co. v. Mast Industries, Inc.* 73 N.Y.2d 111, 7 UCC Rep. Serv. 2d 1380 (1989).
[6] *Clyburn v. Allstate* 826 F.Supp. 955 (D.S.C. 1993).
[7] *Goodman v. J Eban Ltd* [1954] 1 Q.B. 550.
[8] *ibid.* at 557.

In the court's opinion, it was hard to see why some methods of "impressing the mark on paper" would be more valid than others.[9] Indeed, Laddie J. even suggested that if the signature was digitised and later appended to the fax (thus making the fax the first tangible copy of the document), the document (or contract) should be regarded as signed.

As these cases demonstrate, the key concept of signature is the authentication it symbolises rather than its physical manifestation. A signature represents an endorsement of the given document, and whether it is written, typed, or stamped makes no difference.[10] All that matters legally is the person's intention to agree and to authenticate.

Electronic mail signatures

How will contracting parties 'sign' on-line contracts? Under the broad interpretations of signature given above, merely typing one's name at the end of an electronic mail will probably suffice, as long as there was an intention to authenticate. Additionally, the 'signature-file' often automatically or manually appended to electronic mails could be considered as a form of letterhead and thus a signature as well.

3.63

However, as in the case of evidence, admissibility does not equal weight. Just because a court recognises a particular form of signature does not mean that it will give any significant weight to it, and understandably so. The basic electronic signatures mentioned above are can be easily forged: a fraudster need only type another person's name or 'cut and paste' over another signature-file. The forger does not even need to go through the pains of stealing or recreating letterhead and the loops and lines of a 'traditional' signature.

To ensure that the courts give greater legal weight to signatures created on-line, more sophisticated methods are required. Thus, in the future, particularly for larger transactions, merchants may use digital signatures (further discussed in Chapter 5) or other forms of authentication codes. Since these methods utilise secret information known only to the parties involved or only to the signer alone (in the case of digital signatures), they offer a far greater level of non-repudiation.

For example, in *Standard Bank London Ltd v. The Bank of Tokyo Ltd*,[11] the banks involved authenticated money transfers by using telexes with a secret code, or 'validated telexes.' In the case, a fraudster forged three telexes from the Bank of Tokyo, each a letter of credit for several million dollars. The court, however, ruled that a 'validated telex' recipient was entirely entitled to rely on it unless otherwise notified or unless there was reason to believe that dishonesty was involved. This decision places significant responsibility on the sending party to secure the codes or keys since, after all, the sending party is in the best position to protect them.

---

[9] *Re a Debtor (No. 2021 of 1995)* [1996] 2 All E.R. 345 at 351.

[10] Cases in the United States have subscribed to a similar position, holding the validity of signatures that are typed (*Watson v. Tom Growney Equip. Inc.* 721 P.2d 1302 (N.M. 1986)), represented by company letterhead (*Kohlmeyer & Co. v. Bowen* 126 Ga. App. 700 192 S.E.2d 400 (1972)), and faxed (*Beatty v. First Exploration Fund 1987 and Co. Limited Partnership*, 25 B.C.L.R.2d 377 (1988)), though this last case did not involve the U.S. Statute of Frauds.

[11] *Standard Bank London Ltd v. The Bank of Tokyo Ltd* [1996] 1 C.T.L.R. T–17.

Web signatures

3.64   Web-based click-wrap contracts, which may ultimately become the mainstay of electronic commerce, may have difficulties fulfilling signature requirements, though they will seldom arise. Unlike electronic mails, where acceptance is usually accompanied by the signing of a name, with web contracts the customer accepts by clicking a button. While actions like clicking a button can signify acceptance, they clearly do not satisfy a signature's definition of being a name or identifying mark.

One possibility for avoiding this problem is to find the signature elsewhere in the contract. The order form for most on-line contracts has input boxes in which the customer types his/her name, address, electronic mail address, etc. A typed or written name, though not at the bottom of the contract, can be construed as a signature. For example, in *Durrell v. Evans*, the court said:

> "If the name of the party to be charged is printed or written on a document intended to be a memorandum of the contract, either by himself or his authorised agent, it is his signature, whether it is at the beginning or middle or foot of the document."[12]

3.65   However, this extremely broad interpretation of signature may not adequately protect consumers, especially in the case of click-wrap contracts. Thus, as a matter of public policy, the courts may rule that click-wrap contracts are not signed. One of the reasons for requiring a signature is its ceremonial implications. When people sign a document they understand that it represents a more serious legal step and consequently may proceed with greater caution. After all, even though signed contracts are generally not required by law, they are often used for their greater legal weight. For example, according to the court in *L'Estrange v. Graucob*,[13] although in unsigned contracts the plaintiff must prove that the defendant was aware of the contractual terms and conditions, no such requirement exists in signed contracts. As Scrutton L.J. suggests:

> "In cases in which the contract is contained in a railway ticket or other unsigned document, it is necessary to prove that an alleged party was aware, or ought to have been aware, of its terms and conditions. These cases have no application when the document has been signed. When a document containing contractual terms is signed, then, in the absence of fraud, or, I will add, misrepresentation, the party signing it is bound, and it is wholly immaterial whether he has read the document or not."[14]

Based on how the general public currently views on-line 'clicks,' click-wrap contracts offer few of the ceremonial elements found in signed documents. Consequently, click-wraps are far less effective in communicating the danger or legal implications of the situation. Furthermore, unlike in a traditional contract where all terms are immediately visible (albeit in small print), on-line documents often hide the contractual terms by providing a hyperlink reference. Thus, recognising click-wrap contracts as signed contracts may create a system whereby people are unknowingly bound to serious contracts, a situation that the signature requirement was originally intended to prevent.

---

[12] *Durrell v. Evans* (1862) 1 H. & C. 174 at 191.
[13] *L'Estrange v. Graucob* [1934] 2 K.B. 394.
[14] *ibid.* at 403 cited in Cheshire 168.

Model Laws

A number of efforts, most notably the United Nations Commission on International Trade Law (UNCITRAL)'s Model Law on Electronic Commerce 1996,[15] have attempted to remove writing and signature requirements to provide greater certainty to on-line contracts and to promote electronic commerce. The Model Law focuses primarily on broadly redrafting statutes to encompass the electronic equivalents of writing and signatures. It first develops the concept of a 'data message,' the electronic equivalent of a written document, which includes electronic mail, EDI, telex, etc.[16] Thereafter, in articles 6 and 7, it redefines the concepts of writing and signature to fit into the digital world.

3.66

The Model Law reduces writing to its most essential legal property, permanence. Article 6 ensures that data messages qualify as writing so long as they can be retrieved:

> "Where the law requires information to be in writing, that requirement is met by a data message if the information contained therein is accessible so as to be usable for subsequent reference."[17]

Similarly, it reduces signature to its endorsement or authentication property.

> "Where the law requires a signature of a person, that requirement is met in relation to a data message if:
> (a) a method is used to identify that person and to indicate that person's approval of the information contained in the data message; and
> (b) that method is as reliable as was appropriate for the purpose for which the data message was generated or communicated, in the light of all the circumstance, including any relevant agreement."[18]

The Model Law also verifies the enforceability of on-line contracts, providing that both offer and acceptance may be in the form of a data message, and that contracts "shall not be denied validity or enforceability on the sole ground that a data message was used for that purpose."[19]

3.67

From the preceding discussion on on-line contracts, English law appears to agree wholeheartedly with the Model Law on issues such as writing, signatures and the enforceability of the on-line contract. However, one should note that most of the English precedents applicable to writing and signatures are from the period before computers and the Internet. Whether the courts will extend these principles into the digital age remains to be seen. Nonetheless, UNICTRAL's Model Law represents a good baseline and may hold some influence with the court should a dispute over on-line contracts arise.

ON-LINE CONTRACT TERMS AND CONDITIONS

Most on-line contracts will not be formed after lengthy discussions and negotiations over specific terms and clauses. Rather, they will generally be standard form contracts,

3.68

---

[15] UNCITRAL's Model Law has met with some success, including its pivotal role in Singapore's Electronic Transactions Bill 1998.
[16] United Nations Commission on International Trade Law, Model Law on Electronic Commerce, Article 2(a).
[17] UNCITRAL Model Law on Electronic Commerce, Article 6(1).
[18] *ibid.*, Article 7(1).
[19] *ibid.*, Article 11(1).

also called contracts of adhesion. Besides key issues, such as price and type/quantity of goods or services, the terms in these contracts are not negotiated but are offered on a 'take-it-or-leave-it' basis. The standard terms and conditions are predrafted by the merchant to protect its interests, and the customer receives them only at the time of purchase, usually with neither the time nor the desire to scrutinise them.

The terms and conditions in these standard contracts often deal with more supplemental matters, such as payment method, exclusion or limitation of liability, warranties, choice of law, and jurisdiction. While electronic commerce businesses will understandably try to draft these terms to their advantage as much as possible, they must remain mindful of the restrictions imposed by legislation such as the Unfair Contract Terms Act 1977. English law recognises that customers generally bargain from an inferior position and have these standard terms imposed upon them. It requires that many exclusion clauses be reasonable in order to be enforceable.

Although a complete review of these topics is beyond the scope of the book they warrant detailed analysis because of the growing importance of standard form contracts in electronic commerce. The global and virtual nature of the Internet creates new concerns often not considered in the past, such as how to adequately display terms and conditions.[20] On-line merchants will also need to place emphasis on new or different clauses, such as specifying a method of contract formation, limitation of liability, warranties, choice of law, and jurisdiction. This section addresses these issues.

Displaying contract terms on-line

3.69   The terms and conditions in a standard form contract will have no effect unless the customer is given 'notice' of them before the contract is formed.[21] For example, in *Olley v. Marlborough Court Ltd*, a contract for a hotel room, having been signed at the hotel's reception desk, was not subject to terms found on a notice in the bedroom.[22] In general, this 'timing issue' should not pose a significant problem for on-line contracts, because on-line merchants can easily display the standard terms before a customer submits the order.

However, the requirements of 'notice' could pose a greater obstacle to on-line standard form contracts. Unless the customer signs the contract, in which case all specified terms should be effective,[23] merely displaying the terms somewhere may not be sufficient. In *Parker v. South Eastern Railway Co.*,[24] referring to standard terms printed on a railway ticket, the court (as interpreted by the court in *McCutcheon v. David MacBrayne Ltd*) divided the concept of notice into three questions of fact:

(1) Did the passenger know that there was printing on the railway ticket?
(2) Did he know that the ticket contained or referred to conditions?

---

[20] See the Data Protection Registrars concerns about electronic forms not providing warnings to the customers until the end of the form which is acceptable on hard copy forms but less so with on-line forms.
[21] *Chitty on Contracts*, 12–009.
[22] *Olley v. Marlborough Court Ltd* [1949] 1 K.B. 532.
[23] *L'Estrange v. Graucob* [1934] 2 K.B. 394. See paragraph 3.62 Signature Requirement above.
[24] *Parker v. South Eastern Railway Co.* (1877) 2 C.P.D. 416.

(3) Did the railway company do what was reasonable in the way of notifying prospective passengers of the existence of conditions and where their terms might be considered?[25]

Simply put by Lord Denning M.R. in *Thornton v. Shoe Lane Parking*, "the customer is bound by the . . . condition if he knows that the ticket is issued subject to it; or if the company did what was reasonably sufficient to give him notice of it."[26] An on-line merchant must make some reasonable effort, not just to make the terms available but also to inform the customer about the existence and meaning of those terms and conditions. **3.70**

For more onerous conditions, such as ones that deprive the customer of legal rights and remedies, English law demands an even greater effort by the merchant to give notice. In *Thornton*, which dealt with an exemption of liability for personal or bodily injury, Lord Denning M.R. suggested that:

> "It [the exemption] is so wide and so destructive of rights that the court should not hold any man bound by it unless it is drawn to his attention in the most explicit way. It is an instance of what I had in mind in *J. Spurling Ltd v. Bradshaw* [1956] 1 W.L.R. 461–466. In order to give sufficient notice, it would need to be printed in red ink with a red hand pointing to it — or something equally startling."[27]

World Wide Web

The world wide web complicates compliance with these notification requirements. On-line merchants have various means by which they can inform the customer of their standard terms and conditions. The following list describes a number of them in increasing order of substantiality (*i.e.* greater notice to the customer). However, electronic commerce businesses will need to balance legal weight and certainty with the resulting attractiveness of their websites. After all, the web pages are there to promote and sell goods, not as a legal exercise. Dense blocks of 'legalese' could be off-putting. **3.71**

- *Reference Statement without hyperlink* — Merchants could include a statement such as "This contract is subject to Company's standard terms and conditions" at the bottom of the order form. While this small statement may be commercially attractive, it may fail the reasonable notice requirement. The customer may not see the notice and, even if he/she does, there is no access to further information. Making the terms effective in this case would clearly be binding the customer to terms and conditions to which he/she did not assent.

- ,6●*Reference Statement with hyperlink* — The reference statement could be linked to a page containing the standard terms and conditions. This technique is popular with many web merchants because it achieves some legal credibility without substantial disruption to the promotional and commercial aspects of the order **3.72**

[25] *McCutcheon v. David MacBrayne Ltd* [1964] 1 W.L.R. 125 at 129, referencing *Parker v. South Eastern Railway Co.*, (1877) 2 C.P.D. 416, cited in *Thornton v. Shoe Lane Parking* [1971] 2 Q.B. 163 at 171.
[26] *Thornton v. Shoe Lane Parking*, [1971] 2 Q.B. 163 at 170.
[27] *ibid.*

form or web page. Indeed, it may satisfy the reasonable notice requirement for 'usual' terms. In *Parker v. South Eastern Railway*, a notice of 'See back' on the front of a railway ticket with the terms and conditions on the back was held to be sufficient notice. This 'See back' notice is strikingly similar to the hyperlink at the bottom of a web page.[28]

An alternative view, however, is that the hyperlink seemingly hides the terms and conditions from the customer. Just because the terms are somehow accessible does not mean that the user is induced to examine them. For example, in the U.S. case of *Microstar v. Formgen*,[29] the court admonished the merchant for putting the restrictive terms in a separate, non-cross-referenced file that the customer did not necessarily have to view.[30]

For more onerous terms, such as long term financial commitments, the hyperlink method is likely to be inadequate, if one applies Lord Denning's example of using "red ink with a red hand pointing at it." In *Interfoto Picture Library Ltd v. Stiletto Visual Programmes Ltd*,[31] the court ruled that the vendor had a duty to drawn attention to particularly surprising or onerous terms using boldface type or a separately attached note. In that case, the surprising term was a particularly harsh penalty clause for the late return of photographs. Thus, electronic commerce businesses using the hyperlink method of displaying terms might best transfer the surprising terms and exclusion/limitation clauses off the 'legal page' and onto the actual order form.

- *Display Terms at Bottom of Page* — Instead of hyperlinking the standard terms and conditions, the merchant could stream the whole text at the bottom of the order form or web page. Since the terms are conspicuously displayed, this method has greater legal weight in terms of notice. However, it can easily make the web page visually unattractive. Also, the user is still a passive participant, since the web page has not required him/her to actively demonstrate that he/she had the opportunity to read the terms and conditions.

3.73
- *Dialogue Box* — One of the most elaborate display mechanisms is to create a dialogue box that forces the user to scroll through the terms and conditions before clicking 'I agree' or 'I have reviewed these terms.' Notwithstanding the possibility of this 'click wrap' being held as a signature,[32] this rather draconian approach is legally powerful. The customer is not just given the opportunity to review the terms; indeed, he/she is forced to review them and to agree through a positive action (the 'click'). The customer clearly realises that the contract is subject to certain terms and conditions.

Naturally, the most effective method legally is probably the most undesirable and unattractive method commercially. Not only is the customer's dialogue box filled with

---

[28] *Parker v. South Eastern Railway* (1877) 2 C.P.D. 416.
[29] *Microstar v. Formgen*, 942 F. Supp. 1312 (S.D. Cal. 1996).
[30] The court in *Microstar*, however, did not rule on the validity on the license in that case.
[31] *Interfoto Picture Library Ltd v. Stiletto Visual Programmes Ltd* [1989] Q.B. 433, [1988] 1 All E.R. 348.
[32] See paragraph 3.62 argues against the clickwrap signature, but it remains a possibility for the courts.

lines of legalese, but he/she must also waste time scrolling through and clicking the assent button. The process could be off putting to the customer, especially when purchasing only low value goods in services. However, this method is more visually attractive than simply appending the terms to the bottom of the web page or order form. At least here, the legalese is confined to the smaller dialogue box.

As previously mentioned, web merchants will have to balance the legal protection and the commercial desirability offered by the above methods. This last option, the dialogue box, however, appears promising. If it can be incorporated into the ordering process, its unattractiveness may be significantly diminished. For example, in the final stage of the order process, after review of the order itself, the web page could require the customer to scroll through the conditions before clicking on the final "Submit order and agree to above terms."   **3.74**

An alternative method could be only to have first-time customers perform the annoying 'scroll and click process,' assuming that on subsequent occasions the customer is already aware of the standard terms and conditions. As decided in *Spurling v. Bradshaw*,[33] previous dealings can bind a party to standard terms and conditions, even if the party is not presented with the terms on subsequent occasions. Nevertheless, the safest procedure is to present the terms and conditions in every instance.

Electronic mail

Complying with notice requirements in electronic mail contracts probably offers the electronic commerce merchant very little choice. Standard terms and conditions will probably have to be included at the bottom of the electronic mail offer (or invitation to treat) in order to constitute proper notice. Electronic mails with 'phantom' referencing statements such as "this contract is subject to the Company's standard terms and conditions" will not suffice.   **3.75**

Further, placing the terms and conditions in attachments or hyperlinks embedded in the electronic mail will meet similar, if not more substantial, objections to the ones explained above for web contracts. For example, electronic mail attachments often get removed by firewalls, and thus the terms may not even accompany the electronic mail. Additionally, the hyperlinks assume that the electronic mail program will support them and that the user has access to the world wide web (which will not be the case if a text-only connection is being used).

Express, Implied, and Mandatory Terms

Properly drafted and displayed to the customer, expressly stated standard terms and conditions are useful devices for protecting the electronic commerce merchant's best interests. However, just as in the case of 'traditional' contracts, on-line contracts are subject to implied and mandatory terms. These either 'fill in the gaps' between or go beyond the terms expressly stated. This section focuses on these three types of contractual term: express, implied and mandatory. A proper understanding of their distinctions and the issues they raise is essential to any on-line merchant who wishes to construct enforceable on-line contracts to their advantage.   **3.76**

---

[33] *Spurling v. Bradshaw* [1956] 2 All E.R. 121.

Express Terms

3.77 In a standard form contract, express terms are found in the standard terms and conditions. They directly and explicitly specify on what terms the merchant wishes to conduct business. Express terms can also specifically override any undesirable implied terms, protecting the merchant from unwanted liability or responsibility.[34] Under English law, once the parties have expressed some view on a particular matter in the contract, "they have expressed all the conditions by which they intend to be bound under that agreement."[35]

As the party in the position to draft standard terms and conditions, on-line merchants appear to have an inherent legal advantage. However, if they fail to exercise care in drafting their standard terms, this advantage can be easily squandered. When the courts interpret written contractual terms, they will focus almost exclusively on the outward appearances and meanings conveyed, not the actual underlying intention of the parties.[36] The House of Lords confirmed this doctrine in *Deutsche Genossenschaftsbank v. Burnhope*, stating:

> "It is true the objective of the construction [of contract] is to give effect to the intention of the parties. But our law of construction is based on an objective theory. The methodology is not to probe the real intentions of the parties but to ascertain the contextual meaning of the relevant contractual language. Intention is determined by reference to expressed rather than actual intention."[37]

As a result, poorly drafted, and ambiguous terms and conditions could result in judicial interpretations unfavourable to the on-line merchant. Indeed, the interpretations will almost certainly be unfavourable; in the case of vague or ambiguous terms, English law requires the courts to interpret the terms against the party who drafted them.[38] The customer will receive the benefit of the doubt.

Express terms are also subject to legal restrictions such as the Unfair Contract Terms Act 1977. To retain their legal advantage as 'drafter,' vendors will have to carefully craft their standard terms and conditions to avoid these pitfalls.

Implied terms

3.78 On-line contracts, like traditional written contracts, cannot possibly explicitly account for every single possibility. As a result, the law interprets contracts using the customs of society or the relevant commercial sector. These customs and the context they provide necessarily insert implicit contractual terms into areas where the explicit contract is silent. As the court suggested in *Hutton v. Warren*:

> "It has long been settled that, in commercial transactions, extrinsic evidence of custom and usage is admissible to annex incidents to written contracts, in matters with respect to which

---

[34] See paragraph for a discussion of implied terms.
[35] *Aspdin v. Austin* (1844) 5 Q.B. 671 at 684 cited in *Chitty* 12–078.
[36] *Smith v. Lucas* (1881) 18 Ch.D. 531–542.
[37] *Deutsche Genossenschaftsbank v. Burnhope* [1996] 1 Lloyd's Rep. 113 at 122.
[38] *Adams v. Richardson & Starling Ltd* [1969] 1 W.L.R. 1645.

they are silent. The same rule has also been applied to contracts in other transactions of life, in which known usages have been established and prevailed; and this has been done upon the principle of presumption that, in such transactions, the parties did not mean to express in writing the whole of the contract by which they intended to be bound, but a contract with reference to those known usages."[39]

For example, when a customer purchases books on-line it is obviously expected that they will be of 'satisfactory quality' not warped.'[40] No contractual term explicitly states this, but the term is implied by the context of the transaction.

The simple example above demonstrates an obvious case of an implied term. However, like many implied terms arising from commercial customs and practices, the notion of 'satisfactory quality' took decades to develop. For years it was a commercial understanding without any definitive legal basis until it appeared as 'merchantable quality' in 1815 in *Gardiner v. Gray*.[41] The implied term was subsequently codified in the Sale of Goods Act 1893.[42] Since the commercial world of cyberspace is not even a decade old, it has obviously not had the opportunity to develop well recognised practices and customs. Also, since the Internet environment is constantly changing, new and novel industry practices continually arise. What is accepted practice today may not be tomorrow. Thus, what the courts will imply into future electronic commerce agreements is largely unknown. This creates a rather uncertain environment for vendors.

Even extending traditional implied terms into cyberspace often poses problems, particularly for digitised services. For example, does software have to satisfy the implied requirement of satisfactory quality and fitness of purpose for goods? This question is actually one of the few issues the courts have addressed. In *St Albans City and District Council v. International Computers Ltd*,[43] the court indeed held that defective software "would *prima facie* be a breach of the terms as to quality and fitness of purpose."[44] Yet, even this decision leaves questions unanswered. *St Albans* dealt with bespoke software and the damages resulting from its faulty calculations. But what about commercial software that is downloaded as a digitised service? Surely a customer expects that downloaded software will run properly. If the program has minor bugs or is incompatible with the customer's computer, is the customer entitled to a refund because the program failed to meet 'satisfactory quality?' Unfortunately, digitised services are insidiously vulnerable to copying and piracy. Would an implied term to refund provide a loophole which dishonest customers could exploit to obtain free services?

Chris Reed has suggested[45] that contracts for the supply of digitised products should as a minimum have implied terms which cover delivery, ownership and use rights,

3.79

---

[39] *Hutton v. Warren* (1836) 1 M. & W. 466 at 475–476.
[40] The Sale of Goods Act 1979, section states that, unless expressly specified otherwise, customers can imply that the goods they purchase will be of satisfactory quality.
[41] *Gardiner v. Gray* (1815) 4 Camp. 144.
[42] The Sale of Goods Act 1979 replaced the 'merchantable quality' found in the Sale of Goods Act 1893 with the term 'satisfactory quality.'
[43] *St Albans City and District Council v. International Computer Ltd* [1996] 4 All E.R. 481.
[44] *ibid.* at 493.
[45] Paper given to the Third Annual Advanced I.T. Conference on October 16, 1998.

description and quality. However, in the case of digitised products these implied terms will be very different from normal implied terms relating to goods or services. For example, implied terms for delivery of goods or performance of services tend to require performance within a reasonable time unless a specific time is agreed. For digitised products this is unlikely to be specific enough. Chris Reed suggests that if a digitised product is transmitted by a supplier via a website download it should try and transmit it within a reasonable number of hours of receiving payment. Electronic commerce for digitised products will require payment before delivery unless completion of the payment process should trigger the time period. If information is to be collected by providing a customer with a password or creating a customised website with password protected download then it should be made available for inspection within a reasonable time and a reasonable number of hours of payment for these reasons and remain available for collection for a reasonable time. Chris Reed also suggests the addition of the implied terms would also be necessary to deal with communications failures in the file transfer process so that an electronic commerce business would provide for re-delivery if delivery fails or that the electronic commerce business will make a refund if delivery is impossible.

Similar problems arise in other instances of applying traditional rules to cyberspace. The Sale of Goods Act 1979 further implies, unless otherwise stated, that in a sale by sample, "the bulk will correspond with the sample in quality." Many computer games are promoted on-line through the use of 'shareware' demonstration versions that only allow the user to play a limited game. Could this practice be construed of as a sale by sample? If so, creating a shareware version that consolidated the few, high-resolution graphics found in the comprehensive version (to make the game appear more impressive) might form the basis of an action for breach of contract.[46]

3.80   In addition to implied terms arising out of industry practice and/or codifying legislation, the courts themselves may imply terms from the language of the contract. However, the courts' discretion is severely limited to only what will give business efficacy to the contract and what is the obvious intention of the parties.[47] Thus, as Lord Pearson said in *Trollope and Colls Ltd v. North West Metropolitan Regional Hospital Board*:

> "An unexpressed term can be implied if and only if the court finds that the parties must have intended that term to form part of their contract: it is not enough for the court to find that such a term would have been adopted by the parties as reasonable men if it had been suggested to them: it must have been a term that went without saying, a term *necessary* to give business efficacy to the contract, a term which although tacit, formed part of the contract which the parties made for themselves."[48]

At the moment, not much goes "without saying" in electronic commerce. The environment is too new and untested for on-line merchants to rely on implied contractual terms.

---

[46] This practice could also form the basis for an action in misrepresentation, though admittedly, those high resolution graphics do exist in the comprehensive version, just at a different level of frequency.
[47] *Chitty*, 13-004.
[48] *Trollope and Colls Ltd v. North West Metropolitan Regional Hospital Board* [1973] 2 All E.R. 260 at 268.

In almost all areas, either industry practice has not yet been well developed or accepted, or the applicability of traditional customs and practices is unknown. The courts therefore have very little on which to base decisions except for the express terms found in the standard terms and conditions and perhaps their own common sense. Consequently, wherever any doubt exists, the electronic commerce business will wisely state its intentions in express terms.

Mandatory terms

Despite the apparent legal advantage given to electronic commerce businesses as the drafters of standard terms and conditions, they certainly do not have complete freedom. Parliament, recognising the dominant bargaining position held by vendors, has imposed mandatory implied terms which may not be excluded or limited in contracts. Many of the terms have arisen through the recent progress in consumer protection, and almost all are felt to be so fundamental that to exclude them would be unfair or unreasonable.

3.81

An example of a mandatory term is found in the Unfair Contract Terms Act 1977, which, among other things, prohibits the exclusion or restriction of liability for personal injury or death resulting from negligence.[49]

Contract Formation Terms

One of the principal areas requiring express terms in an on-line contract is how the contract itself is formed. In traditional contracts, this topic created less concern, since the 'rules' and business practices are better established. However, in on-line contracts electronic commerce businesses will want to expressly delineate the contract formation process to create greater legal certainty and to give themselves as many options and advantages as possible.

3.82

The "Contract Formation" clause of the standard terms and conditions can encompass the entire contract formation process, including the following terms. The reasons and rationale behind these terms were discussed in great detail in paragraph 3.28 Contract Creation.

(1) What constitutes an offer, as opposed to an invitation to treat;
(2) Whether counteroffers are allowed, prohibition against customer-changed offer terms where there is automated computer acceptance;
(3) If the merchant is making an offer, how long an offer is valid and what constitutes revocation of an offer;
(4) What constitutes acceptance: how, by what method and exactly when an acceptance is effective (postal or receipt rule).

A sample contract creation term is shown in the box below.

---

[49] Unfair Contract Terms Act 1977, s.2(1).

> **Contract Formation**
>
> All communications made by the Company thus far are invitations to treat only. Prices and availability of goods are subject to change. You agree not to change these standard terms and conditions from the form presented by the Company. This Agreement represents an offer of contract from you only, and is not binding until acceptance is sent via electronic mail by the Company and received by you. The Company reserves the right to refuse your offer for any reason.

Limitation and Exclusion of Liabilities

3.83   For on-line merchants of goods and services, limitation and exclusion of liability clauses are quite similar to the traditional case of a direct-mail supplier. Using their standard terms and conditions, electronic commerce businesses will try to exclude as much liability for errors and negligence as possible and limit or cap what cannot be excluded.

> **Liability**
>
> In no event will the Company be liable to you for any indirect, incidental or consequential damages arising out of the services or any products provided under this Agreement, even if the Company has been advised of the possibility of such damages. Except for cases of personal injury or death, arising from the Company's negligence the Company's liability to you for actual damages, regardless of the form of action, will be strictly limited to the price of the services or products sold.

English law, heavily regulates the exclusion or limitation of liability in standard form business contracts and consumer contracts. As previously mentioned, a standard form business contract is where one of the parties deals on his own pre-drafted standard terms and conditions. Overlapping in some respects, a consumer contract is defined under the Unfair Contract Terms Act 1977 using three criteria: first, the customer or consumer does not make the contract in the course of a business, and does not hold itself out as doing so; second, the other party, the supplier, makes the contract in the course of a business; and third, the goods being supplied are ordinarily used for private consumption.[50]

3.84   One of the uncertainties regarding the definition of a consumer contract is whether a buyer is actually making the contract in the course of business. In *R. & B. Customs Brokers Co. Ltd v. United Dominions Trust Ltd,*[51] the court held that "in the course of business" meant that "the transaction must be an integral part of the business carried on or, if only incidental thereto, be of a type regularly entered into."[52] Thus, a bank ordering flowers on-line to send to an important customer would probably involve a consumer contract. The definition given in the judgment, however, still offers considerable room for interpretation.

---

[50] Unfair Contract Terms Act 1977, s.12(1).
[51] *R. & B. Customs Brokers Co. Ltd v. United Dominions Trust Ltd* [1988] 1 W.L.R. 321.
[52] *Chitty,* 14-052.

The Unfair Contract Terms Act 1977 regulates exclusion and limitation of liability clauses in most consumer and standard form contracts for goods and services. It does not, however, apply to a few specific types of contract, including ones for insurance, securities, land, and intellectual property rights (creation, transfer or termination). Interestingly, it also does not apply to the international supply of goods defined as [53] where the formation or performance of a sale of goods contract takes place across international borders.[54]

This definition of international supply contracts poses substantial issues for consumers and electronic commerce business who transact internationally on-line. If a consumer in the U.K. purchases goods or services on-line from a foreign country, the Unfair Contract Terms Act 1977 will not be applicable. The foreign merchant will be able to ignore the Act's provisions (discussed below) to its great advantage. Similarly, a U.K. vendor can ignore the Act in dealing with foreign customers.

Another potential area of debate is whether international sales of digitised services fall under the definition of 'goods' and are thereby excluded from the Act's restrictions. Downloadable software and other digitised services are essentially dematerialised versions of goods, as suggested in paragraph 3.07. This particular interpretation, however, has yet to gain universal acceptance. In any case, international supply contracts will naturally become more popular and important as electronic commerce becomes increasingly global and they may require similar 'unfair term legislation' in the future.

The most serious restriction imposed by the Unfair Contract Terms Act 1977 is found in Section 2(1). Here, the Act renders any contractual term that excludes or limits liability for personal injury or death due to negligence invalid and unenforceable. Unlike other sections of the Act discussed below, this restriction is applicable to all contracts, including non-standard form contracts. Thus contracts should refrain from making any such disclaimers. The example limitation clause above follows this suggestion.

Besides personal injury or death, all other exclusions or limitations of liabilities in standard form contracts are subject to a test of reasonableness. For example, the popular clauses limiting direct damages to the price of product or service and excluding liability for incidental or consequential damages fall under test this test. Schedule 2 of the Act lists five guidelines for determining reasonableness. Though they are neither exhaustive nor always applicable, they are often used by the courts for evaluating contractual terms:

(1) the strength of the bargaining positions of the parties relative to each other, taking into account (among other things) alternative means by which the customer's requirement could have been met;

(2) whether the customer received an inducement to agree to the term, or in accepting it had an opportunity of entering into a similar contract with other persons, but without having to accept a similar term;

(3) whether the customer knew or ought reasonably to have known of the existence and extent of the term (having regard, among other things, to any custom of the trade and any previous course of dealing between the parties);

---

[53] Unfair Contract Terms Act 1977, Schedule 1.
[54] *ibid.* at Section 26.

(4) where the term excludes or restricts any relevant liability if some condition is not complied with, whether it was reasonable at the time of the contract to expect that compliance with that condition would be practicable;

(5) whether the goods were manufactured, processed or adapted to the special order of the customer.[55]

3.86   In addition to these five principles, in House of Lords case of *Smith v. Eric S. Bush*, Lord Griffiths gave a similar set of principles:

(a) Were the parties of equal bargaining power?

(b) In the case of advice, would it have been reasonably practicable to obtain the advice from an alternative source taking into account considerations of costs and time?

(c) How difficult is the task being undertaken for which liability is being excluded?

(d) What are the practical consequences of the decision on the question of reasonableness?[56]

Both Lord Griffith, referring to (d) practical consequences, and the Unfair Contract Terms Act 1977 in Section 11(4) further recommended that the courts consider whether insurance is available to protect the company attempting to limit the liability. As an example, two recent software liability cases hinged significantly on this insurance consideration.

3.87   In *St Albans City and District Council v. International Computers Ltd*,[57] a faulty computer program designed by ICL for St Albans resulted in a loss of nearly £1 million, but a clause in ICL's standard terms and conditions limited its liability to £100,000. In the originating trial court, Scott Baker J. held that this limitation was unreasonable, considering, among other things, that ICL had the resources to remedy the damage as well as an insurance policy of £50 million. The Court of Appeal affirmed this decision.

Similarly, in *Salvage Association v. Cap Financial Services*,[58] the court held that a clause limiting liability to £25,000 was unreasonable. This decision reasoned that, among other things, a supplier can obtain insurance far more easily and cheaply than the customer. Additionally, the supplier already had insurance covering up to £5 million in damages.[59]

The Unfair Terms in Consumer Contracts Regulations 1994[60] apply to all business contracts with consumers for the sale or supply of goods or services. Unlike the Unfair Contract Terms Act 1977 the Regulations cover all terms in a contract not just those that limit or exclude liability. The Regulations only cover contracts with consumers whereas the 1977 Act covers business to business electronic commerce contracts. The Regulations apply to terms which have not been individually negotiated. The Regulations will

---

[55] *ibid.* at Schedule 2.
[56] *Smith v. Eric S Bush* [1990] 1 A.C. 831, [1989] 2 All E.R. 514. Also *Harris v. Wyre Forest District, ibid.* (twin appeal cases).
[57] *St Albans City and District Council v. International Computers Ltd* [1995] F.S.R. 686, [1996] 4 All E.R. 481. (CA).
[58] *Salvage Association v. Cap Financial Services* [1995] F.S.R. 654.
[59] *Chitty Supplement* (1997) 14–074.
[60] Implement the E.C. Directive on Unfair Terms in Consumer Contracts (93/13/EEC) and come into force on July 1, 1995.

therefore apply to all electronic commerce contracts with consumers which are in the electronic commerce businesses standard form even if a consumer has had the opportunity to negotiate specific terms. The Regulations provide that any unfair term does not bind the consumer. However issues on the subject matter and price cannot render a term unfair. The Regulations detail an exhaustive list of the sort of terms which may be regarded as unfair. Finally the Regulations require contracts to be in plain intelligible language.

Warranties

Under the Sale of Goods Act 1979,[61] any contract for the sale of goods has an implied warranty of 'satisfactory quality,' which takes into consideration the description, price, and all other relevant circumstances of the sale.[62] This warranty is strict. There is no defence of having exercised reasonable care in manufacturing, handling and transport of the goods, etc.[63] The goods must also be reasonably fit for the purpose for which they are being bought, though for unusual instances, English law may require that the buyer inform the seller first.[64]

3.88

In contrast to goods, contracts for services have an implied term that the supplier will perform the service with reasonable care and skill.[65] If the supply is for professional services, the level expected is that of a professional person with ordinary skill and expertise. The essential difference between classifying a product as a good or a service hinges on this distinction between satisfactory quality and performance with reasonable care and skill. The law holds goods and services to different standards and, in case of a dispute, one standard may be more easily satisfied than the other.

For the most part in electronic commerce, the traditional distinction between goods and services and the warranties those contracts imply will remain exactly the same. Buying a football from the local sporting goods store is no different from buying it from the on-line version. In order to maintain customer satisfaction and loyalty, most on-line businesses offer generous return and refund policies, just like their high street counterparts. However, even if an on-line merchant wanted to exclude the applicable implied warranties, it would not be permitted in the case of consumer contracts. Under Section 6(2) of the Unfair Contract Terms Act 1977, the implied warranties of satisfactory quality and fitness of purpose cannot be excluded or limited. The on-line merchant might succeed in disallowing refunds without cause, but even then would have to contend with the Distance Selling Directive (Chapter 2) which will require a mandatory seven day withdrawal period for the consumer. Thus, most consumers will not see a substantial change in warranty policy as they move from the high street to cyberspace.

However, one area that continues to pose problems for measurements of quality is digitised services, particularly software. Regardless of whether software is judged to be a good or a service (paragraph 3.07), determining standards for software quality poses a

3.89

---

[61] All references to the Sale of Goods Act 1979 assume that it is as amended by the Sale and Supply of Goods Act 1994.
[62] Sale of Goods Act 1979 (as amended), section 14(2A).
[63] *Chitty*, 41-074.
[64] Sale of Goods Act 1979, s.14(3).
[65] Supply of Goods and Services Act 1982, s.13.

considerable challenge for the courts. Given the complex nature of software programming and execution, all commercial software will almost always have bugs. Do these
bugs constitute a breach of satisfactory quality or reasonable care? A similar argument
may apply to other digitised services, since they typically depend on a software
platform, and bugs in the platform can distort or disrupt the digitised service, whether it
is audio, video, text, etc.

Unfortunately, most of the case law deals with bespoke software rather than
commercially available, packaged software. However, the bespoke cases do offer a view
into the courts' rationale and may be predictive of future decisions on packaged
software. In *Saphena Computing Ltd v. Allied Collection Agencies Ltd*,[66] the court recognised
the bug and defect removal process as a slow and iterative one, and that:

> "Just as no software developer can reasonably expect a buyer to tell him what is required
> without a process of feedback and reassessment, so no buyer should expect a supplier to get
> his programs right first time."[67]

3.90   Thus, software containing bugs were not a breach of satisfactory quality. The supplier
was merely required to fix those bugs in due course. Similarly, in *Eurodynamic Systems v.
General Automation Ltd*,[68] Steyn J. concluded that:

> "The expert evidence convincingly showed that it is regarded as acceptable practice to
> supply computer program (including system software) that contain errors and bugs. The
> basis of the practice is that, pursuant to his support obligation (free or chargeable as the case
> may be), the supplier will correct errors and bugs that prevent the product from being
> properly used. Not every bug or error in a computer program can therefore be categorised
> as a breach of contract."

These two precedents favouring leniency were then followed by *St Albans v. ICL*, where,
as mentioned in paragraph 3.87, the court awarded the plaintiff approximately £1
million in damages stemming from the consequences of a programming error that
breached the requirement of satisfactory quality.[69] Thus, on the whole, the courts appear
to measure software quality on a case by case basis. As *Eurodynamics* suggests, not every
bug is a breach of the implied term to satisfactory quality or reasonable care and skill,
but some, more insidious errors can be. In cases where quality is neglected, the damages
can be startling.

The above cases involved bespoke software where the parties knew the level of
quality expected and the purposes anticipated. Mass-produced application software and
other digitised services will be quite different in this respect. With respect to the
requirement of fitness for purpose, one might expect a legal distinction between
personal use and business use, since errors in business application software can result in
far greater damages. One might see digitised service providers in the future restricting

---

[66] *Saphena Computing Ltd v. Allied Collection Agencies Ltd* [1995] F.S.R. 616.
[67] *ibid.* at 652.
[68] *Eurodynamic Systems v. General Automation Ltd* (1988) Q.B.D., September 6, unreported.
[69] The damages were reduced by the Court of Appeal.

programs for personal use only, or charging a premium for business use in order to cover the added liability risk. If a premium is collected, that 'business' version will naturally be held to a higher and more stringent standard.

Payment and Delivery Terms

Standard terms and conditions will undoubtedly specify the specific payment and delivery terms of the transaction. On-line payment methods such as digital cash and the secure transmission of credit card numbers are covered in Chapter 5, 'Getting Paid in Cyberspace'. However, regarding contractual issues of payment, on-line vendors and customers should keep two legal principles (and their respective nineteenth century precedents) in mind.

    In *Luttges v. Sherwood*,[70] the court held that cash lost in the post consituted non-payment. Thus, the sending of payment is not like the sending of an acceptance; the postal rule does not apply. In order to satisfy the payment terms of the contract, the other party must receive the payment. Applying this rule to cyberspace, digital cash that becomes 'lost' *en route* to the on-line merchant does not constitute payment either. If there is a fault in the line or server connection and subsequently the digital cash disappears, the customer is left with the loss. Due to the rule in *Luttges*, people in traditional commerce rarely ever sent cash through the mail; it is too insecure. Besides, an unscrupulous merchant theoretically could even keep the cash and deny ever having received it. In the future, customers in cyberspace may want two systems, anonymous digital cash for small transactions and privacy, and traceable digital cash for larger transactions and accountability.

    In *Norman v. Ricketts*,[71] however, the court suggested that if the contractual terms described a method of payment and the sender observes the specified procedures, the sender will not have liability for the lost payment. From the customer standpoint, this case rightfully balances the burden of accountability and record keeping imposed by *Luttges*. However, for the on-line merchant, the precedent gives a good reason to exercise caution in specifying a payment method. Instead, vendors should probably add a standard term which denies liability and responsibility for lost credit card numbers and digital cash. Let the customer send the payment at his or her own risk.

3.91

SUMMARY

This chapter has addressed the key issues concerning electronic commerce businesses contracting on-line. Why does an on-line merchant want to select the customer with whom he deals? Does electronic mail fall under the postal rule or the receipt rule of acceptance? Does an electronic document constitute 'writing?' How should an electronic commerce business display its standard terms and conditions on-line? Can a web server constitute a 'place of business?' Many of these issues are made academic if on-line merchants abide by the primary rule:

3.92

---

[70] *Luttges v. Sherwood* (1895) 11 T.L.R. 233.
[71] *Norman v. Ricketts* (1886) 3 T.L.R. 182.

> Specify everything possible in the standard terms and conditions. English law occa-sionally restricts the extent of these standard terms but, for the most part, on-line merchants are free to choose the way by which they contract and do business.

The following is a short list of the key areas which should be explicitly addressed in the terms and conditions of an on-line contract:

(a) Selecting Customers — at whom are the advertisements and contracts directed?

(b) Offer/Invitation to Treat — what do the advertisements and order forms constitute?

(c) Acceptance Methods and Procedures — what constitutes an acceptance? How and when is a contract formed?

(d) Revocations — how can an offer be revoked?

(e) Limitations of Liability/Warranty — for exactly what does the on-line merchant have responsibility?

(f) Applicable Law/Jurisdiction — what law and forum govern the interpretation of the contract?[72]

---

[72] See Chapter 4.

— • 4 • —

INTERNATIONAL ISSUES

> "There is no Government like no Government"[1]

The global and borderless nature of electronic commerce means that contracting parties **4.01**
and customers are just as likely to be from overseas as from the U.K. Consequently,
jurisdictional issues are inevitable. This chapter is divided into three sections. The first
section considers which jurisdiction will be the forum for any dispute. The second
section considers which country's or state's laws will govern the contract the subject of
any dispute, and the third section briefly considers enforcement of judgments overseas.

JURISDICTION (FORUM)

The issue of forum — which country will hear a dispute, resolve it, and enforce the **4.02**
contractual terms — is decided by the laws of jurisdiction. Jurisdictional issues
encountered on-line are not new or novel and are well addressed by legislation and
international conventions drafted before the emergence of electronic commerce.
However, in practice, the borderless nature of electronic commerce has raised the
importance of jurisdictional issues to a far higher level. On-line merchants as well as
customers will need to know how to enforce their contracts against foreign parties in the
global economy.

Jurisdiction in the U.K. is principally governed by the Brussels Convention on
Jurisdiction and the Enforcement of Judgments in Civil and Commercial Matter 1968.
This was implemented into U.K. law by the Civil Jurisdiction and Judgments Act 1982.
With only a few exceptions,[2] the Convention governs all civil and commercial matters,
thereby covering most, if not all, electronic commerce transactions.

The Brussels Convention applies to "Contracting States," members of the European
Union (E.U.). In addition, European Free Trade Agreement (EFTA) countries are brought
under essentially identical rules through the Lugano Convention 1988.[3] In both Conventions, the determination of jurisdiction relies significantly on whether or not a party to

---

[1] The New Barbarians or How to Survive the Information Age — Professor Ian O'Angell.
[2] Exceptions include marriage, wills, bankrupty, social security, customs, taxes, etc. See the 1968 Convention
on Jurisdiction and the Enforcement of Judgments in Civil and Commercial Matters, Article 1.
[3] *The Supreme Court Practice* 1997, Volume 2, para. 8–037.

the contract is domiciled in a Contracting State. If the defendant in domiciled in a Contracting State, the rules of the Convention apply; otherwise English common law will govern the determination of jurisdiction.

Domicile Determination

Persons

4.03   As mentioned above, the key determinant for jurisdiction is domicile. For the Convention to apply, the defendant's domicile must be either in the U.K. or another Contracting State. Interestingly, the Brussels Convention leaves the rules regarding domicile to domestic law. Under English law, domicile is defined under Sections 41-46 of the Civil Jurisdiction and Judgements Act 1982.

A defendant is domiciled in the United Kingdom if he/she is resident in the U.K. and if the nature of that residence indicates a "substantial connection" with the U.K.[4] A substantial connection is automatically presumed, although disputable, if the period of residence is greater than three months.[5] Alternatively, a defendant is domiciled in a Contracting State outside the U.K. if he/she would be so viewed under *that* country's legal system.[6] Under either of these conditions, the Convention rules of jurisdiction will apply.

However, if the defendant does not satisfy either of the above criteria, or if he/she is domiciled in a non-Contracting State, jurisdictional issue questions will be determined by common law. A defendant is domiciled in a non-Contracting State if he/she is resident in that foreign country and his/her residence constitutes a substantial connection.

Corporations

For corporations, the seat of the corporation is defined as its domicile.[7] Again, if the defendant corporation has its seat in the U.K. or another Contracting State, jurisdictional questions will be subject to the Brussels Convention. A corporation has its seat in the U.K. if it was incorporated under U.K. law or if its "central management and control" is exercised in the U.K.[8] Similarly, a corporation has its seat in a Contracting State outside the U.K. if it was incorporated in that State, or its central management and control is exercised in that foreign State.[9] Furthermore, the foreign Contracting State must recognise that the corporation has its seat there.[10]

Just as in the case of a natural person, if a corporation is not recognised as having a seat in the U.K. or another Contracting State, jurisdiction will be determined by common law.

---

[4] Civil Jurisdiction and Judgments Act 1982, s.41(2).
[5] *ibid.*, s.41(6).
[6] Convention on Jurisdiction and the Enforcement of Judgments in Civil and Commercial Matters (1968), article 52.
[7] Civil Jurisdiction and Judgments Act 1982, s.42(1).
[8] *ibid.*, s.42(2).
[9] However, in case of conflict been a seat in the U.K. and one in a foreign Contracting State, the U.K. seat will take precedence. For example, if the defendant is incorporated in the U.K. but has its central management and control in France, the English courts will place its seat in the U.K. Civil Jurisdiction and Judgments Act 1982, sections 42(6)–(7).
[10] Civil Jurisdiction and Judgments Act 1982, s.42(7).

Application of the Brussels Convention

If the Brussels Convention applies, the determination of jurisdiction is greatly simplified. **4.04**
Unless the contract has a jurisdiction clause (paragraph 4.14), jurisdiction will usually lie
in the courts of the defendant's domicile. A defendant has the right to be sued only in
his/her home domicile.

The general rule of the defendant's domicile, however, is subject to a number of
exceptions. For example, the general rule does not apply to certain contracts such as
insurance,[11] land, and intellectual property.[12] In these areas, specific criteria given in the
Brussels Convention grant exclusive jurisdiction to a relevant country. For example, for
contracts concerning the transfer of intellectual property rights, the courts of the country
where those rights are registered or deposited have exclusive jurisdiction.

Expected place of performance

An important exception to the rule of defendant's domicile is that a defendant may be **4.05**
sued in "the place of performance of the obligation in question."[13] This exception has
great relevance to contracts, since most disputes will involve a defendant who has failed
to perform a contractual duty. In the electronic commerce transactions, failure to
perform will often involve failure to pay for the goods or services rendered. According
to *The Eider:*

> "The general rule is that where no place of payment is specified, either expressly or by
> implication, the debtor must seek out his creditor."[14]

This statement implies that when a customer pays an on-line vendor, the place of
performance is at the vendor's location. Thus, if a customer (non-consumer, see
paragraph 4.06) fails to pay, he/she can be sued in the on-line vendor's jurisdiction.

> A French travel agency orders books on-line from an English bookseller who promptly
> delivers them to Lyon. However, the cheque from the travel agency is not honored
> and the travel agency refuses to deliver further payment. Under the 'place of
> performance' clause in the Brussels Convention, the travel agency can be sued in
> the U.K., even though its domicile is France.

However, the converse of the above situation is not true. This may have English
customers slightly unprotected. An on-line vendor who fails to deliver goods or delivers
defective goods cannot be sued in the customer's jurisdiction. Under English law, a
seller only has a duty to ship the goods, not deliver them, to the buyer. Thus, according

---

[11] Convention on Jurisdiction and the Enforcement of Judgments in Civil and Commercial Matters (1968)
articles 7–12.
[12] Convention on Jurisdiction and the Enforcement of Judgments in Civil and Commercial Matters (1968)
article 16.
[13] Brussels Convention, article 5(1). The reader should note that this place of performance rule is different from
the breach of contract rule in common law jurisdiction found in paragraph 4.12. As discussed in that section,
breach of contract can occur in ways other than failure to perform, such as explicit and implicit repudiation.
[14] *The Eider* [1893] P 119, at 136–137 (CA), cited in Dicey 336.

to the House of Lords in *Johnson v. Taylor*,[15] the substantive part of performance occurs at the seller's location, where it ships the goods, rather than at the buyer's. Consequently, an English customer cannot sue a foreign merchant for breach of contract in an English court because the defendant's domicile and the place of performance is overseas. Notably, however, this rule does not protect English on-line merchants in the same way, since foreign countries may locate the place of performance elsewhere.

Consumer Contracts

4.06   Another significant exception to the rule of defendant's domicile rule is in consumer contracts. Under Article 14 of the Convention, a consumer may sue the defendant vendor in either the defendant's domicile or the consumer's own domicile. On the other hand, the consumer can only be sued in his/her own domicile. Recognising the limited resources of consumers, this exemption eases the burden on them when responding or initiating legal action.

One should note, however, that the definition of consumer contract under the Convention is slightly different from that found in the Unfair Contract Terms Act 1977 and other areas of English law. While sales of goods to a consumer are included in entirety, contracts for the supply of services are only considered as consumer contracts if two conditions are satisfied. The consumer contract had to be solicited (*i.e.* direct mailing or advertising) by the merchant in the consumer's domicile and the consumer must have completed all contract formation steps there.

This distinction between goods and services, and the advertising requirement in service contracts can cause problems for on-line commerce. In the case of warranties (paragraph 3.88), for example, whether digitised services are considered as goods or as services will make a substantial difference. If digitised services are goods (as recommended in paragraph 3.07), consumers will be granted jurisdictional protection when they make on-line purchases of software, music, video, etc. However, if digitised services are services, and the consumer was not solicited, no such protection will apply.

The consumer may need to sue the vendor for breach of contract in a foreign court or, worse yet, get hauled into the foreign court.

4.07   But even discounting the situation of digitised services, what exactly constitutes a solicitation in the consumer's domicile? Do e-mail and web pages fall under the definition? The implications could be very significant. For example, if services such as banking and web page design were advertised on the web, subsequent contracts may or may not protected by the consumer jurisdiction clauses. The wording regarding solicitations in Article 13(3)(a) is:

> "In the State of the consumer's domicile the conclusion of the contract was preceded by a specific invitation addressed to him or by advertising."[16]

E-mail solicitations will probably be considered as specific invitations since they are directed solicitations. However, the status of advertisements on web pages is unclear.

---

[15] *Johnson v. Taylor* [1920] A.C. 144.
[16] Convention on Jurisdiction and the Enforcement of Judgments in Civil and Commercial Matters (1968) article 13(3)(a).

Does a "webvertisement" really constitute an advertisement in the consumer's domicile? After all, web pages are never 'directed' at a particular jurisdiction, but instead passively spread all over the globe.[17]

U.K. government agencies have taken a subjective approach to this question of 'directedness'. For example, under the Financial Services Act 1986, all advertising material relating to investment business must be approved by the Financial Services Authority (FSA).[18] However, with respect to a foreign website that advertises investment opportunities, the FSA will consider whether the site is directed at U.K. consumers, by examining a list of factors, and then decide on enforcement measures. A similar method might be applied by the courts in determining whether or not a webvertisement for a service transformed the resulting contract into a consumer contract under the Brussels Convention.

Evasion

Since the emphasis of the Brussels Convention is on domicile, contracting parties will probably be unable to avoid their home jurisdictions by merely using an off-shore web or mail server. In many ways reducing uncertainty and potential confusion, the concept of domicile focuses solely on permanent physical locations, such as a person's place of residence or a corporation's seat. On-line vendors will not be able to 'forum-shop' by placing web servers in countries with more favourable laws.

Common Law Jurisdiction

Where the defendant's domicile is not in a Contracting State or, for other reasons, more generally where the Brussels Convention does not apply,[19] English common law will settle the issue of jurisdiction. This situation will arise when contracts are formed with parties domiciled outside the Europe. In these cases, the principles for claiming jurisdiction are substantially different, providing English courts with a greater opportunity to seize jurisdiction.

4.08

Jurisdiction in personam

The key issue for jurisdiction *in personam* is whether the defendant can be physically served with a writ in England. If the defendant can, then English courts can claim jurisdiction.

Under this doctrine, the courts can exercise jurisdiction over any individual (natural person) present in England, regardless of whether his/her stay is meant to be temporary or permanent.[20] As long as the defendant is served with the writ,[21] the claim of jurisdiction is effective. In addition, according to RSC, Ordinance 81, rule 9, if an individual conducts business in England, the writ may be served at his English place of business, whether or not the individual himself/herself is in England at the time.[22]

---

[17] See Chapter 8 on Webvertising.
[18] See Chapter 2 on Financial Services.
[19] For example, other instances include where the defendant does not satisfy the requirements for being domiciled in a Contracting State, or where the dispute involves non-civil/non-commercial matters.
[20] *Colt Industries Inc. v. Sarlie* [1966] 1 W.L.R. 440 (CA), Dicey 300.
[21] The procedures and means by which writs may be served can comprise a chapter in itself and will not be discussed here. See Dicey and Morris, *Conflict of Laws* Chapter 11.
[22] One exception to this rule is that if the person conducts business in his won name, then jurisdiction cannot be exercised via this means. Dicey 301.

4.09   Similar rules apply to partnerships or corporations. A partnership or firm (under a single name) with a place of business in England may be served a writ at that location, whether the partners are in England or not. The rule also applies regardless of the nationality or residence of the partners, thus allowing the courts to exercise jurisdiction over foreigners who do business in England. Companies incorporated in England or registered under the Companies Act 1985 can be served writs at their registered offices. Even a foreign corporation with no officially registered office can be served a writ at its English place of business if that place has been operational for a sufficient period of time and carries on substantial activities.[23] As the court suggested in *South India Shipping Co. Ltd v. Export-Import Bank of Korea:*

> "We have only to see whether the corporation is "here"; if it is, it can be served. There are authorities as to the circumstances in which a foreign corporation can and cannot be said to be "here"; the best test is to ascertain whether the business is carried on here and at a defined place."[24]

Jurisdiction *in personam* has ramifications for international on-line contracts, though its applicability will only lie where one party is from the U.K. and the other is from a non-Contracting State. Under the doctrine, a foreign party or consumer can easily use the English courts to sue any on-line vendor with a place of business in England, provided the forum is relevant to the contract in question (see below). Similarly, a foreign vendor can sue (in the English courts) an English resident or someone who occasionally visits England, provided that the writ is properly and successfully served. These two instances are straightforward, though one should note that, unlike the Brussels Convention, presence, not domicile, determines jurisdiction.

4.10   One uncertainty that arises under jurisdiction *in personam* is whether a writ can be served on a web server. Some have suggested that if a purely foreign company set up a web server physically based in England and directed at English customers, that server might constitute a 'place of business.' Even though the server is not a traditional form of 'place,' it is nonetheless where substantial advertising and business transactions occur. In fact, one could even argue that a web server exhibits the "degree of permanence or recognisability" required by *Re Oriel Ltd.*[25] If this method of serving writs were possible, English courts would be able to exercise jurisdiction *in personam* over all foreign (non-Contracting State) companies with web servers in England.

The courts would probably be unwise to follow this route. The issue of jurisdiction concerns finding a *forum conveniens*, an applicable forum that will maximise justice for both parties in the dispute. The 'web server as place of business' rule would not be in this spirit. Companies place their web servers all over the world, particularly because many Internet/Access Service Providers are located elsewhere. Thus, the physical location of the Web servers of an electronic commerce business is often completely irrelevant to the contracts being formed. For example, if an English consumer purchased goods from an English on-line merchant, why should the courts care that the merchant's

---

[23] Dicey 306.
[24] *South India Shipping Co. Ltd v. Export-Import Bank of Korea* [1985] 2 All E.R. 219.
[25] *Re Oriel Ltd* [1985] 3 All E.R. 216.

website was physically based in the Cayman Islands? The 'web server as place of business' rule would create these inconsistencies and, in some cases, might even undermine the ability of the courts to exercise jurisdiction over English companies that cunningly base their web servers elsewhere.

The virtual attributes of the Internet offer no reason for English law to change its traditional and physical definition of a 'place of business.' Besides, English law does not need to unnecessarily stretch jurisdiction *in personam* to haul foreign corporations into court. It already has a variety of other potent jurisdiction principles as considered below. **4.11**

Contracts made in England

If a contract is created in England, the English courts can exercise jurisdiction over disputes concerning it. Thus, as already emphasised in paragraph 3.38, the moment of contract creation, whether the courts use the postal rule or the receipt rule, becomes extremely important for jurisdiction purposes.

Breach of contract in England

English courts can exercise jurisdiction in cases where the breach of contract occurred in England, regardless of whether or not the contract was originally formed in England. A contracting party can breach the contract in one of three ways: by explicit repudiation, implicit repudiation; or failure to perform. This common law 'breach of contract' rule varies in scope from the 'place of performance' rule in the Brussels Convention. Breach of contract does not necessarily have to occur at the expected place of performance.

An explicit repudiation occurs when the reneging party expressly informs the other party that it will no longer abide by the contract. The instant at which repudiation occurs is important. According to *Cherry v. Thompson*,[26] for written letters of repudiation, the postal rule is followed. A repudiation by e-mail, however, will probably fall under the receipt rule (see paragraph 3.40). Thus, a defendant who sent an e-mail explicitly breaking a contract to a plaintiff located in England could be sued in an English court, regardless of where the contract would have been performed. **4.12**

Implicit repudiation, on the other hand, involves performing an act that is inconsistent with the contractual performance. For example, if Alice is under contract to sell her car to Bob, selling the car to Cindy would be an implicit repudiation. Where this act of implicit repudiation occurs can form the basis for a jurisdiction claim.

Probably the most common manner of breach, however, is the failure to perform a contractual obligation. If the expected place of performance was in England, the English courts will be able to exercise jurisdiction.[27] This principle is the same as the one found in Article 5(1) of the Brussels Convention, which deals with the 'place of performance' (see paragraph 4.05), except here it is applied to defendants from non-Contracting States.

The issues are very similar to the ones described for Article 5(1). Foreign customers who fail to pay English merchants can face litigation in England because payment is performed at the creditor's (merchant's) location. On the other hand, under this rule English customers cannot sue foreign suppliers in an English court. Supplier performance involves only shipping, which occurs at the supplier's location, not complete delivery. **4.13**

---

[26] *Cherry v. Thompson* (1872) L.R. 7 Q.B. 573 at 579.
[27] Just as in article 5(1) of the Brussels Convention, except that this rule now applies to a defendant from a non-Contracting State.

However, English common law does not provide the consumer protection granted in the Brussels Convention. A consumer from a non-Contracting State who fails to pay an English merchant can be sued in England.

Contracts governed by English law

If the applicable law/choice of law (see paragraph 4.18) of a contract is England and Wales then the English and Welsh courts can seize jurisdiction. However, choice of law does not provide a conclusive determination of jurisdiction. It is a particularly weak factor and, according to Lord Diplock in *Amin Rasheed Shipping Co. v. Kuwait Insurance Co.*, the plaintiff has a burden to show that it could not obtain justice from a more relevant foreign court, or that to do so would require excessive time, resources, or inconvenience.[28] Furthermore, in *Spiliada Maritime Co. v. Cansulex Ltd*, the court held that in determining jurisdiction, choice of law must be considered in light of the context and other facts of the case.[29]

Jurisdiction Clauses

4.14   Relying upon the Brussels Convention or English common law to determine jurisdiction can cause major problems for an electronic commerce business. English common law is a confusing legal labyrinth; the principles for determining jurisdiction often conflict and can result in several countries having jurisdiction rights. For example, if an American customer purchases goods from an English vendor and then fails to pay, both England and America have reason to claim jurisdiction. The breach of contract occurred in England and the standard terms and conditions probably stipulated English law. However, since the English vendor probably made the acceptance, the contract was formed in America under the receipt rule, and the American courts could therefore also claim jurisdiction.[30]

For European commerce, the Brussels Convention makes jurisdictional issues more manageable, but situations can still present problems for electronic commerce businesses. For example, other European laws may provide that suppliers have the duty to deliver the goods, not just ship them (thereby putting the place of performance in the customers' location) Consequently, English on-line vendors who fail to deliver the ordered materials could be sued in foreign courts.

Electronic commerce businesses clearly have good reason to specify jurisdiction explicitly in their standard terms and conditions. For example, the following simple clause could be inserted:

---

[28] *Dicey* 332.
[29] *Spiliada Maritime Co. v. Cansulex Ltd* [1987] A.C. 460 at 480.
[30] N.B.: The arguments in this example only consider jurisdictional issues from an English law standpoint; it does not even touch on the American rules, which are different paragraph 4.17.

> **Jurisdiction**
>
> Each party agrees to submit to the exclusive jurisdiction of the (English) courts as regards any claim or matter arising under this Agreement.

Both English common law and the Brussels Convention attach great weight to express jurisdiction clauses and will usually allow the clause to override all other determinations of jurisdiction. Under RSC, Ordinance 11, rule 2a, if a contract has an explicit term granting the English courts jurisdiction, they automatically have the right to examine any aspect of the contract. Similarly, the Brussels Convention states in Article 17:

> "If the parties, one or more of whom is domiciled in a Contracting State, have agreed that a court or the courts of a Contracting State are to have jurisdiction to settle any disputes which have arisen or which may arise in connection with a particular legal relationship, that court or those courts shall have exclusive jurisdiction."[31]

Recognition of jurisdiction clauses under the Brussels Convention, however, is limited only to non-consumer contracts. The consumer protection measures given in Articles 13-15, including the consumer's right to sue and to be sued only in his/her domicile, cannot be overridden by contractual terms.

For both commercial contracts and consumer contracts the choice of jurisdiction should be relevant, or at least not blatantly irrelevant. Otherwise, the opposing party could prove that some other forum was more appropriate. For example, if a contract between an English vendor and an American supplier listed Brazil as the jurisdiction, either party would have a strong case for claiming that the *forum conveniens* was either England or America.

4.15

Jurisdiction selection in litigation

As previously mentioned, where a contract has no express jurisdiction clause, the plaintiff often has an option as to where to initiate litigation.[32] For example, if common law applies, the plaintiff can choose between the location where the contract was formed or breached, or the defendant's place of business. If the Brussels Convention applies and the contract involves a consumer, the consumer can choose whether to sue the defendant vendor in consumer's domicile or the defendant's domicile. These locations, particularly in electronic commerce, will not be necessarily the same. Thus, the laws of jurisdiction permit the plaintiff to 'forum-shop.' The plaintiff can balance the advantages and disadvantages of the various forums available and make the most advantageous choice. Some factors include:

4.16

- In which jurisdiction is success most probable?

- In what other relevant jurisdictions can a judgment from the chosen forum be enforced?

---

[31] Brussels Convention, Article 17. Understandably, the Convention requires the selection of jurisdiction to be made in writing. (See paragraph 3.58 for a further discussion on writing and on-line contracts.).
[32] Indeed, this possibility of plaintiff 'forum-shopping' alone represents an important reason why there should always be an express jurisdiction clause!.

- Does the forum have procedural rules that will help or hinder the action?
- Is the chosen jurisdiction relevant? *i.e.* Will it accept jurisdiction over the dispute? (see below).

Staying Actions

However, just because a court can exercise jurisdiction does not necessarily mean that it will. The Supreme Court Act 1981[33] and the Civil Jurisdiction and Judgments Act 1982,[34] provide that, whenever necessary in the interests of justice, English courts have the ability to stay or strike out proceedings. The criteria for the granting of a stay are quite strict, as the House of Lords suggested in *Spiliada Maritime Co. v. Cansulex Ltd*:

> "The basic principle is that a stay will only be granted on the ground of *forum non conveniens* where the court is satisfied that there is some other available forum, having competent jurisdiction, which is the appropriate forum for the trial of the action, *i.e.* in which the case may be tried more suitably for the interests of all the parties and the ends of justice."[35]

Thus, while litigating parties may have some choice over forum, the guiding principles of relevance and appropriateness make the choice far more restricted than it may have initially appeared.

Foreign jurisdictions

4.17   An English electronic commerce business will have to compete in a global marketplace knowing that English law is not sufficient. Fortunately, for the most part, the actions of other European courts are predictable, since the members of the European Union and the European Free Trade Agreement abide by either the Brussels or Lugano Convention. However, the principles on jurisdiction outside of Europe can be quite different.

For example, in the United States, jurisdiction is often decided based on whether a person makes a 'purposeful act toward a forum.' For example, in *Minnesota v. Granite Gate Resorts*,[36] the defendant advertised an on-line gambling service on the Internet, and subsequently formed a mailing list which included Minnesota residents. However, no gambling activities *per se* were considered by the court. The Minnesota Court of Appeals held that:

> "[The defendants] are subject to personal jurisdiction in Minnesota because, through their Internet activities, they purposefully availed themselves of the privilege of doing business in Minnesota to the extent that the maintenance of an action based on consumer protection statutes does not offend traditional notions of fair play and substantial justice."[37]

Similarly, in *United States v. Thomas*,[38] the operators of a pornographic electronic bulletin board[39] in California were convicted of criminal obscenity laws by a Federal

---

[33] Supreme Court Act 1981, s.49(3).
[34] Civil Jurisdiction and Judgments Act 1982, s.49.
[35] *Spiliada Maritime Co. v. Cansulex Ltd* [1987] A.C. 460 at 476.
[36] *Minnesota v. Granite Gate Resorts*, 568 N.W.2d 715 (Minn. Ct. App. 1997).
[37] *ibid.*
[38] *United States v. Thomas*, 1996 FED App. 0032 P (6th Cir.).
[39] An electronic bulletin board (BBS) is the predecessor to a web site, and was a popular medium among computer enthusiasts in the 1980s. Users do not access it via the Internet, but rather directly call up the computer using their modem.

court in Tennessee based on Tennessee standards of decency.[40] The Sixth Circuit Court of Appeals held that the material was 'sent' to Tennessee and subject to local standards, despite the 'sending' being electronic and the bulletin board being essentially accessible world-wide.

In both of these cases, the actions of the defendants were active. In *Granite Gate*, the defendant complied a mailing list and had even spoken on the phone to the undercover consumer investigator, assuring him that the betting service was legal. In *Thomas*, the defendants charged $55 and required an application requiring age, address, and telephone number. However, U.S. courts may not construe mere passive activity as a "an act purposefully directed toward the forum."[41] In *Blackburn v. Walker Oriental Rug Galleries*,[42] the court held that a website with no purchasing option and only an e-mail response mechanism was 'passive' and thus warranted no claim on jurisdiction.

APPLICABLE LAW/CHOICE OF LAW

Although often confused together, applicable law or choice of law (the law that governs the contract), is not equivalent to jurisdiction (the right to hear a contractual dispute). Jurisdiction deals with issues of forum, whereas applicable law deals with what legal principles that forum applies. The country that claims jurisdiction does not necessarily have to apply its own laws to the case. For example, the High Court in England could resolve a contractual dispute according to French law.

    4.18

Electronic commerce does not result in any particularly new or novel issues regarding applicable law. Much of the doctrine has already developed over the past century with the growth of international commerce and shipping. However, in the past, only specialised international importers, exporters, and shippers dealt with these issues on a regular basis. In the global world of electronic commerce, applicable law will become a common problem faced by all on-line merchants.

The Rome Convention

In England the issue of applicable law is governed under the Contracts (Applicable Law) Act 1990. The Act implemented the 1980 Rome Convention which harmonised applicable law principles throughout the European Union.[43] The primary interpretative document of the Convention is the Report by Professors Giuliano and Lagarde.

    4.19

The Rome Convention broadly applies "to contractual obligations in any situation involving a choice between the laws of different countries."[44] Thus, all contracts will fall under its scope, except in a few explicitly stated areas in Article 1(2) such as legal capacity, land, family matters, trusts and procedural law. The Giuliano-Lagarde Report

---

[40] *United States v. Thomas*, 1996 FED App. 0032 P (6th Cir.), II.C.2.
[41] *Blackburn v. Walker Oriental Rug Galleries Inc.* (E.D. Penn. 7 April 1998).
[42] *ibid.*
[43] N.B.: A few terms of the Rome Convention, notably article 7(1) were not implemented by the U.K. Since they are not particle of English law, they will not be discussed here.
[44] 1980 EEC Convention on the Law Applicable to Contractual Obligations ("The Rome Convention"), article 1(1).

also interprets the Convention as excluding intellectual property issues,[45] though this exclusion most likely only concerns proprietary rights, not contracts licensing or selling copies of intellectual property (*e.g.* books and software).

Before the passage of the Contracts (Applicable Law) Act 1990, except in specific cases governed by international treaties, common law principles typically governed applicable law disputes in England. However, for all intents and purposes, the Rome Convention now supersedes those principles. Notably, unlike the Brussels Convention and jurisdiction, English courts must apply the Rome Convention in all contractual disputes, irrespective of whether or not the parties are from Contracting States. No connection with a Contracting State is necessary. The Rome Convention universally applies and there are no residual applications for common law.

Despite some suggestions to the contrary,[46] parties most likely cannot 'contract out' of the Rome Convention through a contractual clause excluding the 1990 Act. To do so would undermine the whole harmonisation and uniformity purpose that the members of the European Union sought to achieve.

Scope of Applicable Law

4.20 The choice or determination of applicable law can be critical in a contractual dispute. By defining the rules and principles by which the courts will interpret the contract, applicable law can mean the difference between a breach and no breach, or enforceable and unenforceable. The following list, albeit not exhaustive, shows some of the issues that applicable law governs.

- Material validity[47] — the courts will judge the existence or validity of a contract using the law that would govern it if the contract were valid (called 'putative proper law' under English common law).[48] Applicable law will govern areas such as mistake, misrepresentation, and contract formation, probably including whether the postal rule or receipt rule is applied under the circumstances. (Paragraphs 3.39 and 3.40)

- Public policy — the contract can be held unenforceable because it is manifestly incompatible with public policy (both either to the applicable law or to the forum).

- Formal validity[49] — applicable law governs the formal requirements of a contract, such as writing, signature, "every external manifestation required on the part of a person expressing the will to be legally bound."[50] English law has few formal requirements for contracts and, as discussed in paragraph 3.58, is likely to accept the electronic forms of writing and signature anyway. However, other countries may not as willing to interpret their formal requirements so broadly. One notable

---

[45] Giuliano and Lagarde, p. 10.
[46] Mann (1991) 107 L.Q.R. 353, cited by *Dicey* 1205.
[47] Rome Convention, article 8.
[48] *ibid.*, article 8(1). See *Current Statutes Annotated* [1990] 36–31.
[49] *ibid., article 9.*
[50] Giuliano and Lagardge, p. 29.

exception to this rule is in consumer contracts. Under section 9(5), formal requirements in a consumer contract are governed by the law of the consumer's habitual place of residence, not the applicable law.

- Capacity — The Rome Convention is essentially silent on questions of legal capacity,[51] leaving those determinations to the individual countries. Under English law, the legal capacity of a minor, or any natural person, is governed by applicable law.[52] However, in this particular case, applicable law means "the law objectively ascertained, without taking account of any choice of law in the contract itself."[53] (See paragraph 4.27 on Absence of Choice).

- Performance[54] — applicable law determines the expected conditions of performance, such as the diligence required, place, and reasonable time period.

- Consequence of Breach/Damages[55] — under the Rome Convention, the remedies and damages available for breach of contract are governed by the applicable law. Although the actual quantification of damages (as a question of fact) remains under the procedural laws of the forum (*lex fori*),[56] limitations on damages and the principle used in measuring damages will be provided by applicable law. In addition to determining remedies for breach, applicable law will also govern how contractual obligations can be extinguished.[57]

- Presumptions of Law/Burden of Proof [58] — to the extent that the principles are substantive and not procedural, the presumptions of law and the burden of proof in a contractual dispute are governed by applicable law. For example, two parties, one from England, the other from Italy, form an on-line contract for the transport of goods. The goods are damaged in transit. Under English law, the carrier must take "reasonable care" of the goods, whereas under Italian law, the carrier must take "all the necessary measures" to prevent damage.[59] The determination of applicable law may make the difference between whether the carrier is liable for damage or not.

- Illegality — if a contract is illegal under the applicable law, the court will not enforce it, regardless of whether it is legal in the court's forum.

However, despite all these conditions, where applicable law governs the interpretation and enforcement of a contract, the court may refuse to adhere to it under certain

---

[51] Except for the rare and narrow case discussed in Article 11 of the Rome Convention, which states that "In a contract concluded between persons who are in the same country, a natural person who would have capacity under the law of that country may invoke his incapacity resulting from another law only if the other party to the contract was aware of this incapacity at the time of the conclusion of the contract or was not aware thereof as a result of negligence."

[52] In this case, applicable means "the law objectively ascertained, without taking account of any choice of law in the contract itself."

[53] *Chitty*, 30–091.

[54] Rome Convention, article 10(1)(b).

[55] *ibid.*, article 10(1)(c).

[56] *Chitty*, 30-098.

[57] Rome Convention, article 10(1)(d).

[58] *ibid.*, article 14(1).

[59] *Dicey*, 1209. The Italian law is found in Civil Code, article 1681.

conditions. For example, the court may not have the procedural powers to execute the remedy required by applicable law. If the applicable law calls for periodic payments of damages (rather than a lump sum), and an English court has no mechanism for issuing such payments, the court may legally ignore the applicable law's provision under Article 10(1)(c) of the Rome Convention.[60]

Additionally, irrespective of a contract's validity, if the contract is illegal in the country of performance, an English court will not enforce it under the doctrine in *Ralli Bros. v. Compania Naviera Sota y Aznar*.[61] Much debate has arisen over whether the *Ralli* doctrine applies only to situations where the applicable law is English, or to all cases.[62]

As a general principle of the conflict of laws, "a forum will not apply a foreign law which is contrary to the public policy of the forum."[63] An on-line contract for gambling activities or the distribution of pornography that is illegal under English law will not be enforced by an English court just because the applicable law is of a foreign (and more lenient) country.

Express or Implied Choice

4.23   The Rome Convention, following English common law, allows almost complete freedom of choice in selecting applicable law. This freedom applies even in consumer contracts, except for the restrictions discussed at paragraph 4.29. Article 3(1) of the Rome Convention states:

> "A contract shall be governed by the law chosen by the parties. The choice must be express or demonstrated with reasonable certainty by the terms of the contract or the circumstances of the case."

Similarly, in *Vita Food Products Inc. v. Unus Shipping Co. Ltd*, Lord Wright (for the Privy Council) held that:

> "Where there is an express statement by the parties of their intention to select the law of the contract, it is difficult to see what qualifications are possible, provided the intention expressed is bona fide and legal, and provided there is no reason for avoiding the choice on the ground of public policy."[64]

As seen in Article 3(1) of the Convention, this choice of law can be made either explicitly or implicitly. Each of these possibilities is discussed in turn.

Express Choice

4.24   The specific contractual term or even the standard terms and conditions can expressly select the law which governs the contract. Obviously, express choice is by far the best option for an electronic commerce business. The following is an example of an applicable law clause.

---

[60] *Current Statutes Annotated* 1990, pp. 36–34.
[61] *Ralli Bros. v. Compania Naviera Sota y Aznar* [1920] 2 K.B. 287.
[62] For further discussion on this debate, see *Chitty on Contracts* 30–108.
[63] *Chitty*, 30–109.
[64] *Vita Food Products Inc v. Unus Shipping Co. Ltd* [1939] A.C. 277 (P.C.) at 290.

Applicable Law

This Agreement shall be governed by, construed, and interpreted in accordance with the laws of England and Wales.

The chosen law need not have any connection with the contract. As the court held in *Vita Food Products Inc. v. Unus Shipping Co. Ltd*, a contract does not need a connection to England in order for a selection of English law to be valid.[65] Indeed, reasons often exist for selecting a governing law, which is not directly or visibly connected to the contract. For example, an underlying intermediary, such as an on-line auctioneer, may be located elsewhere and select the local laws instead. Alternatively, the auctioneer may choose neutral laws, totally devoid of any connection, on the basis that they are well-constructed for governing auctions. In either case, the purpose of the chosen law is to standardise the contract, so that the other parties know what to expect and the applicable laws do not change from transaction to transaction. However, the chosen laws have no 'connection' with the contract *per se*.

However, although the parties have the freedom to choose the applicable law, the Rome Convention imposes a few specific restrictions. These are described in paragraph 4.29. Additionally, in the effort to standardise, choice of law clauses may not select non-national legal systems or 'general principles of law.' Those choices would probably not constitute an express choice of law under the Rome Convention.

Implied Choice

As is the case for other contractual terms, where no choice of law is explicitly made, it can be inferred from the circumstances under which the contract was formed. The Rome Convention acknowledges this possibility by accepting implied choices of law where the choice is "demonstrated with reasonable certainty."[66]

4.25

However, according to the Giuliano-Lagarde Report, although choice of law may be inferred, a court may only infer it when "the parties have made a real choice of law, although this is not expressly stated in the contract."[67] But in no case does the Rome Convention allow the court to infer a choice of law if the parties had no original intent to choose.[68] This distinction is a fine and tenuous one, and thus the Report suggests a number of situations where the court may infer an intended choice of law. This list is by no means exhaustive, but instead offers examples where an intended choice may be most apparent.

- Standard Contract: If the contract is a commonly-used standard form contract where the applicable law is known, the courts may infer the choice of law. A typical example of this type of contract is Lloyd's policy of maritime insurance. In electronic commerce, one can imagine that if a particular form became the standard on-line sale of goods contract in England, the courts may infer that English law was chosen by the parties.[69]

---

[65] *Vita Food Products Inc v. Unus Shipping Co. Ltd* [1939] A.C. 277 (P.C.) at 290.
[66] Rome Convention, article 3(1).
[67] Giuliano-Lagarde, p. 17.
[68] *Dicey*, 1224.
[69] One would hope, however, that the contract that becomes the standard on-line contract in the future will already have an express choice of law clause to eliminate this uncertainty!.

- Previous Dealing — If previous contracts or dealings between the parties left no doubt as to the choice of law, the court may infer that choice law into the present contract.

- Choice of Forum — If a contract expressly grants jurisdiction to a specific forum, it implicitly chooses the law of that forum as well. However, choice of forum is only one factor which must be considered in light of other facts in the case.[70]

- Reference to a Specific Legal System — If a contract references legal provisions or statutes from a particular country's legal system, the court may hold those laws as the implied choice. For example, mention of the Unfair Contract Terms Act 1977 or the Sale of Goods Act 1979 in a contract might provide grounds for an inference that English law is to apply. Nevertheless, references alone are by no means conclusive. A court must decide if they really imply a particular choice of law.[71]

4.26   To infer an intended choice of law, the courts will naturally try to consider as many pre-contractual circumstances as possible. One question, however, is whether the courts can account for conduct after contract formation. In *Whitworth Street Estates (Manchester) Ltd v. James Miller and Partners Ltd,* the House of Lords did not allow post-contractual considerations.[72] However, under the Rome Convention and the interpretation in the Giuliano-Lagarde Report, the position reverses, allowing the court to consider factors after contract formation. English courts will probably consider post-contractual conduct in the future, but only to the extent that it depicts the parties' state of mind prior to contract.

     In the absence of an express clause or a definitively implied choice of law, the contract has an 'absence of choice.' In that case, the court will use different principles to determine applicable law, as described below at paragraph 4.27.

Absence of Choice

4.27   In the absence of a choice of law, the contract is governed by the law of the country most closely connected to the contract.[73] This rule generally applies, the only notable exception being in consumer contracts where an absence of choice will result in the contract being governed by the laws of the country in which the consumer is habitually resident.[74]

     Exactly which country is 'most closely connected' is often unclear. Article 4(2) of the Rome Convention therefore provides a presumption:

---

[70] The situation described here is the exact reverse of that described in the previous section on jurisdiction. There, an express choice of law aided the court in determining jurisdiction, although again, it was only a factor and had to be considered in light of other facts.

[71] For example, the court must determine whether (a) the reference to an English statute implies a choice of English law; or (b) the reference is merely a 'shorthand' for a contractual term (*e.g.* the parties seek to include the English standards of satisfactory quality) but the choice of law is a different country altogether (e.g. France).

[72] *Whitworth Street Estates (Manchester) Ltd v. James Miller and Partners Ltd* [1970] A.C. 583.

[73] Rome Convention, article 4(1).

[74] *ibid.,* article 5(3).

"It shall be presumed that the contract is most closely connected with the country where the party who is to effect the performance which is characteristic of the contract has, at the time of conclusion of the contract, his habitual residence or, in the case of a body corporate or unincorporate, its central administration."[75]

Article 4(2) changes the presumption slightly for commercial contracts. In the case of a party effecting characteristic performance during the course of a trade or business, "the country shall be the country in which the principal place of business is situated."[76] Obviously, this latter case is particularly relevant for electronic commerce.

The above presumption can be overruled if the place of characteristic performance is undetermined or the circumstances suggest that the contract is more closely connected to another country.[77] However, one can imagine that the courts will usually apply this presumption and thus the definition and determination of characteristic performance becomes critical.

Characteristic Performance

Characteristic performance is defined in the Giuliano-Lagarde Report as:

"The performance for which payment is due, . . . the delivery of goods . . . which usually constitutes the centre of gravity and the socio-economic function of the contractual transaction."[78]

Consequently, in the on-line environment, examples of characteristic performance will include the delivery of goods and the supply of services or digitised services. Those goods and services, not the payment exchanged for them, constitute the essence of the contract.

4.28

However, the Rome Convention emphasises not the actual place of characteristic performance, but the habitual residence or place of business of the party who performs. Therefore, since the vendor executes the characteristic performance in the typical commercial on-line contract (non-consumer), the applicable law will be the law of his/ her country, not the customer's. The Rome Convention gives the advantage to the vendor.

Since applicable law in the absence of choice will fall to the vendor's place of business, vendors may wonder if the location of the web server could be considered as a place of business. This interpretation would give vendors the flexibility to 'forum shop' between their actual physical place of business and the location of the web server. However, as suggested at paragraph 4.09 (Jurisdiction *in personam*), defining a web server as a place of business would be an over extension of the concept and contrary to the spirit of the law. Companies can place their web servers virtually anywhere in the world and the physical location of the web server is often totally irrelevant to how the merchant conducts business. 'Place of business' is a holistic determination, not one based on minute objective criteria that may lead to distortion.

---

[75] *ibid.*, article 4(2).
[76] *ibid.*
[77] *ibid.*, article 4(5).
[78] Giuliano-Lagarde Report, p.20.

In any case, electronic commerce vendors are advised to always make a choice of law in their standard terms and conditions. For non-consumer contracts, the rules on applicable law in the absence of choice may be automatically favourable to vendors, but for consumer contracts they are not. Besides, why take chances? Express choice of law solidifies the governing law in nearly all cases, including, surprisingly enough, consumer contracts (subject to the few restrictions set out below at paragraph 4.29.)

Mandatory acts

4.29   Although the Rome Convention allows contracting parties considerable freedom in making their choice of governing law, it does impose a number of restrictions. These restrictions, however, are very limited in scope. They do not prohibit or prevent a choice of governing law under any circumstance; they only ensure that the choice of law does not pre-empt or evade mandatory rules. Although electronic commerce business establish a great deal of legal certainty by expressly specifying a choice of law, they may therefore still be subject the mandatory laws of other forums.

Domestic evasion of mandatory acts
Article 3(3) of the Rome Convention states:

> "The fact that the parties have chosen a foreign law, whether or not accompanied by the choice of a foreign tribunal, shall not, where all the other elements relevant to the situation at the time of the choice are connected with one country only, prejudice the application of rules of law of that country which cannot be derogated from by[sic] contract, hereinafter called 'mandatory rules'. "[79]

This clause has an extremely narrow application. Its essential purpose is to prevent an otherwise purely domestic contract from evading mandatory rules by specification of a foreign applicable law. Article 3(3) is only applicable if all elements of the contractual situation (not just the contract itself, but the surrounding circumstances) involve only one country. If the circumstances involved other countries, it will not apply. If, however, the clause does apply, the contract will be subject to all the mandatory rules of the forum. For example, two English parties create what is otherwise a purely domestic sales contract, but specify French law as the governing law. The courts will honour the choice of law as French, but will also impose English mandatory rules, such as the Unfair Contract Terms Act 1977.[80]

Superseding mandatory rules
Article 7(2) also deals with mandatory acts:

---

[79] Rome Convention, article 3(3) from Current Statutes Annotated (1990) 36–16.
[80] The Unfair Contract Terms Act 1977 does not apply to international supply contracts. However, in the given case, the contract is of a purely domestic nature and no goods pass between borders. On a more curious note, the Act will not apply if the example in the text were reversed. If two French parties stipulated English law, normally all the English mandatory rules would apply, since applicable law is English. However, the Unfair Contract Terms Act 1977, section pecifically stipulates that if the choice of law is English but aside from the choice the applicable law would be a foreign country (in the latter example, France), then the Act's provision will not apply. Unfair Contract Terms Act 1977, s.27(1).

"Nothing in this Convention shall restrict the application of the rules of the law of the forum in a situation where they are mandatory irrespective of the law otherwise applicable to the contract."

Normally, a country's mandatory laws apply only if a contract is governed by those laws. For example, the Unfair Contract Terms Act 1977 is a mandatory law if the applicable law is English, but will not apply if the applicable law is French (except under special provisions).[81] However, Section 7(2) recognises the possibility of creating "mandatory rules of a higher order,"[82] rules that would apply to a contract even if it were international in nature and governed by a different law. The Giuliano-Lagarde Report suggests that future rules concerning competition or consumer protection might fall under this category, provided that they are explicitly legislated to be applicable irrespective of a contract's governing law.

4.30

Consumer contracts

The most substantial application of mandatory acts in the Rome Convention is where it grants consumers protection against choice of law clauses:

". . . a choice of law made by the parties shall not have the result of depriving the consumer of the protection afforded to him by the mandatory rules of the law of the country in which he has his habitual residence."[83]

However, this consumer protection clause is not automatically applicable. In order to qualify for protection, the contract must satisfy any one of three conditions.

The first condition is that the consumer contract was solicited (*i.e.* by direct mailing or advertising) by the vendor in the consumer's domicile, and the consumer completed all contract formation steps there. This definition of consumer contract is the same as the one found in the Brussels Convention for jurisdiction. (See discussion on issues at paragraph 4.06.) It is also probably the most relevant for on-line contracts.

4.31

The second condition is where the vendor received the consumer's order through an agent in the consumer's country. 'Agent' in this context represents anyone acting on behalf of the vendor and not a principal-agent relationship.[84] One potential area of dispute is determining whether an agent is involved, particularly if a website is operated by a third party from the consumer's country. In most cases, as explained earlier, neither the web server not the third party provider would be considered an 'agent' or 'place of business.' Since the server can be located anywhere and essentially serves as a communications medium, its location is not related to the supplier's business or business practices. However, if the third party operator took active steps, such as order processing, then it might be construed as an agent.

The third condition, which concerns cross-border excursions for the purchase of goods, is not relevant to electronic commerce.

---

[81] For example, where the contract falls under Section 3(3) of the Rome Convention (above).
[82] *Chitty*, 30–041.
[83] Roman Convention, article 5(2).
[84] *Dicey* 1290.

If the contract is a consumer contract, the Rome Convention will not allow the choice of law to deprive the consumer of the mandatory protections offered by his/her place of habitual residence. However, this requirement defines the minimum level of protection. If the choice of law in the contract offers the consumer greater protection, the consumer will receive that higher level instead.

ENFORCEMENT

4.32   If one cannot enforce a court judgment, concerns about forum and applicable law become meaningless. Normally, in a domestic case, enforcement flows naturally from jurisdiction. An English court will enforce its own judgment. However, the international nature of many on-line contracts may require that a judgment obtained in one country be enforced in other countries in which the defendant owns assets.

Enforcement is an extremely broad issue since each foreign country may have its own unique enforcement laws.[85] English judgments can be enforced in many foreign countries through international conventions, particularly the Brussels Convention,[86] but some other countries (notably the United States) have no reciprocal enforcement agreements with England.[87] In the latter case, enforcement will depend on the specific laws of each country, analysis of which is beyond the scope of this book. This section focuses on enforcement within members of the E.U. and EFTA.

Enforcement under the Brussels Convention

One of the primary purposes of the Brussels Convention was to harmonise the jurisdictional and enforcement laws within members of the European Community. This same mission was continued in the Lugano Convention which brought similar harmonisation to members of the EFTA.

4.33   In the spirit of harmonisation and legal certainty, the Brussels Convention leaves very little room for interpretation and decision-making in matters of enforcement. In Article 31, it states that:

> A judgment given in a Contracting State and enforceable in that State shall be enforced in another Contracting State when, on the application of any interested party, the order for its enforcement has been issued there."[88]

A person seeking to enforce a judgment need only to make an application to the forum. The enforcing country has very little discretion. Applications can only be denied for a limited number of reasons such as if the judgment is contrary to public policy or if it irreconcilably conflicts with another decision involving the same parties in the enforcing

---

[85] For a more detailed discussion on enforcement, particularly concerning foreign judgments in the U.K., see *Dicey* Chapter 14.

[86] 1968 Brussels Convention on Jurisdiction and the Enforcement of Judgements in Civil and Commercial Matters, discussed extensively at paragraph 4.02 concerning jurisdictional issues.

[87] *Dicey*, 460.

[88] Brussels Convention, article 31.

forum. The Convention further prohibits review of the judgment in terms of substance,[89] and binds the enforcing court to the jurisdictional rulings of the original court. In other words, the enforcing court cannot refuse to enforce a ruling because it feels the original court improperly exercised jurisdiction.

As a result of these strict conditions regarding enforcement, there is little difficulty (despite the inconvenience) in enforcing an English judgment in another Contracting State.

Enforcement outside the Brussels Convention

Outside of Europe, the situation regarding enforcement is far less certain. Some countries, particularly in the Commonwealth, have reciprocal enforcement agreements given effect under the Administration of Justice Act 1920 or the Foreign Judgments (Reciprocal Enforcement) Act 1933.

However, where a defendant's country has no reciprocal agreement with the U.K., a plaintiff seeking to enforce an English judgment in that foreign country will need to commence a new court action there. This process will be far more complicated; the foreign court may wish to re-assess the merits of the case or re-assess the English court's assumption of jurisdiction before giving effect to the decision.

CONCLUSION

With most consumer electronic commerce transactions being for sums of £100 or less, it is unlikely that the application of the complex rules of jurisdiction, governing law and enforcement will be worthwhile considering. However, as the amount of business to business electronic commerce increases, it is inevitable that disputes for larger amounts of money will arise where it is necessary to consider which law applies and which forum should hear the dispute. For the electronic commerce business, as this chapter shows, the importance of well drafted terms and conditions which contain express choice of law and jurisdiction clause can not be overstated.   **4.34**

---

[89] *ibid.,* article 34.

— • 5 • —

PAYMENT MECHANISMS: ENCRYPTION AND DIGITAL SIGNATURES

> "The cheque is in the mail"[1]

GETTING PAID IN CYBERSPACE — INTRODUCTION

Associated with electronic commerce are new ways of paying for goods and services.[2]   **5.01**
These are the logical development of the conventional cheque which is a type of bill of
exchange. Under the Bills of Exchange Act 1882[3] a bill of exchange is defined as being:

> "An unconditional order in writing, addressed by one person to another, signed by the
> person giving it, requiring the person to whom it is addressed to pay on demand or at a
> fixed or determinable future time a sum certain in money to or to the order of a specified
> person, or to bearer."[4]

A cheque is defined in Section 73 of the Bills of Exchange Act 1882 as a bill of
exchange, drawn on a banker payable on demand. Combining this definition with
Section 3 produces the following definition of a cheque:

> "An unconditional order in writing, addressed by one person to a bank, signed by the
> person giving it, requiring the bank to whom it is addressed to pay on demand a sum certain
> in money to or to the order of a specified person, or to bearer."

All of these elements can now be contained in an electronic analogue of the cheque
which is confusingly referred to as digital money or digital cash or virtual cash (rather
than the more logical term "digital cheque"). Each of the key features of a bill of

---

[1] Anon.
[2] For current methods of payment using credit cards and the regulatory structure of Distance Selling and
credit card transactions see Chapter 2.
[3] Referred to by MacKinnon L.J. in *Bank Polski v. K.J. Mulder & Co.* [1942] 1 K.B. 497 at p. 500 as "the best
drafted Act of Parliament ever passed".
[4] Bills of Exchange Act 1882, Section 3.

exchange can be converted into an electronic form through the use of sophisticated cryptography. This allows the creation of digital signatures, authentication of electronic messages and verification of the integrity of electronic messages (confirming that the message has not been tampered with and is received in the same form in which it was sent). If digital money is to replace cheques and bills of exchange, however, the U.K. Government will have to introduce legislation (see below).

Background to the Emerging Legal Regime

5.02   Over the past twenty-five years the world banking system has developed a number of different networks and services for the transfer of funds. Some of these, referred to as wholesale EFT (Electronic Funds Transfer), are closed systems which can only be used between regulated financial institutions.[5] The best known system is SWIFT — the Society for Worldwide Interbank Financial Telecommunications. SWIFT is a co-operative organised under Belgian law, with headquarters in La Hulpe, near Brussels. SWIFT provides communications services to the international banking industry, including payments and administrative messages and, more recently, securities settlements. SWIFT is owned by the member banks (approximately 1,600) including the central banks of most countries. The U.S. Federal Reserve is not a member, but participates in certain types of payments. Securities brokers and dealers, clearing and depository institutions, exchanges for securities, issuers of travellers cheques also participate in SWIFT.

The profits from the global transfer of funds are vast. Consequently, SWIFT has had a turbulent life as its members have sought to gain advantages over each other by producing their own international funds transfer systems. Additionally, SWIFT has always been little more than a secure closed messaging operated under strict rules between banks. Under its rules, payment instructions sent by SWIFT are irrevocable guaranteed unconditional payments. But in electronic terms these are nothing more than messages which are stored and forwarded by one closed e-mail system to another. With the deployment of real-time systems throughout banking and commerce, the SWIFT store-and-forward technology is obsolescent. There are plans to upgrade it but the question of who will pay for such a development in an age of commodity telecommunications and cheap computer power remains unresolved. SWIFT has said that it is going to have to have interactive, query-and-response, as well as store-and-forwarding file transfer, and a new standards paradigm. In time, it says that it will also have to move to an Internet Protocol infrastructure.[6] But the issues of security, of migration to the new systems and how SWIFT intends running incompatible networks together remain unanswered. Since SWIFT pays for its developments out of the profits it earns from its funds transfer activities and these profits are already under serious attack from rival products, it may be the case that SWIFT does not have a future in the electronic commerce marketplace. Instead its role will be taken over by some form of digital money.

---

[5] In the U.K. the main regulatory legislation for financial institutions is contained in the Banking Act 1987 as amended by the Banking Coordination (Second Council Directive) Regulations 1992 (S.I. 1992 No. 3218) which implement, *inter alia*, the Second Banking Directive (89/646/EEC).
[6] Interview with Leonard Schrank, chief executive officer of SWIFT in "Global Custodian"; http://www.assetpub.com/archive/gc/97-04gcwinter/winter97GC036.html.

Retail EFT

The real revolution in funds transfer was started by bank to customer systems known as   **5.03**
retail EFT. These, to date, have been corporate cash management systems (allowing
businesses to give instructions to their banks either by the use of dedicated terminals or,
today, using standard PCs over the Internet), and consumer EFTPOS (Electronic Funds
Transfer Point of Sale systems) which allow customers to make payments directly from
their bank account to merchants. SWITCH is the main U.K. brand in this sphere. During
the 1990s, national EFTPOS systems have become international through their links to
VISA and MasterCard credit cards to become universally accepted payment mechanisms
around the world. This has contributed to a change in international business practices
driven not from the multinationals doing business with each other but by tourists
travelling and spending. The payment mechanisms developed for tourists are now being
adapted for electronic commerce and may become serious alternatives to conventional
bank to bank funds transfer.

Emerging funds transfer systems such as Mastercard-owned Mondex and Visa Cash
use smart cards to store "virtual cash". The idea is that a customer loads up a card from
an Automatic Teller Machine (ATM), a payphone, or a personal computer (if fitted with
a smart card reader), and uses it to pay for anything that would otherwise be paid by
cash. Mondex was trialled in Swindon and at several universities in the U.K. Visa Cash
was tested in Leeds. Both have also been on trial elsewhere in the world. The advantage
is that transactions go direct from site to site in an instant, rather like handing over cash.
Virtual cash is in reality a virtual bearer cheque and adoption of the technology has so
far been slow. It should also be noted that while payment by personal cheque is in
decline in the High Street through the growing use of EPOS, Switch and credit cards,
quite the opposite is happening in the use of cheques between businesses — cheque
usage by businesses is growing. This is not because electronic technologies are unable to
supplant cheque payments but rather because all banks are able to charge businesses for
every cheque drawn on the businesses' accounts and there is no current consensus
regarding the charging regime for electronic payments.

Digital Cash and Micropayments

The fact that the cost of a single credit card transaction can be fairly high (up to 7.5 per   **5.04**
cent of the value of the transaction for small businesses plus a minimum charge) has led
to a parallel development of digital cash and what is termed "microtransactions".
Several schemes exist on the Internet which allow customers to 'buy' cash with a once-
only credit card deduction. The customer can then use the cash to pay out very small
sums online. This is alleged to be an efficient way of paying for subscription sites, but
the promoting companies lack the backing of major banks at this stage. CyberCash,[7]
which recently merged with the pioneer, First Virtual, is a leading contender in this field
along with DigiCash,[8] the Dutch company set up by the cryptographic expert David
Chaum. For very small purchases , less than a penny, Digital Equipment have developed
Millicent, a technology which lets customers 'buy' a money substitute called scrip. There
are currently no commercial implementations of Millicent.

---

[7] http://www.cybercash.com.
[8] http://www.digicash.com.

These systems have only been made possible through a standardising and formalisa-
tion of the content of funds transfer messages which has been part of a larger process —
the move towards Electronic Document Interchange (EDI) in all commercial documentation. EDI is the process of replacing the paper media on which trade data were
traditionally communicated by computer-to-computer transfer of structured information.
Such trade data may comprise, as on paper, contractual or trade-related information
such as orders, invoices, specifications or parts lists, and increasingly also the EFT
information required for the settlement of invoices. Therefore, worldwide message
standards have been developed under the auspices of the U.N., and constantly
expanded. U.N./EDIFACT (United Nations/Electronic Data Interchange for Administration, Commerce and Transport) was aimed to enable the worldwide exchange of large
volumes of data regardless of the language of origin or the communications and
computer systems employed. Its work, which was supported by the American National
Standards Institute (ANSI), on technical standardisation and legal standardisation led to
the most definitive treatment of the issues for international electronic commercial
transactions: the United Nations Commission on International Trade Law Model Law on
Electronic Commerce (the UNCITRAL Model Law), adopted by UNCITRAL during its
29th Session in December 1996. Since then, a number of countries and 40 U.S. states have
enacted electronic commerce legislation to address the issues of dematerialization of
commercial documents and to give effect to digital signatures which are created using
encryption technology. The UNCITRAL Model Law is supported by what is termed a
"living document" called the GUIDEC from the International Chamber of Commerce.
GUIDEC[9] (General Usage for International Digitally Ensured Commerce) is a set of
international guidelines which aims to draw together the key elements involved in
electronic commerce, to serve as an indicator of terms and an exposition of the general
background to the issue. It also addresses one of the key problems with electronically
signed messages — they are not signed physically but require the intervention of an
electronic medium. This in turn alters the function of the signer and introduces problems
which a physical signature does not encounter, most especially the possibility of use of
the medium by a third party.

   The OECD too has also been active in this field: in March 1997 it adopted Guidelines
for Cryptography Policy,[10] setting out principles to guide countries in formulating their
own policies and legislation relating to the use of cryptography. The Recommendation is
a non-binding agreement that identifies the basic issues that countries should consider in
drawing up cryptography policies at the national and international level. The Recommendation culminates one year of intensive talks to draft the Guidelines.

The role of the European Commission

5.05   Naturally the European Commission has also tried to be active but its work has not been
at the leading edge. In 1994 the Commission published "Europe and the Global
Information Society, Recommendations to the European Council (the Bangemann
Report) and "Europe's Way to the Information Society: An Action Plan".[11] These gave

---

[9] http://www.iccwbo.org/guidec2.htm.
[10] http://www.oecd.org/dsti/sti/it/secur/prod/e-crypto.htm.
[11] COM (1994) 347 final).

the development of electronic commerce within the European Union a high priority. Following a call for tenders in 1996[12] regarding the security of information services, in October 1997 it published "Towards a European Framework for Digital Signatures and Encryption"[13] In this document the Commission recognised that digital signatures and encryption are essential tools in making "good use of the commercial opportunities offered by electronic communication via open networks." With respect to harmonisation, it suggests that "Divergent legal technical approaches would constitute a serious obstacle to the Internal Market and would hinder the development of new economic activities linked to electronic commerce. An E.U. policy framework for ensuring security and trust in electronic communication and safeguarding the functioning of the Internal Market is therefore urgently needed." It followed this up in May 1998 with a draft Directive on a Common Framework for Electronic Signatures[14] to "ensure the proper functioning of the Internal Market in the field of electronic signatures by creating a harmonised and appropriate legal framework for the use of electronic signatures within the European Community and establishing a set of criteria which form the basis for legal recognition of electronic signatures."

However, some European Union states have not waited for the Commission. Germany and Italy have both introduced digital signature laws.[15] The U.K., in contrast, has delayed legislation "to ensure that our policy development is compatible with that outlined in the Commission's Communication on Encryption and Electronic Signatures".[16] At the end of April 1998 the U.K. Government indicated that it intends to implement legislation to establish a legal framework for digital signatures. The DTI published a paper[17] which concluded ". . . electronic commerce offers tremendous opportunities to us all; but unless we harness those opportunities in policies that are both balanced and internationally compatible then trust and security will be the losers." The paper set out the basis of the Government's proposed regulatory regime. Before attempting to explain this, it is necessary to say a little about encryption and the science of cryptography.

---

[12] The Interdisciplinary Centre for Law & Information Technology from the University of Leuven was awarded a contract in mid-1996 by the European Commission D.G. X.V. to conduct a study on the Legal Aspects of Digital Signatures. A draft report has been issued, which gives an overview of national and E.U. policies, existing and envisaged rules and regulations, as well as practices concerning digital signatures in the Member States and the E.U.'s main trading partners. The Study is not yet available to the general public, but the Table of Contents and further information are available at their website: http://www.law.kuleuven.ac.be/icri/projects/digisig—eng.htm.

[13] COM (1997) 503).

[14] (COM (1998) 297).

[15] Germany has passed the *Information and Communication Services Act of 1997*. This legislation was enacted on June 13, 1997. Article 3 of the Act governs digital signatures. It requires the licensing of certification authorities. See http://www.kuner.com/data/sig/digsig4.htm for an unofficial translation and commentary by Christopher Kuner. In Italy the *Italian Digital Signature Legislation* was enacted on March 15, 1997 (Italian Law No. 59, Art. 15, c. 2, March 15, 1997). The Regulations were promulgated on November 10, 1997 (Presidential Decree No. 513). An English language translation of the law (http://www.aipa.it/english/law(2/law5997.asp) and regulations (http://www.aipa.it/english/law(2/pdecree51397.asp) is available at the website of the Autorita per l'Informatica nella Pubblica Amministrazione/Authority for IT in the Public Administration (AIPA). The law gives binding and legal effect to electronic documents, and the regulations enacted November 10, 1997 give the same legal effect to digital signatures attached to such documents as if they were manually signed.

[16] http://www.dti.gov.uk/CII/ana27p.html.

[17] http://www.dti.gov.uk/CII/ana27p.html.

Encryption's escape

5.06 Encryption is the process of disguising a message in such a way as to hide its substance. It sounds easy but the problem is that the intended recipient of the message has to turn the message back into a readable text. Cryptography is the science which has developed over centuries around this problem. Until recently, developments in cryptography were a highly secret topic and ordinary people did not have access to sophisticated technologies. All this changed twenty years ago when the U.S. security services arrived too late to stop a public lecture on "public key cryptography" which heralded a breakthrough in the science by providing a solution to the key distribution problem (see below).

A Cryptographic Primer[18]

5.07 All discussion of cryptography begins with three characters: Alice, Bob and Eve. Alice is the sender of a message, Bob is the receiver and Eve is the eavesdropper. In the basic example Alice wants to send a message to Bob. She takes the message (which is referred to as the *plaintext*) and *encrypts* it. The encrypted message is called the *cyphertext*. Eve who intercepts the cyphertext cannot read it. Bob can *decrypt* the message to convert the cyphertext back to plaintext using an algorithm.

An algorithm is a mathematical transformation. Alice uses an encryption algorithm to convert the plaintext into cyphertext. Bob uses a decryption algorithm to convert the cyphertext back into plaintext. At its simplest level an algorithm might be a rule saying "Shift all characters 5 along in the alphabet". So applying the encryption algorithm to the word "safe" would produce the cyphertext "weji". The decryption algorithm is the rule "Shift all characters 5 back in the alphabet".

Until recently the security of this type of system depended upon keeping the algorithm secret. This has not been easy. The problem became unmanageable when large numbers of people needed to communicate with each other securely. Each one would need to have their own unique algorithm.

The solution to this problem comes through the use of keys. Again using the simple example, the encryption algorithm might be put into a general form "Shift all characters X along in the alphabet" where X is the key. Alice now encrypts the message using the algorithm and the key. Eve may know the algorithm but so long as she does not know and cannot guess the key the message is secure. Bob is able to decrypt the message using the key.

The Data Encryption Standard (DES)

5.08 The above example is obviously simplistic. In practice designing algorithms is a major activity. A good real world example is DES, the Data Encryption Standard. In the early 1970s the U.S. Government sought candidates for their proposed federal encryption standard. IBM submitted a variant of an algorithm called Lucifer. The U.S. National Security Agency evaluated the algorithm and DES, as it was called, was adopted by the

---

[18] For further information look at the Counterpane site **http://www.counterpane.com/** which maintains a detailed bibliography. The best textbook on the subject is *Applied Cryptography* (Second Edition by Bruce Schneier John Wiley & Sons, 1996).

U.S. National Institution of Standards and Technology in 1976 and became an inter-national standard. It has been widely analysed by cryptoanalysts around the world. DES is an *iterated block cypher*, which means that it encrypts plaintext in block sized chunks — each block being 8 bits in length — and applies its algorithm again and again to the block until it outputs the cyphertext. DES has 16 iterations. As a general rule using more iterations provides greater security. However, DES is constructed in such a way that more than 16 iterations do not increase the security of the cyphertext.

So, if Alice sends a message to Bob using DES, she encrypts the plaintext on her computer. The encryption breaks the message down into 8-bit blocks and, using the key, applies the DES algorithm to each block 16 times before outputting the cyphertext.

Exchanging Keys and Public Key Encryption

But there remains the problem of getting the key to Bob. If Alice and Bob have never met and yet want to exchange secure messages; historically they have always needed to exchange keys. This problem was solved through the development of public key cryptography which is based upon the inherent mathematical difficulty in factoring prime numbers.[19] Public key encryption is also referred to as RSA encryption (after Rivest, Shamir, Adleman — the inventors of public key encryption and the owners of the U.S. patents relating to this development)   **5.09**

In public key encryption there are two different keys, one for encryption and the other for decryption. They come in pairs: a specific encryption key comes with a specific decryption key. Everyone has a pair of keys. Alice and Bob each publish their encryption keys which are called their public keys. They keep their decryption keys private. When Alice wants to communicate securely with Bob she encrypts her plaintext using Bob's public key to produce the cyphertext. Bob is able to decrypt it using his private decryption key.

Public key encryption also provides the solution to digital signatures. If Alice creates a key pair, publishes one key and keeps the other secret, she can "sign" electronic messages. Here the plaintext is encrypted using Alice's private key. Anyone is able to decrypt the cyphertext using Alice's public key. This proves that the person who encrypted the text was Alice since only Alice would know her private key.

In practice these key pairs tend to be used together. Alice will take a piece of plaintext   **5.10** and encrypt it with her private key. The resulting cyphertext can only be decrypted using her public key. She then takes the cyphertext and encrypts it again using Bob's public key. The resulting cyphertext can only be read by Bob who, to do so, must go through a two stage process decrypting the text with his private key and then Alice's

---

[19] Public key cryptography owes its existence to a branch of mathematics known as computational number theory, and involves techniques such as modular reduction, discrete logarithms, factoring of large prime numbers, and, most importantly, one way functions. A one-way function furnishes security by providing a relatively easy computation in one direction, but an extremely difficult computing problem when trying to reverse the original computation. As an example, the value of Y where:
A = 2, x = 5, P = 7, and $Y = A^x$ mod P, can be computed relatively easily. This is simply the remainder when A^x is divided by P. For this particular example:
$Y = A^x$ mod $P = 2^5$ mod $7 = 32$ mod $7 = $ remainder $[32/7] = 4$.
However, given: A = 2, Y = 4, P = 7, and $Y = A^x$ mod P, it is not easy to determine the correct value of x. This is especially true when the values typically range anywhere from 512 bits to 2048 bits.

public key. By this means the message been securely transmitted from Alice to Bob without either of them having to exchange keys. Additionally, Bob knows that the message is authentic since it had to be decrypted using Alice's public key.

The complexity is not finished. Public key cryptography is not suitable for encrypting long e-mail messages since the task of encryption and decryption would take too long and long public key encrypted messages could be vulnerable to cryptographic attack.[20] Instead it is always used as a method of communicating a conventional symmetrical key from Alice to Bob — the key that is to be used by both parties when encrypting and decrypting using an algorithm (such as DES) on a particular occasion. Cryptographic systems also use what is termed one way hash functions to generate a kind of fingerprint which proves that messages which "hash" to this value have not been tampered with. The most popular one-way hash function in current use if called MD5.[21]

The complexity is actually handled by electronic mail security programs. All Alice has to do is indicate that she wishes to send an encrypted message to Bob and the program does the rest. It generates the secret session key, encrypts the message, finds Bob's public key, encrypts the secret session key, concatenates them together and ships the whole thing off to Bob. On the receiving end, Bob's program automates the decryption process in a similar manner.

The most popular encryption program which in its latest commercial versions does all these things, is called PGP which stands for Pretty Good Privacy. It has been through a number of developments but today it uses IDEA[22] for data encryption, RSA[23] for key management and MD5[24] as a one way hash function. PGP also compresses files before encrypting them. It is very secure — so secure that governments resist its use by the general public.

Secure Electronic Transactions and the Microsoft Patent

5.11   In late 1995 MasterCard and VISA, who had each been working independently on secure technologies for use in electronic commerce, joined together to develop and promote the Secure Electronic Transaction (SET) protocol as a technical standard for safeguarding payment card purchases made over open networks. SET was published as an open specification for the industry with the statement "this specification is available to be applied to any payment service and may be used by software vendors to develop applications. Advice and assistance in the development of this specification have been provided by GTE, IBM, Microsoft, Netscape, RSA, SAIC, Terisa, and VeriSign."[25] It

---

[20] But a short message such as a 2048 bit key is totally secure.

[21] Invented by Ron Rivest at MIT in 1991. A hash function is a computation that takes a variable-size input (such as the total number of characters and their value in a document) and returns a fixed-size string called the *hash value*. A one-way function is a function that is significantly easier to perform in the forward direction than in the inverse direction — *e.g.* seconds to compute forward, years to calculate in reverse.

[22] International Data Encryption Algorithm. It was invented in Switzerland in 1991 and has been patented in Europe (patent pending in the USA). It has a 64 bit block and a 128 bit key size. It only uses 8 iterations and on most microprocessors a software implementation of IDEA is far faster than a software implementation of DES. It appears to be extremely secure.

[23] Rivest, Shamir, Adleman — there was been a long running patent dispute regarding PGP's use of the RSA algorithm but this has now been resolved.

[24] See note 16 above. For the full mathematical proof of the strength of MD5 see in Internet RFC (Request for Comment) 1321 which explains MD5 with sample code.

[25] Full documentation on the SET protocol in both postscript and Word format is available at **Error! Reference source not found.**

might therefore be thought that this specification was for public consumption. However, on August 4, 1998, Microsoft were granted U.S. *Patent 5790677: System and method for secure electronic commerce transactions.* This appears to be a patent covering the underlying technology in the SET protocol in a series of 83 claims. It is difficult to reconcile the invitation given out by MasterCard and Visa in publishing the specification with the patenting of the underlying technology by Microsoft. The latter's conduct would suggest that it was planning to use the technology as part of a Patent Pool agreement with various U.S. partners.

Microsoft's patenting in the United States of the underlying cryptographic technology may lead to problems in any commercial developments arising out of the major European Commission funded research project in this area called SEMPER (Secure Electronic Marketplace for Europe). This has been executed by an interdisciplinary consortium, combining experts from social sciences, finance, retail, publishing, I.T. and telecommunications, with the aim of providing an infrastructure for a secure electronic marketplace in Europe. SEMPER not only supports electronic advertising and sale of goods but also provides the means for a complete electronic market transaction, involving factors like electronic payment, non-repudiation of electronic contracts and exception handling within electronic systems. The fact that the patent has only been granted in the U.S. is unlikely to stop U.S. courts claiming jurisdiction over all transactions on the Internet which pass through servers located on U.S. territory.

SET offers banks the potential for a reduction in fraud owing to the fact that in one implementation of the protocol the customer's credit card number does not have to be revealed to the merchant in the transaction but remains at all times within a secure encrypted environment. However, this implementation is not compatible with existing merchant payment systems which require access to the customer's card number. Merchants cannot therefore integrate this way of working into their existing operations. Instead they have been insisting on an alternative implementation which can reveal the card number to the merchant on a merchant by merchant basis. Unfortunately, this second implementation is considerably more complex and expensive to implement. It also removes one of the main security advantages of SET by permitting merchant personnel to have access to customer credit card numbers.

5.12

Additionally, to initiate SET transactions, credit card holders have to obtain digital certificates which are used to sign orders with merchants. The obtaining of a digital certificate remains a non-trivial task. Once obtained, the credit card holder has to manage the certificate in accordance with a proper understanding of the risks and liabilities which could arise if his digital certificate is misused or lost or stolen. Very few bankers, let alone cardholders, are aware of the risks which can flow from the misuse of a customer's digital certificate.[26]

Because the additional security benefits which come from use of SET appear to benefit banks more than the merchants or the customers, there is relatively slow growth in the use of SET in general electronic commerce. It is unlikely that this situation will change in the near future.

---

[26] See later in this chapter "Liability Issues concerning Digital Signatures and Cryptography".

Government Regulation of Cryptography

5.13   Many governments are concerned about the widespread use of cryptography, claiming that it interferes with law enforcement and intelligence gathering. However little public evidence in support of their claims has been produced. Privacy advocates[27] suggest that legitimate law enforcement and intelligence gathering is not genuinely inhibited by the availability of strong cryptography to the general public since conventional surveillance using hidden microphones, informers, wiretaps and covert actions can always fulfil the real needs of law enforcement and intelligence gathering.

The U.K. position

5.14   The U.K. Government changed its position during the 1990s. In 1995 its position was that it had no intention of legislating against data encryption. In 1996, the G7 Summit considered the threat posed by criminal and terrorist use of strong encryption. Following the G7 communiqué, the U.K. Government, in June 1996, announced support for key escrow (discussed below), in the form of a system of Trusted Third Parties[28] ('TTPs' discussed below). This was ostensibly aimed at protecting the commercial sector, whilst giving the authorities some ability to obtain decryption where deemed necessary. The proposal mixed two separate justifications for TTPs, one appealing to private organisations and the other to law enforcement officials. In March 1997 the Government issued a "Public Consultation Paper on Licensing of Trusted Third Parties for the Provision of Encryption Services" which was said to be the prelude to legislation and which set out policy proposals for the mandatory licensing and regulation of TTPs to provide a range of information security services to their clients. 260 responses, 102 from organisations, and 158 from individuals were received by the Government most of which "expressed their views very strongly."[29]

5.15   On April 16, 1998 the Department of Trade and Industry (DTI) released a report with a preface by the Prime Minister called "Our Information Age," a general statement about future plans and current activities regarding uses of I.T. in education, government and electronic commerce. In support of this report, on April 27, 1998, the DTI Minister for Small Firms, Trade and Industry released her "Statement on the Legal Framework for Secure Electronic Commerce."[30] This policy statement announced that the DTI had begun the process of drafting legislation to license Certification Authorities and other TTPs, and Key Recovery Agents. The statement says "We intend that licensed Certification Authorities — conforming to the procedural and technical standards which such licensing will confer — would be in a position to offer certificates to support electronic signatures reliable enough to be recognised as equivalent to written signatures; an

---

[27] See, *e.g.*, Dr Ross Anderson's paper at **http://www.cl.cam.ac.uk/users/rja14/dtiresponse/dtiresponse.html**.
[28] See **http://www.coi.gov.uk/coi/depts/GTI/coi9303b.ok**.
[29] For a summary of the responses received see **http://www.dti.gov.uk/CII/respons.html** For a criticism of these U.K. proposals in peer reviewed legal paper see *Cryptography and Liberty: 'Can the Trusted Third Parties be Trusted ? A Critique of the Recent U.K. Proposals'* by Yaman Akdeniz, Oliver Clarke, Alistair Kelman, Andrew Oram at **http://ltc.law.warwick.ac.uk/jilt/cryptog/97—2akdz/akdeniz.htm**.
[30] Available at **http://www.dti.gov.uk/CII/ana27p.html**.

essential ingredient of secure electronic commerce." It appeared that the licensing scheme for the use of secure cryptography was not intended to be mandatory but a voluntary system which would be given procedural support in legislation. This statement was followed on July 1, 1998 by a White Paper containing the Government's proposals for a new legislative framework for strategic export controls and export licensing, with particular emphasis on the export of military equipment and technology. In section 3.2, "Transfer of technology by intangible means," the paper proposed legislation to provide the Government with the power to control transfers of technology by electronic means. The new laws would provide that "documents transferred abroad containing controlled technology should be subject to export licensing requirements, whether exported physically or in electronic form," and would also govern the posting of information on electronic networks such as the World Wide Web. For the time being, the definition of "controlled technology" is to be limited to that involving weapons of mass destruction and long-range missile systems. But one leading academic has stated that this proposed legislation would "instantly terminate our research in computer security" and is unworkable.[31]

International Controls

The basis of international controls over the use of cryptography was formally the subject **5.16** of COCOM and is now the subject of the Wassenaar Agreement.[32] The Wassenaar Arrangement controls the export of cryptography as a dual-use good, *i.e.* one that has both military and civilian applications. Software containing cryptography may be subject to controls as a dual-use item although confusingly Waasenaar provides an exemption from export controls for mass-market software. The interpretation of Waasenaar is thus open to interpretation.

Internationally, governments currently use two methods to control the use of cryptography by citizens. Some, such as France and Russia, restrict the domestic use of cryptography. In France a government authorisation[33] must be obtained in order to use any cryptography for confidentiality purposes (as opposed to authentication purposes). Only if very weak encryption is used will the use of encryption be authorised. The user

---

[31] Dr Ross Anderson of the Cambridge Computer Laboratory in a Usenet message " Export Licensing of Intangibles" — August 7, 1998, where he suggests that it would be impossible to implement since "a minimum . . . would have to include . . . numerically controlled machine tools and fibre winding equipment, semiconductor design and test equipment, robots, high performance computers (even top end PCs), optical amplifiers and software radios, aero engine control software, flight management systems, as well as many lasers, gyros, accelerometers and similar components. ... It will also be illegal to communicate, by demonstration or orally, information relevant to 'weapons of mass destruction and long range missiles'. This is not precisely defined. Will it force the removal of standard textbooks such as Fieser and Fieser's Organic Chemistry (which contains the recipe for mustard gas) and the Feynman Lectures in Physics (which describe how atom bombs work)?".
[32] Coordinating Committee on Multilateral Export Controls (COCOM), a grouping of Western nations that was abolished in 1994 and replaced by the Wassenaar Arrangement which has been signed up to by Argentina, Australia, Austria, Belgium, Bulgaria, Canada, the Czech Republic, Denmark, Finland, France, Germany, Greece, Hungary, Ireland, Italy, Japan, Luxembourg, the Netherlands, New Zealand, Norway, Poland, Portugal, the Republic of Korea, Romania, the Russian Federation, the Slovak Republic, Spain, Sweden, Switzerland, Turkey, Ukraine, the United Kingdom and the United States.
[33] Based on Decree 92–1358 of December 28, 1992.

may also be required to deposit his private key. Russia[34] has similar draconian controls over the internal use of cryptography but also uses the method used by the United States and many other countries — export controls in accordance with the Waasenaar Agreement. These in general require a licence to be obtained from a government agency in order to export cryptographic products and technical data.

U.S. Controls on the export of cryptography

5.17 The U.S. ban on the export of cryptographic products does not cover everything — there are exceptions for weak cryptographic products. As we have seen, the strength of a cryptosystem depends partly on the security of the algorithm and partly on the length of the key. The export ban means that while U.S. companies can use standard commercial cryptosystems with 128 bit keys within the U.S. (such as the encryption built into the Netscape browser's Secure Sockets Layer (SSL)), if people or companies outside of the U.S. wish to use a U.S. cryptographic product they are only legally allowed to have a version which uses keys of a maximum of 40 bits (eg the International version of Netscape's SSL). These weaker products can be broken in days.[35]

The present U.S. restrictions on the export of strong encryption are generally considered to be completely unworkable as a means of stopping widespread foreign use of unbreakable cryptography. The controls have not stopped strong U.S. cryptography from getting out of the country because the software has been illegally exported over the Internet.[36] The restrictions have also driven cryptographic development outside of the U.S. and provided markets for non.U.S. cryptographic companies who are not bound by such restrictions, even though their countries are signatories to the Waasenaar Agreement.[37]

However, the U.S. export restrictions have a secondary purpose. Not only are they intended to stop foreigners using unbreakable cryptography, they are designed to encourage the development of an international key recovery infrastructure. How this

---

[34] Upon the disintegration of the U.S.S.R., the President of Russia issued five degrees of February 22, March 27, April 11, May 12, and July 5, 1992 (Nos. 179, 312, 388, 469, and 507), which, together with the Law on Defense Industry Conversion, laid down certain legal foundations for a national armaments and military technologies control system. These decrees were consolidated in 1994 by the "Statute on Controls of Exports from the Russian Federation of Certain Types of Raw and Processed Materials, Equipment, Technology, Scientific and Technical Information Which Can Be Used in the Production of Weapons or Military Equipment" as ratified by the President of the Russian Federation under Decree 74, dated February 11, 1994. Included in this statute is a list of commodities, which require an individually approved license, issued by the Ministry of Foreign Economic Relations for export from Russia. Cryptographic equipment and software (including mass-market) is identified in the list of commodities requiring individually approved export licenses. Section 5 of Edict Number 334, of April 3, 1995, issued by the President of Russia prohibits the import of cryptographic products without a license. Section 4 of Edict Number 334, of April 3, 1995, issued by the President of Russia prohibits all activities in the development, sale, and use of cryptography without a license issued by the Federal Agency for Government Communications and Information (FAPSI).

[35] Note that because of the use of session keys every message has to be broken separately and can only be done through use of a substantial amount of computing resources.

[36] Indeed one enterprising crypto freedom advocate famously produced the best selling PGP T-shirt which had the source code of the strong cryptography software printed on the T-shirt. The T-shirt was advertised as not only being "machine readable" but also "machine washable".

[37] E.g. The Swiss government is providing 128-bit encryption plug-ins for browsers for download off of the Internet to secure its Telegiro Internet payment system. Downloads and more information are available at: http://www.swisspost.ch/E/21.html.

infrastructure works in the commercial arena and the legal implications of doing business utilising this infrastructure is an important aspect of electronic commerce (see the following sections: "Trusted Third Parties, Certification Authorities and Key Recovery Agents" and "Liability Issues concerning Digital Signatures and Cryptography")

THE ADMINISTRATIVE INFRASTRUCTURE OF ENCRYPTION

Public key encryption is an elegant technology which leaves one major problem: how does one correspondent know whether he has the right key for the other correspondent? If two individuals have a secure channel over which they can pass a key — for instance, by sealing a piece of paper or diskette in an envelope and sending it through the mail — they can then communicate in confidence. But if they wish to rely simply on electronic media, they have no such secure channel. No one can trust an e-mail message saying, 'Here is my public key,' because the very message containing that key may be sent by an eavesdropper. The problem arises whenever two people who do not previously know each other wish to communicate. It comes to the fore most often in on-line commerce, where a customer wants to know whether he can trust someone who is claiming to offer goods and is asking for payment.

5.18

Trusted Third Parties ('TTPs') may be the solution that allows an initial contact to be made. If you and your desired correspondent are both known by an intermediary, and you both entrust it with your public keys, you can obtain each other's public key from this trusted intermediary and start your communications. For worldwide communication, the TTP will probably be a large organisation with the same public visibility, quality controls, and sense of responsibility as a bank; in the case of electronic commerce it may very well be a bank.[38] The precise duties of a TTP are the crux of the debate between civil libertarians and law enforcement concerning encryption.

At the moment there are no regulations establishing who or what can be a TTP. The U.K. Government has now committed itself to introducing a voluntary system which will ensure that the TTP can, in fact, be trusted by correspondents. It has done so by establishing a clear policy differentiation between digital signatures and encryption.

Certification Authorities

The first group who will be affected will be TTPs who are in the business of certifying the identity and nature of communicators. It may be the case that a bank may wish to issue digital signatures to its best commercial customers, a digital signature which will indicate not only that it belongs to the high value customer but also that that customer has maintained, say, a £20,000 credit balance in its account over the past year. If a customer wants to do business on-line with another person, the customer sends that person an order signed with his bank-issued digital signature. The person who receives the order looks up the public half to the digital signature on the bank's website and is then in receipt of an instant credit reference as well as reliable proof of the identity of the

5.19

---

[38] Although this does not have to be the case. Global law firms and major accountancy practices have expressed an interest in getting into the TTP business along with well known systems houses.

customer. On the basis of this information the person can instantly decide whether to do business with the customer. The bank which issues the certificate is a special type of Trusted Third Party called a *Certification Authority* (C.A. for short). Under the forthcoming legislation the C.A. will have to be licensed and will have to show that it is conforming to the procedural and technical standards which such licensing will confer. At a minimum it must be in a position to offer certificates to support electronic signatures reliable enough to be recognised as equivalent to written signatures. It may well be required to do more to secure consumer and business confidence in the security of its signature mechanism.

Key Recovery Agencies

5.20   Everyone who uses encryption in the U.K. will be affected by the other provisions of the legislation. If any person uses cryptography for confidential communications he/she will be subject to new powers which will require him/her to hand over his/her private key on receipt of a judicial warrant or a warrant issued by a Secretary of State in accordance with the legislation. Most customers will not generate their own encryption keys but will obtain them from a special type of TTP known as a *Key Recovery Agent*[39] who, under the proposed legislation, will keep in *escrow* a copy of the customer's private key.[40] Key Recovery Agents will be required to hand over a copy of its' customer's private encryption key within one hour of receipt of a judicial warrant or a warrant issued by a Secretary of State. However, this part of the legislation will be specially restricted to encryption keys; it will not include cryptographic keys used solely for digital signature purposes. The new powers will apply to those holding such information (whether licensed or not) and to all users of encryption products.

Associated with this change in the law there will also have to be legislation to make it an offence not to hand over the private key needed for decryption of a cryptographic message when the same has been lawfully requested.

It should not, however, be thought that Key Escrow is solely a last ditch attempt by governments to regain control over secret communications between its citizens. A major reason why Key Escrow schemes are necessary in the commercial world is recovery of information when a private key has been lost, stolen or hidden. If a businessman dies it will be necessary for his executors to be able to decrypt financial records made using his private key. If a senior employee of a company is fired, the company will need to be able to read all correspondence written by the employee while working for the company and encrypted using his/her private key. It may be thought, therefore, that electronic commerce could be unable to safely function without Key Escrow systems being used.

---

[39] Unlike every other term of art this has not been shortened to its abbreviation "KRA". A possible reason for this is that for legislation to say that "all secret cryptographic keys have to be deposited with the KRAs" could be misunderstood since the Krays or Kray Twins were a notorious gang of villains who ran major London crime in the early 1960s.
[40] Key escrow or key recovery has been the subject of very heated debate around the world as can be shown by putting either of the two words into any Web search engine.

LIABILITY ISSUES CONCERNING DIGITAL SIGNATURES AND CRYPTOGRAPHY

Doing business using digital signatures requires a different mindset to conventional contract management because there are different risks. When a digital signature is incorporated in a document it signs every single part of it and links the authority of the signer with every single comma and colon. In practical terms it is far more than signing the end of a document and initialling every page. Yet the digital signature, unlike a physical signature, does not come from a human hand but from an artefact. Unauthorised access to this artefact can lead to the production of signed contractual documents and payment orders which are the same as the genuine articles. The obvious way of controlling such abuse is to make the holder of the digital signature (referred to as the *keyholder*) liable for all signatures generated by the artefact unless and until the keyholder has revoked the digital signature's authority with the C.A.

5.21

It is not easy to establish this new system of working. One business model involves the use of smart cards with the customer's signing and encryption keys recorded in the chip as a replacement for conventional magnetic stripe credit cards. If such a regime were to be grafted onto a U.K. credit card, thereby making the keyholder liable for all transactions made using the card, this would run counter to the current practice whereby a credit card holder is only liable for misuse of his card up to £100. This will not happen. To deal with the problem all credit card companies will instead have to maintain comprehensive, up-to-date lists of stolen or compromised cards. These will have to be far more extensive than today's "stop list" and will require a global infrastructure to enable instant checks to be made every time the credit card is used in a transaction.

New risks arise through the multiple functions of smart credit cards. If the customer's signing and encryption keys are recorded on the cards when the customer requests a revocation of the card, the credit card company not only has to invalidate the credit card, but also invalidate the public halves of the personal signing and encryption keys recorded on the cards.

5.22

> Paul, a noted investigative journalist, has his home burgled. His smart credit card is stolen along with his PC containing his personal electronic organiser. Paul's digital signature is recorded on the smart card with other secret information recorded on the PC. Paul notifies his credit card company to revoke his credit card and his digital signature. The credit card company fails to do so. A few days later a major foreign newspaper publishes a highly defamatory article allegedly written by Paul. The subject of the article sues the newspaper for libel. The newspaper says it relied upon Paul's digital signature. Paul says he relied upon the credit card company revoking his digital signature. The credit card company tries to rely on limitation of liability clauses in the contract with Paul to absolve it from liability for the defamation arising through its failure to revoke Paul's digital signature.

If a customer is using his smart card not just to buy goods and services but also as the repository of his digital signature, the credit card company could find itself liable for damages which lie well outside of the scope of electronic commerce.

There is also the problem of distinguishing between digital signatures (used for authentication of on-line messages) and encryption (used for keeping messages secret). They are both generated by the same mathematical functions and based upon the same mathematical principles in computational number theory. The U.K. Government has correctly seen that it should not require the handing over of private keys which are solely used in digital signatures.[41] But there is going to be a major difficulty in explaining to citizens how to manage their signing keys and their encryption keys. Bank staff have been known to treat a simple check digit system as an encryption system.[42] A citizen could easily need to have several cryptographic keys: a personal signing key used for all correspondence written by that person in a personal capacity; a commercial signing key (supplied to him as part of his employment which permits him to make binding statements on behalf of his employer limited to a pre-defined value of a transaction; a board level commercial signing key for use in transactions in excess of the pre-defined level made on behalf of company which may inherently incorporate features such as credit reference warranties; a corporate encryption key used when sending private communications in an employed capacity; and a board level corporate encryption key used when sending private communications in the capacity of being a member of the board. The use of each of the keys and the security needed to be associated with each of them is different. This will inevitably lead to disputes and raise the question of how the courts would decide the case of an employee using a corporate key for personal purposes. Current English law suggests that the company would be liable for the employee's actions on the basis of ostensible authority unless the recipient of the signed message knew or ought to have known that the employee was on a frolic of his own. Such cases are likely to become complicated as questions regarding whether the company had an adequate system of internal control over the misuse of corporate signing keys and of whether such misuse was condoned at senior levels as a illegitimate boardroom perk but condemned at junior levels, will have to be addressed by the court.

Problems with managing encryption

5.23   Companies are also likely to demand, as part of their employment terms, that any employee has to place in escrow with the company any private encryption key he may use in personal correspondence. Were the employer to be unable to demand the private encryption keys of its employees there would be a risk that a disgruntled employee could pass confidential information and trade secrets to rivals secure in the knowledge

---

[41] One very significant reason for this is if governments were allowed to have the private keys used in digital signatures of citizens the police and security services could fabricate signed evidence allegedly produced by the citizens.

[42] In 1979, Dr Lawrence C. Galitz was commissioned by the Committee of London Clearing Banks (CLCB) to develop a "test key" system for the verification of bank messages. This was intended to verify messages and warn against simple errors like the substitution of one digit for another, or the transposing of digits. The key he developed was based on "patterns" and "shapes" of 3-digit groups. It was not intended to be used as a authentication system, proving the identity of the sender in a cryptographically secure manner. Most significantly, because the system was intended to be universal, and applicable around the world where varying and very limited technology was then available, it had to be a manual system. Yet despite clear statements to the contrary the "test key" was treated by many bankers at the time as a secure method of message authentication.

that cryptography would hide the infamy from the employer. Such a measure would have to be carefully considered, however. Confusion and litigation could result if this practice were badly implemented and was used as a means of company surveillance over its employees' lifestyles and relationships. Furthermore, corporate ignorance could lead to companies demanding not only the personal private encryption key but the employee's private signing key. This would be totally unjustified.

Digital Certificates

> "A gentleman's agreement is an agreement which is not an agreement, made between two people neither of whom are gentlemen, whereby each expects the other to be strictly bound without himself being bound at all"[43]

The digital certificates which are currently in general circulation might be termed "gentleman's digital certificates" (see the above definition). They come with sweeping disclaimers of liability. Both the 40 and 128 bit Netscape SSL encryption that are used for secure Web connections rely in part on digital signatures to identify the server and the browser to each other. No one actually guarantees the server's public key. All that the user gets is the practical assurance that if the response back is the same each time he logs on, it is unlikely that he is communicating with an impostor. But nobody is accepting liability for the user who is being misled.

    The same situation applies with other current Internet-based certificates, including the "authenticode" certificates used to identify the authors of Java-like ActiveX programs. The certificates offer no "bankable" reassurance for Internet users who are understandably reluctant to let code written by strangers gain access to their computer's operating system.[44]

5.24

Growing jurisdictional conflict

The problem is that existing digital signature legislation does not address the liability issue in the same manner from jurisdiction to jurisdiction. If, for example, a comparison is made between the digital signature laws of Utah and Washington, important differences can be found. Both states require a C.A. to suspend a certificate if the C.A. gets a call from the keyholder saying the private key has been compromised. But to guard against fraud or anti-competitive practices (*e.g.* "Let's hinder our rival in this contract race by faxing its bank and getting its signing key suspended"), the C.A. can't suspend for long without checking to make sure the suspension request really came from the keyholder. Under Utah law, the check has to be done within two days, but the certificate is automatically suspended whenever the C.A. gets a request from someone claiming to be the keyholder. Under Washington law, the caller can ask for a four-day suspension but the C.A. can only suspend the certificate if the CA is sure that the caller really is the keyholder.

5.25

---

[43] Mr Justice Vaisey — an unreported interlocutory observation in *Bloom v. Kinder* [1958] T.R. 91 quoted by Sir Robert Megarry in *A Second Miscellany at Law* (Stephens, 1997).
[44] See Stewart A. Baker "International Developments Affecting Digital Signatures", October 1997 at **http://www.steptoe.com/WebDoc.nsf/Law+&+The+Net-All/All**.

Mr Stewart A. Baker of Steptoe & Johnson LLP has considered this point[45] and has commented that while there is the same basic idea in both states ". . . what if you are a C.A. doing business in both states and you get a suspension request from someone who doesn't sound very much like the keyholder? In Utah, you must suspend; in Washington, you can't. Or suppose the caller asks for three days to come in and verify his identity? In Utah, you can't wait that long; in Washington, you must. C.A.s simply can't obey the laws of both states."

This lack of consensus regarding the correct balance of risk between the keyholder and the C.A. runs though all U.S. states that and can be found in all national systems. "How much risk should the keyholder bear and how much should fall on the C.A.? Different states, and certainly different countries, will arrive at different answers to such questions. But, if C.A.s must change their practice in each country or each state, there will be very few C.A.s in 10 years, and digital signatures will not live up to their promise"[46] Clearly digital signature legislation requires a great deal more thought than simply trying to bring in measures to deal with the de-materialisation of written documents. Somebody has to accept the risk and be adequately compensated for such acceptance. Businesses engaged in electronic commerce using digital signatures appear to need similar rights to those given to consumers using credit cards for their payments — a clear limit on their losses when the digital signature is misused.[47] But the speed of modern business may suggest that businesses should also be able to recover unlimited damages for failure of their C.A. to provide them with round-the-clock services and for failure to supply the business with an instant replacement to a signing key which has been compromised, as well as instantaneous revocation of the compromised key.

5.26   There is a further problem which has to be resolved before a global system of electronic commerce using digital signatures can become a reality. In its White Paper, the U.K. Government has made it clear that it will legislate to ensure that a C.A. will have to be licensed and will have to show that it is conforming to the procedural and technical standards which such licensing will confer. As a corollary it will have to be illegal for an organisation to issue a digital certificate to a U.K. citizen or company when that organisation has not been licensed or recognised by the U.K. authorities. Where does this leave Netscape SSL encryption, "authenticode" certificates and other similar products which are all over the Web today? Will every organisation which uses these "gentlemen's digital certificates" have to register? According to Stewart A. Baker: "The German digital signature law implies that no one may issue certificates without meeting strict standards for security; these standards include a requirement that private keys be stored only on a smart card — they cannot be sent over the Internet, and they cannot be stored on a magnetic swipe card or 3.5-inch floppy."[48] In Malaysia, under Section 4 of the Malaysian Digital Signatures Act 1997, any organisation issuing digital certificates

---

[45] *ibid.*
[46] *ibid.*
[47] See Chapter 2 for the discussion on the Distance Selling Directive and Consumer Credit Legislation.
[48] Cited above. Since Mr Baker published his paper the German position appears to have been modified. See Christopher Kuner of Gleiss Lutz Hootz Hirsch, Frankfurt at **http://www.kuner.com/data/new/gov—digsig—recognition.html**.

must register with the Malaysian authorities.[49] Singapore, requires Certification Authorities to be regulated by an appointed Controller of Certification Authorities, who will be responsible for licensing, certifying, monitoring and overseeing certification activities. Licensing will be voluntary, but certificates issued by licensed C.A.s will be entitled to greater presumptions of validity and limitations on liability. Closed networks may use unlicensed C.A.s if they choose.[50] None of these systems regulatory systems are compatible with the system used in the U.S. of voluntary registration by C.A.s.

Conclusion

In the light of these problems perhaps the U.K. was right not to rush ahead with digital signature legislation but to shape the debate in the European Union towards a minimalist but mandatory regulatory solution for C.A.s. But in 1999 the U.K. can no longer safely wait on consensus developing within the European Union. Having consulted and considered matters (and seen the errors made by other nations) it seems clear that Parliament should press ahead to establish a regulatory regime for electronic commerce to protect U.K. business and industry and create an attractive environment in which to trade electronically.

5.27

---

[49] "Section 4(1) No person shall carry on or operate, or hold himself out as carrying on or operating, as a certification authority unlessthat person holds a valid licence issued under this Act.
Section 4(2) A person who contravenes subsection (1) commits an offence and shall, on conviction, be liable to a fine not exceeding five hundred thousand ringgit or to imprisonment for a term not exceeding ten years or to both, and in the case of a continuing offence shall in addition be liable to a daily fine not exceeding five thousand ringgit for each day the offence continues to be committed. . . .".
[50] Section 43 of the Singapore Electronic Transactions Act 1998.

EVIDENCE AND SECURITY

"Trust me, I'm a lawyer"[1]

INTRODUCTION

It is an unfortunate fact of life that people do not always tell the truth. Sometimes people **6.01**
forget, sometimes they lie or circumstances change which leads one party to remember
matters differently. Any modern system of commerce depends partly on trust but
mainly on the fact that agreements between the parties are documented. In electronic
commerce this situation is crucial since the parties to the agreement may never have
physically met or spoken to each other by telephone. In most cases the only evidence of
the agreement between the parties will be documents evidencing the transaction. But
there may be particular problems because the documents will be computer-generated.

TYPES OF EVIDENCE

Computer-generated documentary evidence will be of three types. First will be calcula- **6.02**
tions or analyses which are generated by the computer itself through the running of
software and the receipt of information from other devices such as built-in clocks and
remote sensors. This type of evidence is termed *real evidence*. Real evidence arises in
many circumstances. If a bank computer automatically calculated the bank charges due
from a customer based upon its tariff, the transactions on the account and the daily
cleared credit balance, this calculation would be a piece of real evidence.

Then there are documents and records produced by the computer which are copies of
information supplied to the computer by human beings. This material is treated as
hearsay evidence. Cheques drawn and paying-in slips credited to a bank account are
hearsay evidence.

Finally there is *derived evidence* which is information which combines real evidence
with the information supplied to the computer by human beings to form a composite

---

[1] A version of a line said by the actor Robin Williams in the Stephen Spielberg movie "Hook".

record. This too is treated as hearsay evidence in modern evidence statutes.[2] An example of derived evidence is the figure in the daily balance column of a bank statement since this is derived from real evidence (automatically generated bank charges) and hearsay evidence (individual cheque and paying-in entries).

REAL EVIDENCE

6.03 With rapid improvements in forensic science, real evidence is of growing importance in criminal investigation. Fingerprints, DNA samples and bloodstains are all common examples of real evidence which are used to convince a court of the guilt or innocence of a defendant.

Automatic Records

The law has not imposed any barriers on the use of automatic records as evidence, despite them being only a recent development. Quite early on, the recordings from automatic recording devices were accepted as real evidence. In *The Statute of Liberty*,[3] the case turned on a record of radar readings showing the location of two ships involved in a collision. The recording was made by a mechanical device without human intervention. Simon P held that such a recording was admissible as real evidence. He cited *R. v. Maqsud Ali*[4] which was authority on the admissibility of tape recordings:

> ". . . if tape recordings are admissible, it seems equally a photograph of radar reception is admissible — as indeed, any other type of photograph. It would be an absurd distinction that a photograph should be admissible if the camera were operated manually by a photographer, but not if it were operated by a trip or clock mechanism. Similarly, if evidence of weather conditions were relevant, the law would affront common sense if they were to say that those could be proved by a person who looked at a barometer from time to time but not by producing a barograph record . . . The law is bound these days to take cognisance of the fact that mechanical means replace human effort."

6.04 In 1981 Professor Smith in a learned article on computer evidence developed the ideas put forward in *The Statute of Liberty* and came up with a rule which was later accepted by the courts:

> "Where information is recorded by mechanical means without the intervention of a human mind, the record made by the machine is admissible in evidence, provided of course, it is accepted that the machine is reliable"[5]

"Mechanical" in the above statement means "automatic" and is meant to include electrical, electronic and chemical methods of recording as opposed to just mechanisms

---

[2] Although this is not so clear if older statutes are considered. See the section "Hearsay in Northern Ireland" below.
[3] [1968] 1 W.L.R. 739.
[4] [1966] 1 Q.B. 688.
[5] J.C. Smith "The Admissibility of Statements by Computer", (1981) Crim L.R. 390. This statement was quoted with approval by the Court of Appeal in *R. v. Spiby* (1990) 91 Cr.App.Rep. 186.

made up of machines. In *R. v. Wood*,[6] the case, concerning the alleged theft of certain metals, turned upon the computer printouts put forward by a chemist who had performed an analysis of the metal found in the possession of the accused. The court found that the evidence was admissible as real evidence since the computer was used as a calculator:

> "This computer was rightly described as a tool. It did not contribute it own knowledge. It merely did a sophisticated calculation which could have been done manually by the chemist"[7]

In *R. v. Spiby*,[8] the appellant had been convicted of being knowingly involved in the unlawful importation of cannabis. In support of the allegation of knowledge the prosecution used telephone printouts from the hotel's PBX computer to that a particular guest at that hotel had called the appellant at his home. At his appeal against conviction his counsel tried to have the printout ruled as inadmissible evidence. The Court of Criminal Appeal held that the printouts were real evidence since the computer had automatically logged the lifting of the phone receiver and the making of the call. It cited and approved Professor Smith's statement (above). The Court of Criminal Appeal also applied the principle that if an instrument was one of a kind which, to common knowledge, are more often than not in working order, then in the absence of evidence to the contrary, the courts will presume that the machine was in working order at the material time. This effectively transfers the burden of proof that the machine was not working properly onto the defendant.

6.05

Replication of Errors

While the above conclusion may be reasonable for the consideration of individual instances — the reliability of a log of the making of a telephone call or the readings of a speedometer in a motoring offence — it is not an appropriate conclusion where an error in any single instance is replicated and modifies another record: a derived record. Thus, if a telephone system records the number of minutes expended in a telephone call correctly in 99 calls out of 100, the total billing record at the end of a period where 1,000 calls had been made will not be correct since it will contain ten incorrect call records each of which will have affected the total.

In statistical terms[9] with a one in a hundred 'single instance' error it is a near certainty that the total billing record will contain errors when it is made up of 1,000 records. If the

6.06

---

[6] (1982) 76 Cr. App. Rep. 23.

[7] *ibid.*

[8] (1990) 91 Cr.App.Rep. 186.

[9] The relevent statistical equation to prove this is Bayes' Theorem which has been the basis of statistical analysis for two hundred years. See: Robertson B and Vignaux GA, *Interpreting Evidence: Evaluating Forensic Evidence in the Courtroom*. Chichester: John Wiley & Sons,1995. For the approach of the U.K. Court of Criminal Appeal to statistical evidence and how juries are meant to approach it see *Michael Gordon* [1995] 1 Cr.App.R. 290, *R. v. Docherty* [1996] T.L.R. 504 (August 16, 1996) and *R. v. Denis Adams* [1996] 2 Cr.App.R. 467. The Court of Criminal Appeal in these cases appears to have fairly comprehensively rejected the use of probability calculations in English criminal law and dashed the hope expressed by Robertson and Vignaux that logic, probability and inference would provide the language in which lawyers and scientists would communicate with each other. What is not plain is whether the decision in Denis Adams precludes the presenting to a jury of expert evidence explaining the calculations of the statistician as to the effect of his application of Bayes theorem to the evidence. That would seem to be a matter of expert evidence which a jury could consider and accept or reject. Such is the situation in Scots criminal law, see *Welsh v. H.M. Advocate* [1992] S.L.T. 193.

total number of calls made is 300 then there is a better than 95 per cent chance that the total billing record contains errors. If the total number of calls made is 70 then on the balance of probabilities it is more likely than not that the total billing record will contain errors.

Number of Records	Likelihood of Errors
1000	99.9956829%
300	95.0959106%
70	50.516134%

To date, the case law on computer evidence has failed to appreciate this important distinction and the consequences which flow from the aggregation of small errors into high probabilities of error. Indeed, the Law Commission accepted a statement by a non-technical legal academic that "most computer error is either immediately detectable or results from errors in the data entered into the machine."[10] — a statement which a practitioner who regularly works with computer evidence in criminal cases would find is not supported by the facts.

ADMISSIBILITY AND HEARSAY EVIDENCE

> "People were formally frightened out of their wits about admitting evidence lest juries go wrong. In modern times we admit the evidence and discuss its weight"[11]

6.07　When matters are litigated the court has to find that certain facts exist before pronouncing on the rights, duties and liabilities of the parties. Proving the existence of certain facts is done by evidence which is either admitted by the parties as not being disputed or the disputed facts (termed the facts in issue) which have to be established by the court. In this determination the court has historically been required to exclude certain evidence under the hearsay rule although the main general rule regarding evidence is that all evidence which is sufficiently relevant to an issue before the court is admissible and all that is irrelevant or insufficiently relevant should be excluded.[12]

The hearsay rule

6.08　The hearsay rule says that: "any assertion other than one made by a person while giving oral evidence in the proceedings is inadmissible as evidence of any fact asserted."[13]

---

[10] Tapper, "Discovery in Modern Times: A Voyage Around the Common Law World" (1991) 67 Chicago-Kent Law Review 217–248. Quoted in the Law Commission Consultation Paper "Evidence in Criminal Proceedings" No. 138, 1995, para. 13.7.

[11] Coburn C.J. in *R. v. Birmingham Overseers* (1861) 1 B. & S. 763 at 767.

[12] *Per* Goddard L.J. in *Hollington v. Hewthorn & Co. Ltd.* [1943] 1 K.B. 587.

[13] A formulation of the rule as approved by the House of Lords in *Sharp* [1988] 1 W.L.R. 7–11, *per* Lord Havers, with whom Lord Mackay of Clashfern L.C., Lord Keith of Kinkel, Lord Bridge of Harwich and Lord Griffiths concurred. This formulation was also approved in *Kearley* [1992] 2 A.C. 228, 254H–255A, *per* Lord Ackner, with whom Lord Bridge of Harwich agreed.

Thus, if a witness to a road accident had told a friend that a person with blue hair was driving the car, under the hearsay rule the friend could not be called to give evidence of that fact because the friend had not witnessed the accident but was only relaying what he/she had been told. Cross-examination of the friend could not test the underlying reliability of the evidence, it could only test the reliability of the friend's recollection of what he/she had been told by the witness.

Many modern commercial lawyers will not be familiar with the hearsay rule since it has been largely ignored in English civil cases over the past thirty years (although it remains of great importance in criminal cases). But the hearsay rule remains part of the general law throughout the common law world and serious difficulties can be expected if litigation is brought in a jurisdiction where the evidence statutes have not been modernised. For this reason we outline the scope of the rule and its recent U.K. legislative history in some detail to enable the reader to made reasonable extrapolations when considering electronic commerce litigation in foreign and Commonwealth jurisdictions.

It will readily be appreciated that the hearsay rule is extraordinarily inconvenient and **6.09** is capable of being used to exclude a great deal of good reliable evidence from trials in breach of the main rule that all evidence which is sufficiently relevant to an issue before the court is admissible. In the nineteenth century in England the business community sought and obtained a statutory exemption to the rule which covered documents created in the course of a trade or business from information supplied by a person who might reasonably be supposed to have personal knowledge of the matters contained therein and where the person in question could not reasonably be expected to have any recollection of the matters contained in the record. Thus, if a clerk working in a business made a note of a sale in a ledger the ledger, could be produced in court as evidence of the sale even if the clerk who had made the entry could no longer recall the matters contained in the ledger. The ledger entry was a business record, part of the books of account of the business, which were subject to the requirements laid down by the revenue authorities. Implicit in this exception to the hearsay rule was a requirement that the exempted evidence was prepared and kept in accordance with the rules laid down by the revenue authorities for the keeping of business records.

The inconvenience of the hearsay rule also led to the creation of a number of common law exemptions which developed in haphazard manner because, when the rule proved highly inconvenient in a particular kind of case, it was relaxed just sufficiently far to meet that case, and without regard to any question of principle.[14] In the United States Thayer,[15] Wigmore,[16] Morgan[17] and Maguire[18] all attempted to find a golden thread in the "rats' nest" of exceptions without real success. In the last quarter century has there

---

[14] See Lord Reid in *Myers* [1965] A.C. 1001, and 1020B–C.

[15] *A preliminary treatise on evidence at the common law* by James Bradley Thayer, Boston, 1898.

[16] *A treatise on the Anglo-American system of evidence in trials at common law, including the statutes and judicial decisions of all jurisdictions of the United States and Canada* by John Henry Wigmore, Boston, Little, Brown and Co., 1940, (10 volumes).

[17] Edmund M. Morgan, *Hearsay Dangers and the Application of the Hearsay Concept*, 62 HARV. L. REV. 177 (1948).

[18] John MacArthur Maguire, *The Hearsay System: Around and Through the Thicket*, 14 VAND. L. REV. 741 (1961).

been some codification in the United States regarding hearsay evidence[19] but its' approach has not found favour elsewhere.[20]

The decision in *Myers v. DPP*

6.10 The position of hearsay evidence in England is today still governed by the majority decision of the landmark House of Lords case in 1965, *Myers v. DPP*[21] which concerned an alleged conspiracy to deal in stolen motor cars. The defendant would buy a wrecked car and its log book, and then steal an almost identical car. He would then convert the stolen car so that the details matched the log book and proceed to sell it for profit. Evidence produced by the car manufacturers at the time of the production of the cars was critical to the prosecution's case. As the cars moved along the production line, workers recorded details of the serial numbers of the various components fitted to a particular car. These details were recorded on a card by the worker responsible. Eventually the completed card was photographed and recorded on microfilm. The prosecution sought to put the microfilm records in evidence at the trial under the exception to the hearsay rule under the Evidence Act 1938 which covered business records. The Evidence Act 1938 did not mention microfilm as a type of business record (because the product was not in common use by business in the 1930s). By a majority of 3:2 the House of Lords held that the evidence was inadmissible as hearsay because any exemption to the hearsay rule had to be construed restrictively. Furthermore, the majority ruled, that any further exceptions to the hearsay rule should be introduced by Parliament, not the judiciary.

Lord Reid giving the majority judgment:

"To admit the evidence is to admit hearsay evidence. Further, the records could only go to prove the truth of the assertions contained therein. They did not corroborate any other witness and it was not relevant to show that they had been made unless it was also accepted that the records were true."[22]

Lord Pearce (dissenting) said:

---

[19] The U.S. addressed the question of hearsay evidence by attempting to codify the evidence law with the publication of the Model Code of Evidence by the American Law Institute in 1942. The Code failed and was not adopted in any jurisdiction in the United States. In 1953, the National Conference of Commissioners on Uniform State Laws promulgated the Uniform Rules of Evidence which was based on the Model Code. The Uniform Rules influenced the development of evidence law in several states. The U.S. Congress then enacted the Federal Rules of Evidence in 1975. The Federal Rules are based on the Model Code and the Uniform Rules and are applicable in the federal courts. More than 30 states have adopted codes of evidence which are modelled on the Federal Rules and a revised version of the Uniform Rules. The Federal Rules of Evidence affirms the rule against hearsay and lists the recognised exceptions by reference to whether the declarant is available as a witness in *Rules 803* and *804(b)*.

[20] The Federal Rules have been criticised for being too complex. There are 27 specific exceptions and two general exceptions. The Scottish Law Commission were of the view that codification on the American model would not reduce but would in fact increase the complexity of the law. Scottish Law Commission, *Evidence: Report on Corroboration, Hearsay and Related Matters in Civil Proceedings* (Scot. Law Com. No. 100, 1986), para. 3.30. The New South Wales Law Reform Commission also thought that the American approach was conservative and "retain far too much of the technicality and distortion-riddled quality of the present law", New South Wales Law Reform Commission, *Report on the Rule Against Hearsay* (L.R.C. 29, 1978), Appendix B, para. 1.5.

[21] *Myers v. DPP* [1965] A.C. 1001.

[22] *ibid.* at page 1022.

"In my opinion, where the person who from his own knowledge made business records cannot be found, and where a business produces some proper servant, who can speak with knowledge to the method and system of record-keeping, its records reliably kept in the ordinary way of business, they should be admitted as prima facie evidence. I say reliably kept because the judge must clearly have a discretion to exclude from a jury (as he would reject from his mind in adjudicating) records so ill kept as not to be worthy of credit. If any question arose about that, he would hear the evidence or argument about it in the absence of the jury, as is done, for instance, in the case of confessions."[23]

Over the years the views of Lord Pearce have gained support. They appear to have a great deal in common with the U.S. approach and although *Myers v. DPP* is still good law in England it was not followed in Scotland where the Lord Chief Justice in *Lord Advocate's Reference (No. 1 of 1992)*[24] considered the judgment in *Myers* and concluded that the judgments of the dissenting minority more accurately reflected Scots Law. It was not followed by the Supreme Court of Canada either.[25] **6.11**

Conclusion on "Myers"

The net result of this situation is that, while the binding authority in English law says that evidence statutes have to be restrictively construed and that it is Parliament alone which can create new categories of admissible hearsay evidence, this is less likely to be the law in other common law jurisdictions on the construction of evidence statutes. Crown colonies and members of the Commonwealth whose evidence statutes were drafted before computers came into common use are today more likely to be construed in accordance with Lord Pearce's dissenting judgment in *Myers* than in accordance with Lord Reid's majority judgment. Indeed, since the House of Lords is no longer bound by its earlier decisions it is possible that the majority decision in *Myers* could be overruled today if the right case were appealed before the House of Lords.

Hearsay in England

In 1993 the Law Commission published a report on the hearsay rule in civil cases[26] in which it made the following points: **6.12**

(a) Evidence should not be excluded on the ground that it is hearsay. Multiple hearsay as well as simple hearsay should henceforth be admissible.

(b) Existing statutory provisions making hearsay evidence admissible should not be affected by the proposals.

(c) Parties intending to rely on hearsay evidence should be under a duty to give notice of that fact to other parties wherever it is reasonable and practicable in the circumstances to enable those parties to deal with any matters arising from its being hearsay. This duty should be subject to any agreement, or any rules of court, to the contrary. Failure to comply with this duty should not affect the admissibility of the evidence but might attract costs or other sanctions at the court's disposal.

---

[23] *ibid.* at page 1044.
[24] 1992 S.L.T. 1010.
[25] *Ares v. Venner* [1970] S.C.R 608.
[26] Law Commission, *The Hearsay Rule in Civil Proceedings* (Law Com. No. 216, Cm 2321, 1993).

(d) A party should be allowed to call a witness whose evidence has been tendered as hearsay by another party, and to cross-examine him on the statement.

(e) Statutory guidelines should be provided for the courts to assist them to assess the weight they should attach to hearsay evidence.

(f) The requirement that the maker of a statement which is adduced as hearsay should be competent to give direct oral evidence should be retained, and that the date on which the statement was made should be the date on which the statement maker is required to satisfy this condition.

(g) Evidence should continue to be admissible to impeach or support the credibility of a person not called as a witness, and evidence tending to show that such a person made previous or later inconsistent statements should also continue to be admissible.

(h) Previous consistent or inconsistent statements of a person called as a witness should continue to be admissible as evidence of the matters stated.

6.13   The Government fully accepted these conclusions and, in consequence, the *Civil Evidence Act 1995* was enacted in November 1995 to implement the recommendations of the Law Commission. The relevant provisions in this Act are Sections 8, 9 and 12.

Civil Evidence Act 1995

Section 8(1):
"Where a statement contained in a document is admissible as evidence in civil proceedings, it may be proved:

    (a) by the production of the document, or
    (b) whether or not that document is still in existence, by the production of a copy of that document or of the material part of it,

authenticated in such manner as the court may approve . . ."

Section 8(2):
"It is immaterial for this purpose how many removes there are between a copy and an original. . ."

Section 9(1):
"A document which is shown to form part of the records of a business or public authority may be received in evidence in civil proceedings without further proof . . ."

Section 12:
" 'document' means anything in which information of any description is recorded . . . 'copy', in relation to a document, means anything onto which information recorded in the document has been copied, by whatever means and whether directly or indirectly . . ."

However no statutory guidelines regarding the weight to be attached to hearsay evidence have yet been produced. This should be of grave concern[27]

---

[27] For a discussion on how Codes of Practice will help, see *Principles of Good Practice — The BSI and DISC Codes* and *The Reliability of Computer Evidence* later in this chapter.

Hearsay in Scotland

Scotland addressed the matter of hearsay evidence at little earlier than England: The   **6.14**
Scottish Law Commission published a report on corroboration and hearsay in civil
proceedings in 1986[28] which were substantially implemented by *Civil Evidence (Scotland)
Act 1988*. Under this Act:

(a) The rule against hearsay was abolished and evidence is not be excluded solely on
the ground that it was hearsay. Both first-hand and multiple hearsay are
admissible under the Act.

(b) Assertive conduct as well as oral and documentary hearsay are covered by the
Act.

(c) There is no requirement of notification of intention to use hearsay evidence.

(d) The court does not have power to exclude evidence solely on the ground that it is
hearsay, nor can a party insist that an available witness whose statement is
challenged should attend and give direct oral evidence.

(e) The court has power to allow a witness to be recalled or an additional witness to
be called before the commencement of closing submissions when hearsay
statements are challenged.

(f) No statutory guidelines are given to the courts to assist them in assessing the
weight of the hearsay evidence.

(g) No special provisions are made for computer records.

(h) Statements by witnesses which are consistent (or inconsistent) with their evidence
in court are be admissible for the purpose of supporting (or challenging) the
witnesses' credibility, and statements proved for such purpose are also be
admissible as evidence of any matter contained therein.

During the Parliamentary debate[29] concerning this legislation the Scottish Office was
of the view that to allow the courts to refuse to admit hearsay evidence if the associated
notice procedure had not been complied with could have the effect of reintroducing the
hearsay rule.[30] If a party was taken by surprise, it could ask that the witness involved be
called. If the witness was available but not called, it would be taken account of by the
court in assessing the weight of the evidence. But the lack of statutory guidelines on
assessing the weight of computer evidence remains a major concern.[31]

Hearsay in Northern Ireland

The courts in Northern Ireland still recognise the rule against hearsay and, until the law   **6.15**
has been amended, problems can be expected in litigating electronic commerce cases.
Modern networks made up from a myriad of interconnecting systems which have

---

[28] Scottish Law Commission, *Evidence: Report on Corroboration, Hearsay and Related Matters in Civil Proceedings*
(Scot. Law Com. No. 100, 1986).

[29] These matters can now be put before the court in argument since the judgment in *Pepper v. Hart* [1992] 3
W.L.R. 1032, where the House of Lords held that the rules excluding reference to parliamentary materials
should be relaxed on certain conditions.

[30] *Hansard* (House of Commons), May 16, 1988, col. 743–4.

[31] For a discussion on how Codes of Practice will help, see *Principles of Good Practice — The BSI and DISC Codes*
and *The Reliability of Computer Evidence* later in this chapter.

copied the original evidence again and again will be a good source of legalistic point taking if one party wishes to take issue with the admissibility of the evidence.

The main statutory exceptions to the rule against hearsay can be found in the Evidence Act (N.I.) 1939, the terms of which are almost identical to those of the Evidence Act 1938, and the Civil Evidence Act (N.I.) 1971 which bears considerable similarity to the repealed Civil Evidence Act 1968.[32] These provide for the admissibility of statements contained in documents which form part of a record and statements produced by computers. However the terms of the Civil Evidence Act (N.I.) 1971 reflects its age:

6.16

> "Section 2 (1) In any civil proceeding a statement contained in a document produced by a computer shall . . . be admissible as evidence of any fact stated therein of which direct oral evidence would be admissible, if it is shown that the conditions mentioned in subsection (2) below are satisfied in relation to the statement and computer in question.
>
> (2) The said conditions are:
>
> (a) that the document containing the statement was produced by the computer during a period over which the computer was used regularly to store or process information for the purposes of any activities regularly carried on over that period, whether for profit or not, by any body, whether corporate or not, or by any individual;
>
> (b) that over that period there was regularly supplied to the computer in the ordinary course of those activities information of the kind contained in the statement or of the form which the information so contained is derived;
>
> (c) that throughout the material part of that period the computer was operating properly or, if not, that any respect in which it was not operating properly or was out of operation during that part of that period was not such as to affect the production of the document or the accuracy of its contents; and;
>
> (d) that the information contained in the statement reproduces or is derived from information supplied to the computer in the ordinary course of those activities.
>
> (3) Where over a period the function of storing or processing information for the purposes of any activities regularly carried on over that period as in subsection (2)(a) was regularly performed by computers, mentioned whether:
>
> (a) by a combination of computers operating, over that period; or
>
> (b) by different computers operating in succession over that period; or
>
> (c) by different combinations of computers operating in succession over that period; or
>
> (d) in any other manner involving the successive operation over that period in whatever order, of one or more computers and one or more combinations of computers,

---

[32] Most of the criticisms made in following paragraphs concerning the Northern Ireland legislation were also made by the Law Commission of the equivalent English legislation in paras 3.61 to 3.68 of Consultation Paper No 117, entitled *The Hearsay Rule in Civil Proceedings* November 1990. A further critique of the equivalent English legislation making all the points made by the Law Commission in an accessible format can be found in *The Computer in Court* by Alistair Kelman and Richard Sizer (Gower 1982) ISBN: 0566034190 which was based upon a British Computer Society Report to the Home Office on computer evidence written by the two authors.

all the computers used for that purpose during that period shall be treated for the purposes of this Part as constituting a single computer, and references in this Part to a computer shall be construed accordingly.

(4) In any civil proceedings where it is desired to give a statement in evidence by virtue of this section, a certificate doing any of the following things, that is to say:

(a) identifying the document containing the statement and describing the manner in which it was produced;

(b) giving such particulars of any device involved in the production of that document as may be appropriate for the purpose of showing that the document was produced by a computer;

(c) dealing with any of the matters to which the conditions mentioned in subsection (2) relate,

and purporting to be signed by a person occupying a responsible position in relation to the operation of the relevant device or the management of the relevant activities (whichever is appropriate) shall be evidence of any matter stated in the certificate; and for the purposes of this subsection it shall be sufficient for a matter to be stated to the best of the knowledge and belief of the person stating it.

(5) Notwithstanding subsection (4) in any civil proceedings the court may for special cause require oral evidence to be given of any matter of which evidence could ordinarily be given by means of a certificate under that subsection.

(6) For the purposes of this Part:

(a) information shall be taken to be supplied to a computer if it is supplied thereto in any appropriate form and whether it is so supplied directly or (with or without human intervention) by means of any appropriate equipment;

(b) where, in the course of activities carried on by any person, information is supplied with a view to it being stored or processed for the purposes of those activities by a computer operated otherwise than in the course of those activities, that information, if duly supplied to that computer, shall be taken to be supplied to it in the course of those activities;

(c) a document shall be taken to have been produced by a computer whether it was produced by it directly or (with or without human intervention) by means of any appropriate equipment.

(7) Subject to subsection (3), in this Part "computer" means any device for storing and processing information, and any reference to information being derived from other information is a reference to its being derived therefrom by calculation, comparison or any other process."

6.17

The computer evidence provisions of the Civil Evidence Act (N.I.) 1971 were drafted in an age of punched cards and paper tape. Computers then always worked using batch processing, taking in a hopper full of cards, processing the data and outputting the results. They were very simple machines which were little more than sophisticated adding machines. This fact is reflected in the legislation which talks of information being supplied "to" the computer and does not consider the situation where evidence is supplied "by" a computer from sources known to itself alone.

6.18   The unsuitability of the Civil Evidence Act (N.I.) 1971 to contemporary computers suggests two major problems for the development of electronic commerce in Northern Ireland. First, since *Myers*[33] means that Parliament alone can create new exceptions to the hearsay rule and any evidence statute must be restrictively construed, then the status of derived evidence which is made up of real evidence (*e.g.* information supplied by the computer from sources known to itself alone) and admissible hearsay evidence (*e.g.* key entries made by operators) remains questionable. A sales account record may, for example, contain a running total on the amount allegedly due from a customer for goods and services supplied. The goods may have been ordered by telephone and keyed in by operators (admissible hearsay). The services may have been downloads of software from a restricted area of the vendor's site (computer generated records produced under program control — a type of real evidence). A strict construction of the Civil Evidence Act (N.I.) 1971 would suggest that the invoice total, derived from mixing the admissible hearsay with the real evidence, would be inadmissible evidence as being a novel form of derived hearsay evidence. The Northern Irish courts would have to refuse to follow the majority decision in Myers for the evidence to be admitted. This would be following the approach taken in Scotland. Yet there is some indication that such a route might not find favour in Northern Ireland: In 1990 the Law Reform Advisory Committee for Northern Ireland rejected the approach implemented in the Civil Evidence (Scotland) Act 1988 on the grounds that (a) it was a breach of the basic principle that a party is entitled to insist on the production of the best reasonably available evidence against him and (b) it did not safeguard the right of a party to cross-examine the direct source of the hearsay evidence. In their opinion, the Scottish Act did not provide sufficient safeguards.[34]

6.19   This conveniently brings us to the second serious problem in the Civil Evidence Act (N.I.) 1971; the requirement that for computer evidence to be admissible there has to be a certificate showing "that the computer was operating properly". With a relatively simple machine like a calculator it is possible for a person to look at the input data and the output data and say, on a knowledgeable basis, that so far as he/she could see the calculator was working properly. But with a modern personal computer, multitasking through its operations, connected into networks and linked to the Internet, it is impossible for a person to say, in a trustworthy sense, that the computer was operating properly. The statement required by the legislation is clearly meant to be a means by which defective evidence could be filtered out of court proceedings.[35] Even Lord

---

[33] *Myers* [1965] A.C. 1001.
[34] Law Reform Advisory Committee for Northern Ireland, *Discussion Paper No. 1: Hearsay Evidence in Civil Proceedings* (1990), at paras 5.39–5.41.
[35] See also *R. v. Minors, R. v. Harper* 2 All E.R. 208. In *Harper*, the appellant had been convicted of handling stolen goods in the form of a London Transport travel pass. Details of the pass were recorded on a computer operated by London Transport and a printout was supplied to the court. The printout was produced by a revenue protection official who had no knowledge of the manner in which the computer functioned and could not testify as to its reliability. The judge ruled that this evidence satisfied the requirements of Section 69 of the Police and Criminal Evidence Act 1984 (PACE) on admissibility of computer evidence. The Court of Appeal disagreed, holding that the witness was not suitably qualified to testify to matters coming within the ambit of Section 69. See *also R. v. Shepherd* [1993] 1 All E.R. 225, where Lord Griffith stated that no authority existed for the proposition that where a computer was merely used to perform functions of calculation, no question of hearsay was involved and the requirements of Sections 68 and 69 of PACE did not apply. The application of Section 69, it was held, extended to all cases where the admissibility of computer-generated evidence was at issue, not merely cases when the evidence was hearsay in nature.

Pearce's dissenting analysis in *Myers*[36] required the deponent to put forward someone would could "speak with knowledge to the method and system of record-keeping".[37] With modern computers their operation and "truthfulness" has to be taken on trust by the great mass of business users.

Undoubtedly, as a matter of urgency, Northern Ireland needs to have a new civil evidence statute. But it is to be hoped that the rush to simplify the admissibility of all computer evidence does not lead to the omission of important procedural safeguards to keep unreliable computer evidence out of the courtroom.[38]

THE RELIABILITY OF COMPUTER EVIDENCE

Computers would be useless if they were not able to record information with a fair degree of reliability. But determining the reliability of a piece of computer evidence is no easy task. The adversarial system of litigation causes problems because it will always be in the interests of one side to suggest that unreliable evidence is reliable and vice versa. Without independent inquisitorial resources to determine reliability the court has a task which it rarely addresses.

6.20

As a starting point the court follows a common law presumption:

> "In the absence of evidence to the contrary, the courts will presume that mechanical instruments were in order at the material time."[39]

Computers have tended to be considered in many cases as little more than a type of filing cabinet. In *R. v. Blackburn*[40] the Court of Criminal Appeal made it clear that they would be extremely reluctant to accept a document produced on a word processor as computer evidence rather than as a written statement from a human author. This would appear to limit the sources of error to be addressed in determining weight solely to inaccurate keying by the human author and would refutably assume the fact that the data had not been corrupted or damaged while being stored on the computer through action by the computer or third parties.[41]

This assumption needs to be looked as in detail and it is necessary to consider the physical record or artefact which is placed before a court. Documentary evidence in the courtroom consists of printouts which may look like pages from a loose leaf file found in manual systems. But the document may never have existed as a single document, being passed intact from hand to hand. Instead, it may be created "on-the-fly" from an

6.21

---

[36] *Myers* [1965] A.C. 1001.
[37] *Myers* [1965] A.C. 1001 at page 1044.
[38] For a discussion on how Codes of Practice will help, see *Principles of Good Practice — The BSI and DISC Codes* and *The Reliability of Computer Evidence* later in this chapter.
[39] *Phipson on Evidence* (14th Edition 1990), para. 23–14, approved by the Divisional Court in *Castle v. Cross* [1984] 1 W.L.R. 1372, 1377B, *per* Stephen Brown L.J.
[40] *R. v. Blackburn, The Times,* December 1, 1992.
[41] But note: The modern practice of allowing a personal computer to insert the creation date in a document while also permitting it to update the same automatically every time the document is opened by a computer can lead to wrongly dated printouts of correspondence bundles in civil litigation.

enquiry being made of a database. An error on the part of the computer in conducting the search of the database needed to create the document is unlikely to produce any evidence on the face of the document to indicate that an error has taken place.

It is useful to open this discussion by considering patients records in medical practices since the problems these produce (reliability, discovery, data protection etc) are a more acute form of the problems that are encountered with customer records in electronic commerce.

In *R. v. Sinha*[42] the defendant, a doctor, was convicted of perverting the course of justice. A patient had consulted him, complaining of palpitations and the defendant had prescribed a course of beta blockers without ascertaining from her medical records that she was an asthmatic. The following day, the patient took one of the beta blockers and later died as a result of an acute asthma attack. The coroner requested that the senior partner at the defendant's practice supplied him with the patient's records. The senior partner could not find the written records, so he sent the computerised version. A later analysis of this computerised version found traces of earlier versions of the patient's records which had been deleted. This led to enquiries and finally the defendant admitted that on three occasions, following the patient's death, he had altered her computerised therapy records which had previously contained four separate references to her asthmatic condition. It was accepted at the trial that it is dangerous to prescribe beta blockers to asthmatics. He was sentenced to six months imprisonment.

6.22   Consider this facts of this case in the context of a civil action for medical negligence. The estate of the dead patient brings an action against the medical practice for causing the death of the patient. In the course of the action it would seek discovery of documents which would include the medical records of the practice. Under normal legal discovery practice this would be a printout from the computer system. Such a printout would not have shown the alterations made by the doctor after the death of the patient. Only if the patient's lawyers had promptly insisted on discovery of an "image copy" of the medical practice's computer system and thereafter employed an independent computer expert to review the material would the activities of the errant doctor come to light. Yet to insist upon electronic discovery of documents would be likely to require a special appointment before a Master to argue the relevance of the material with considerable risks of costs being awarded to the other side and any delays in obtaining the order in any event resulting in the loss of all traces of the alterations.[43]

But the supply of an "image copy" of the database in discovery is unlikely to occur in civil litigation unless the decision in *Derby & Co. Ltd v. Weldon*[44] were reviewed by the

---

[42] *R. v. Sinha* [1995] Crim. L.R. 68.

[43] For a variant on how this situation could occur in practice, where journal records stored on a computer could corroborate witness statements or prove them to be false see the fictional tale "Sam's story" in Chapter 1 where Sam is required to go through the automatic journal entries and compare these with draft witness statements. Users of programs such a Microsoft Outlook may find that, unknown to them, Microsoft Outlook keeps a running journal of work being created or edited on every workstation; recording when documents were produced and when they were modified, when telephone calls were made etc. Coupled with the caching facilities built into modern Web browsers a great deal of corroborating evidence is capable of being found on ordinary business workstations in the course of a forensic examination. There is a good case for requiring this material to be discoverable in all civil litigation as a matter of course, particularly since it can be analysed electronically without creating mountains of paper.

[44] *Derby & Co. Ltd v. Weldon* [1991] 2 All E.R. 901.

court and distinguished. In that case, the defendants applied for discovery of a computerised database held by the plaintiff which contained details of transactions which were the subject of the litigation. Vinelott J. held that a computer database which forms part of the business records of a company is, in so far as it contains information capable of being retrieved and converted into readable form, a "document" for the purposes of making discovery. However the court ruled that party seeking discovery is not entitled to unrestricted access to the database and the court will only permit discovery in the light of expert evidence as to the extent to which the relevant information was available on line or from back up systems. The court allowed the defendants to access the database subject to agreement or expert evidence as to what information was or could be made available, to what extent inspect was necessary and whether the provision of print-outs would be sufficient.[45]

Computers used for storing patient records have tended to be small closed networks **6.23** of standard personal computers running customised software. With the common law assumption that mechanical devices tend to work properly, it is not considered likely that these standard computers used for record taking and the production of prescriptions are not working properly. But the question of weight will turn upon whether the computer records have been altered and whether those alterations could have been made without trace.

In a civil action based on the facts of the *Sinha*[46] case the defendant medical practice would have a strong motive to tamper with the evidence prior to discovery. To re-edit a patient's records and remove all traces of the original on the computer system would be relatively easy to do using standard utility software.

But the task of altering records gets a lot harder once the small computer network is part of a large wide area network on which duplicate copies of the data are recorded. The errant doctor has to alter not only the local copy of the record but also the copies which are held and replicated throughout the network. He has to be able to cover his tracks by altering the time and date stamps of his alterations through editing all the log files in a coherent fashion. This many not in fact be possible.

Forensic Computing

Beyond the above introduction a detailed determination of the reliability of computer **6.24** evidence is outside of the scope of this book. The topic is now being properly addressed in the new science of forensic computing.[47] This complicated discipline starts by considering reliability as a combination of two elements:

---

[45] See also T–11/95 *B.P. Chemicals v. Commission* CFI 2CH September 15, 1998, where in a complaint concerning an Italian state capital injection to EniChem the Court ordered the Commission to produce the original calculation it had made to support the decision that the cashflow from the investment would have been satisfactory to a private investor over a ten year period. The Commission produced a table but after the hearing it informed the Court that it was not from its file but was reconstructed. The Commission submitted a second table and at a second hearing asked the Court to disregard the first. In the course of the judgment the Court noted several inconsistencies between the Commission's tables and explanations given to the Court. The Court could not ascertain what calculations had been made at the time and was not in a position to decide that no state aid was involved at the initial stage.

[46] *R. v. Sinha* [1995] Crim. L.R. 68

[47] For an introduction to the topic of Forensic Computing, see *Downloads, Logs and Captures: Evidence from Cyberspace* by Peter Sommer, Computer Security Research Centre, London School of Economics & Political Science in The Journal of Financial Crime [1997] 5 J.F.C.2 pp. 138–151.

(1) the trustworthiness of the *content* of a piece of computer-derived evidence (*content* is what you see with your eyes);

(2) the trustworthiness of the *process* by which it was produced (*process* is what produced it).

6.25   Together the trustworthiness of content and process form the actual reliability of the evidence. Factors which have to be taken into account in determining this trustworthiness can include the quality of the original source, the quality of the internal computer manipulations, the strength of any control or audit mechanism which might reduce error or provide corroboration, the integrity of the way in which an exhibit — what the court actually considers — has been derived, and integrity of the way in which the exhibit has been handled by or brought into being by investigators. All of these factors will interact with each other. For example, a classic fraud scenario involves a dishonest internal auditor discovering a small fraud by a member of staff involving the putting through of unauthorised transactions for cash and posting the unbalanced transactions to a suspense account which is not monitored on a regular basis. The dishonest auditor adopts this fraud and posts a series of additional transactions for his own benefit, withdrawing the money and creating a false trail to the staff member. He then reports the staff member for prosecution. The staff member's denials regarding the scale of his fraud are rarely believed and the dishonest auditor has an illegal profit which is not subject to further investigation. One role of a forensic computing expert in this situation is to analyse the environment in which the transactions have been created and stop the court or jury from jumping to conclusions by highlighting the fact that the evidence does not reliably point to the staff member as the author of all the unauthorised transactions.

How long must records be kept and what records need to be kept?

6.26   It is well known that under the Companies Act 1985 accounting records have to be kept for six years by a public company and three years by a private company.[48] Other statutes and business risks also raise important questions regarding what falls within the scope of the accounting records in electronic commerce transactions and whether there are any "long tail" situations which suggest that it would be prudent for companies to keep their business records for longer than the statutory minimum period.

The underlying business model and its controls

Historically, accounting records have been considered to be the books of account of the business. In early times these books of account were kept in bound ledgers and clerks would make entries in ink in the bound ledgers whenever transactions took place. This primitive method of record keeping had certain hidden controls:

(1) it was possible to identify which clerk wrote a record through his handwriting characteristics;

(2) the accounting entry in a bound ledger in ink meant that any alterations left a visible trace;

---

[48] Section 222, Companies Act 1985.

(3) the inclusion of the record within a bound book meant that it was not possible to substitute entries;

(4) a practice developed whereby a clerk who made an alteration to a record initialled it to signify that the change was authentic.

As technology permitted new ways of keeping business records other than bound books, legislation was brought in to make this possible. But the hidden controls were not forgotten and modern company law contains important restrictions regarding the keeping of accounting records in Section 722(2) of the Companies Act 1985.   **6.27**

Companies Act 1985 — Form of Company Registers etc.

722(1) Any register, index, minute book or accounting records required by the Companies Act to be kept by a company may be kept either by making entries in bound books or by recording the matters in question in any other manner.

722(2) Where any such register, index, minute book or accounting records is not kept by making entries in a bound book, but by some other means, adequate precautions shall be taken for guarding against fabrication and facilitating its discovery.

722(3) If default is made in complying with subsection (2), the company and every officer of it who is in default is liable to a fine and, for continued contravention, a daily default fine.

With electronic commerce it is necessary to find analogues for the traditional controls but these are not easy to implement or particularly obvious. If an accounting record has been digitally signed (as opposed to being physically signed or initialled) the provisions of Section 722(2) appear to indicate that the company needs to be able to associate the digital signature with a particular person. Merely having a smart card and a PIN is unlikely to be sufficient since the signing will have been done by the artefact rather than by a characteristic human hand and that artefact is capable of making unauthorised accounting records when in the wrong hands.   **6.28**

In 2004 Company X sends an e-mail message to Company Y saying "Your shipment is ready for collection". "What shipment?" replies Y to discover that Company X says that it received, in 2001, an official electronic commerce order for 3 Million gallons of Frozen Orange Juice for delivery in 2004 allegedly digitally signed by "Company Y". Company Y has no knowledge of any such order and has destroyed and replaced the signing key it was using 2001. Company Y finds that its C.A. does not have a record of Company X's signing key for the year 2001. It does not know and cannot demonstrate that the order was not a genuine irrevocable order for which it is now liable.

It is quite likely that a company will have to revoke and replace its signing keys and encryption keys several times a year because they have been compromised, staff have left or there have been management changes. To enable the historic accounting records to be verified as genuine a separate archival record will have to be maintained which is able to show which particular cryptographic and signing keys were current at particular times. Companies will turn to their Certification Authority[49] for this information and, if the C.A. is unable to supply the information, serious consequences will follow.

It is also true that legal disputes involving documentary evidence can arise long after the original events. In *Brian S. Grave v. Leslie & Godwin Financial Services Limited*[50] an insurance broker was held to have been in breach of contract and negligent in not retaining documents that would have identified the reinsurers of the plaintiff's risk. The only document that had been given to the plaintiff was a cover note which did not identify the reinsurers. In that case the reinsurances had been effected nearly thirty years before the plaintiff wished to make a claim under them. The slips could not be found. The court held that there was a duty to take reasonable care of any documents owned by the insured and not to destroy them without first obtaining instructions as to whether to do so or not. The court further held that in the particular circumstances there was a duty not to destroy a slip without the consent of the insured, even if the slip was not the property of the insured.

Modern archival storage

6.29   With improvements in digital storage media it is now possible to keep archival business records in a reproducible form in very little space and at relatively low cost. It would therefore be sensible for a record retention policy to be applied throughout a business as part of the company's risk management strategy. Archival copies of old business records held offsite on inexpensive WORM[51] media for use in limited circumstances would appear to be an appropriate and cost effective means by which a company could continue have evidence to defend itself when faced with "long tail" claims and liabilities. Such a record management policy needs to be considered in the light of the provisions of the Data Protection Act 1984 and the Data Protection Act 1998 which require a business to consider the length of time it holds personal records as well as the amount of personal data it holds on data users. It can also be argued that the Subject Access Provisions of Data Protection legislation applies to this archival information.[52]

PRINCIPLES OF GOOD PRACTICE — THE BSI AND DISC CODES

6.30   In 1993, two academics, Mayon-White and Dyer, published a ground breaking set of principles on good practice for the operation of systems making use of "imaging" technology.[53] They established the Legal Images Initiative (LII) as a consortium of mainstream business organisations which sought to achieve a position where an imaged

---

[49] For discussion on Certification Authorities and their regulation, see *Trusted Third Parties, Certification Authorities and Key Recovery Agents* in Chapter 5 herein.
[50] Queens Bench Division — reported in *The Times*, May 16, 1995.
[51] 'Write Once Read Many', being storage media such as CD–ROMs, which used to be referred to as Optical Disks. CD–ROM writers are now relatively inexpensive products which can work on standard personal computers.
[52] For a fuller discussion on this topic see Chapter 7 on Data Protection.
[53] Mayon-White W.M. and Dyer B. *The Legal Images Initiative: Towards a Voluntary Code of Practice*, 1993 (available from the Image and Document Management Association c/o the Department of Information Systems. The London School of Economics, Houghton Street, London WC2A 2AE).

document would be treated in law as equivalent to the typed, printed or hand-written document. In their report they said that "The primary objective of the LII is to create a framework which, if followed by users of electronic document management systems, will give them confidence in the security of the storage and retrieval processes and in the acceptability of such records in any court of law, should a dispute arise in which the documents stored in this way may be required as evidence."

Mayon-White and Dyer's work became the basis of a British Standard Code of Practice, now published by the British Standards Institute (DISC PD0008). This takes as its starting point their 'Five Principles of Good Practice':

1. Recognise all types of information;
2. Understand the legal issues and execute "duty of care" responsibilities;
3. Identify and specify business processes and procedures;
4. Identify enabling technologies to support business processes and procedures;
5. Monitor and audit procedures.

Each of these principles has been expanded upon. Thus the first process, recognition of information, is subdivided into classification, storage and evaluation. Classification draws upon the skills of both the librarian or information scientist and those of diligent office administrators. Storage considered the life cycle of the information following its receipt. Evaluation requires the organisation to take appropriate steps to protect its information resource. **6.31**

This expanding process continues throughout the principles. In relation to the legal issues the code requires the organisation to establish a chain of responsibility and consequently of accountability in relation to information handling within the organisation.

The current position is that there are now two British standards publications[54] and one general publication[55] which can provide courts and lawyers with guidance regarding the management of computer evidence and hence the reliability of such evidence.[56]

The significance of BS7799

But before considering the weight to be attached to evidence it is necessary to consider what weight to attach to BS7799 — The Code of Practice for Information Security Management. The early work, which led to BS7799, came from the Commercial Computer Security Centre of the U.K. Department of Trade and Industry (CCSC). In the late 1980s the CCSC and the DTI, inspired by work done by the U.S. Department of Defence in producing their "Orange Book" classification of computer security, published **6.32**

---

[54] BS 7768 : 1994 *Management of Optical Disk (WORM) System for the Recording of Documents that may be Required as Evidence* and BS7799 : 1995 *Code of Practice for Information Security Management.*
[55] Image and Document Management Association (IDMA) *Principles of Good Practice for Information Management*, London 1995 (available from IDMA, c/o the Department of Information Systems, The London School of Economics, Houghton Street, London WC2A 2AE).
[56] These documents are likely to be merged into a "Best Practice" document — see later in this section.

three worthy documents on computer security.[57] These were developed within Europe[58] but, although great efforts were made to harmonise the security classification criteria, the work remained mainly of academic interest partly because the developers were starting from a military rather than a business point of view. Nevertheless, the business need for a consensual approach to computer security led a number of major commercial users[59] to look at the work and set about turning the European work into a code which was both meaningful and practical from a user's point of view.[60] Public consultation on these revisions led to the British Standards Institute publishing the code as a guidance document[61] and, following a further period of public consultation, this code was recast as British Standard BS7799:1995.

6.33   BS7799 was submitted for acceptance into the International Standards Organisation (ISO) "Fast Track" procedure in order to become an International Standard, in 1996. ISO were unable to agree on it proceeding by this route and it is still not an International Standard. There are concerns that BS7799 is seriously flawed in its mandatory approach to particular issues which might be better cast as recommendations rather than formal requirements.

However the broad thrust of BS7799 has been generally accepted. Australia and New Zealand accepted it, changed the U.K. legislative references to corresponding Australian and New Zealand references and re-published it as AS/NZS 4444. The Netherlands fully accepted the approach and went considerably further by establishing a certification scheme in early 1997. This is considered by many within the BSI process[62] to be too radical a step given the developing nature of the work and the likelihood of an elementary low cost certificate giving a false impression of security.

One key weakness within BS7799 is the fact that it is very much a document which focuses on information technology quite narrowly. While it contained a great deal of information on technologies such as passwords and access control it is nearly silent on

---

[57] U.K. Systems Security Confidence Levels, CESG Memorandum No. 3, Communications-Electronics Security Group, United Kingdom, January 1989 and DTI Commercial Computer Security Centre Evaluation Levels Manual, V22, February 1989; DTIFN DTI Commercial Computer Security Centre Security Functionality Manual, V21, February 1989.

[58] The naming of these reports became rather farcical. After the U.S. Orange Book the American authorities published a revised report on networked systems called "the Brown Book". The U.K. authorities published their Green Book (see above). The French authorities published their "Blue-White-Red Book" (Catalogue de Critres Destins valuer le Degrde Confiance des Systmes d'Information, 692/SGDN/DISSI/SCSSI Service Central de la Security des Systmes d'Information, Juillet 1989). Only the Germans failed to colour their reports with the ZSIEC Criteria for the Evaluation of Trustworthiness of Information Technology (I.T.) Systems, ISBN 3–88784-200-6 German Information Security Agency (Bundesamt fr Sicherheit in der Informationstechnik), Federal Republic of Germany, January 1989.

[59] i.e. BOC, British Telecom, Marks & Spencer, Midland Bank, Nationwide Building Society, Prudential Assurance Corporation, SEMA, Shell and Unilever.

[60] One of the problems faced by the commercial users arose from the original military model of computer security which was hierarchical and did not match the horizontal or departmental team working approach of modern business which, in the mid 1990s, was being driven by groupware technologies such as Lotus Notes. In a parallel development in a European Union funded project French military security consultants initially specified a security model for a university library system where the students were only allowed to read books on a "need to know" basis. It took a long time for the Project Reviewer to convince the military that students at university should not have to study in such a restricted manner.

[61] PD 0003, A Code of Practice for Information Security Management.

[62] Private communication from members of the "Best Practice Project" team in IDMA.

topics such as the Internet. Generally, BS7799 appears to have been oversold by the understandable desire of business to be able to measure their security compliance against independent objective criteria — the standard is not yet a mature product.

A broader treatment of information security is necessary in the form of a revised code which looks strategically at all aspects of information security in a central document with detailed guidance by reference to other documents, thereby ensuring that the code is capable of handling technological developments without constant revision. Work is currently underway in the production of such a revised code of practice. It is thought, by some,[63] that PD0008 rather than BS7799 could be the foundation of this revised approach and new discussion documents will be appearing during 1999.[64]

The significance of the Codes of Practice — an Analogy

So far as lawyers are concerned the existence of BS7799 "A Code of Practice for Information Security Management", along with DISC PC 0008 "A Code of Practice for Legal Admissibility of Information Stored on Electronic Document Management Systems" presents lawyers with essential material to cross-examine corporate executives who wish to place computer-generated evidence before the court. The long term legal consequences of codes of practice in information security are interesting if an analogy is drawn.

6.34

In September 1983 the Accounting Standards Committee the Institute of Chartered Accountants of England and Wales commissioned Mr Leonard Hoffman Q.C. and Mary Arden to supply them with a joint opinion of the meaning of 'true and fair' with particular reference to the role of Accounting Standards. Leonard Hoffman, who has since become a Law Lord. Mary Arden is now a Chancery High Court Judge and Head of the Law Commission. In their 1983 Opinion the two barristers stated that:

(1) The application of the 'true and fair view' involves judgment in questions of degree. There may sometimes be room for differences of opinion over the method to adopt to give a true and fair view. Because questions of degree are involved when a company is deciding on how much information is sufficient to make its financial statements true and fair, it may take account of cost effectiveness amongst other factors.

(2) It is for the court to decide whether financial statements give a true and fair view in compliance with the Act. But the courts will look for guidance to the ordinary practice of accountants. This is principally because the financial statements will not be true and fair unless the quality and quantity of the information they contain is sufficient to satisfy their readers' reasonable expectations. Those expectations will have been moulded by accountants' practices.

(3) Statements of Standard Accounting Practice have a two-fold value to the court. First, they constitute an important statement of professional opinion. Second, because accountants are professionally obliged to comply with SSAPs, the readers

---

[63] Certain corporate members of IDMA as well as Alistair Kelman.
[64] One of the authors, Alistair Kelman, has been commissioned by IDMA to produce the discussion document in 1999 on *Legal Awareness* as part of the revised Code of Practice termed "The Best Practice Project" which aims to merge all the codes together.

of financial statements expect those statements to conform with the prescribed standards. Departure from a SSAP without adequate explanation may therefore result in the financial statements not showing a true and fair view.

6.35   (4) Consequently, the courts will treat compliance with accepted accounting principles as prima facie evidence that the financial statements are true and fair, and deviations from accepted principles will be prima facie evidence that they are not true and fair. These presumptions will either be strengthened or weakened by the extent to which the SSAP is accepted and applied in practice. A SSAP has no direct legal effect, but it will have an indirect effect on the content the courts give to the 'true and fair' concept.

   (5) The fact that Accounting Standards can change over time does not alter the effect they have on the true and fair view. The concept of true and fair is dynamic; its content changes but its meaning remains the same.

In our view it is a short step from the existence of a code of practice to the establishment of a rule of law that information which is handled in accordance with the code of practice should *prima facie* be considered as evidence in legal proceedings and conversely that information which was not handled in accordance with the code of practice should *prima facie* not be considered as evidence in legal proceedings. This would mirror the approach the courts take regarding the meaning of "true and fair" in the keeping of business records and the consequences of failing to comply with a Statement of Standard Accounting Practice.

CONCLUSIONS

6.36   In consequence, a good tactic in electronic commerce litigation would be to ask the opponent to specify with full particularity how each and every piece of computer evidence has been handled to be in accordance with BS7799 and DISC PD0008 (or their successor documents). Failure to respond could reasonably lead to a request to have all the evidence excluded.

But such a draconian request should not be complied with by a court unless and until there is near universal acceptance of the codes of practice throughout the business community. The current limitations of BS7799 suggest that it, and PD0008, needs to evolve before such a position is arrived at.

There is a well known saying in the software industry: "Never buy a commercial software package until it has reached Version 3.0". The rush to release the first version and the pressure of bug fixing on the second version conspire to create a situation where programmers may only start getting things right in the third release of the software. A similar conservative approach to reliance on codes of practice on information security and legal reliability in the courtroom would appear to be warranted.

— • 7 • —

DATA PROTECTION

Businesses are increasingly using the Internet as another medium through which to attract customers. In some cases they trade directly from their websites, although in other cases detailed business transactions are conducted by e-mail, post or telephone. The Data Protection Act applies to personal data obtained and processed over the Internet as it does to information obtained by more conventional sources for automatic processing.[1]

The fast growth of electronic commerce gives rise to many privacy issues. In every electronic commerce transaction a user is forced to trust the security of the world wide web. Personal data, such as on individual's name, address and credit card number, may be routed wide via countries with little or no data protection legislation. There is no single authority which controls the web and every message sent can be intercepted at any site it passes and then traced, forged, suppressed or delayed. Every electronic mail message contains a header with information about the sender and the recipient (for example name and I.P.-address, host name and time of the mailing) and the routing and subject of the message. Increasingly, electronic commerce businesses are moving towards tailoring their offering to an individual's preferences raising even more privacy and data protection issues.

Virtually every electronic commerce transaction will involve the transfer of personal data and will be regulated in Europe by data protection laws. This chapter examines the law on data protection.

The Data Protection 1998 (DPA) was enacted in July 1998 and implements the E.U. Data Protection Directive.[2] The Government has announced that it will come into force late, probably, in phases during 1999. For the purposes of the Chapter it is assumed that the DPA is fully in force.

7.01

BACKGROUND AND FRAMEWORK

Fear about the information gathering ability of computers and the power which they could have over citizens has been fully appreciated by commentators since the 1960s.

7.02

---

[1] The 14th Annual Report of the Data Protection Registrar published on July 14, 1998.
[2] European Directive 95/46 E.C.

Prior to our present legislation there were a series of Parliamentary Bills, Reports and White Papers from 1961 onwards. In the late 1970s the United States, Sweden and West Germany introduced data protection legislation. The Council of the Organisation for Economic Co-operation and Development (OECD) adopted on September 23, 1980 Recommendation with Guidelines on the protection of privacy and transborder flows of personal data (The OECD Guidelines).

The Council of Europe produced its Convention on Data Protection which the U.K. signed up to in 1981. This indicated support for the principles but did not commit the U.K. to bringing in any legislation. That came about once a critical number of countries had also signed up to the legislation. By 1983 major British businesses were asking the Government to bring in data protection legislation. It is unusual for businesses to ask a Government to bring in new legislation to regulate them. But industry perceived that the lack of data protection legislation in the U.K. was hindering economic activity.

A good example of what was happening arose when a multinational oil company in the early 1980s wanted to centralise its data processing operation for petrol distribution in England. Some of its customers were in Sweden. Most of them were limited companies. But a couple were sole traders — people trading in their own name. The Swedish Authorities indicated that they would not permit the multinational oil company to export the personal data concerning these two sole traders because the U.K. did not have any data protection legislation.

7.03   Business lobbied Parliament to introduce data protection legislation so that it could fully ratify the Council of Europe Convention. As a consequence the Data Protection Act 1984 was introduced and came into force on October 1, 1985. It was the first piece of legislation in the U.K. to address the use of computers. But, being business driven, the approach to data protection in the U.K. was to do the very bare minimum to comply with the Convention. This situation needs to be contrasted with other states such as Germany who have developed the concept of data protection to a much greater extent, seeking to elevate the interests and wishes of the individual above those of data users.

The discrepancies between national data protection statutes were identified by the European Commission as constituting an impediment to the attainment of the Single Market. In 1990 the Commission submitted a package of proposals to the Council aimed at promoting the free movement of data within the Community. Included in this was a proposal for a Directive on the topic of data protection.

In addition to the importance of data flows for the attainment of the Single Market, the proposal was also founded in the Treaty of Rome's provisions relating to consumer protection and the promotion of fundamental human rights. In these fields, the Treaty obliges the Community to ensure that harmonisation of national laws occurs at a 'high level'.

7.04   But there were problems. During the course of its five year passage through the European legislative processes, the Directive was criticised, both by countries such as the U.K. which considered that its requirements marked too great an advance over current data protection statutes, and by those such as Germany which were concerned that European legislation might lead to a diminution in the level of protection provided under existing national regimes. A further factor complicating E.U. action is that its legislative competence generally does not extend to matters coming within the fields of criminal law and national security — owing to the concept of subsidiarity.

Additionally, while the Directive was making its slow way through the European legislative process, the Internet appeared. At the start of the process there was no World Wide Web — but by the time the "Framework Directive" was adopted by the European Union on October 24, 1995 the whole computer and data processing industry had been revolutionised by browser technology and hotlinking. Some lawyers have said that the legislation was unworkable and out of date before it became part of U.K. law.[3]

It is not however sensible to look at the U.K. or Europe in isolation. Before we go forward to look at the current British legislation and then to the future of Data Protection we need to return to look again at the history. As technology has developed over the past thirty years, the legal imperatives have changed with them

THE FOUR AGES OF DATA PROTECTION[4]

The legislative perception of data protection and the nature of the legislation has changed over the past forty years and it is possible to roughly divide the legislation into four ages.

7.05

The First Age of Data Protection viewed computers as part of a dismal world where all personal data files were centralised in gigantic national databanks. In the 1960s the Western world had recovered from the Second World War and was bringing in massive social reforms and extensive social welfare legislation. Europe was rapidly creating 'cradle to the grave' social security systems which required a sophisticated system of government planning. Government bureaucracies had to constantly collect increasing amounts of information from citizens to fulfil its tasks and to plan for the future. By the late 1960s in Sweden, census and registration records had already been merged, and tax data was stored in centralised tax data banks. Sweden's legislature proposed to merge all these information sources into one national information bank.

The legislation during this First Age concentrated not on the direct protection of individual privacy but on the function of data processing in society. The use of computers itself endangered humane information processing. Data protection was seen as a tool to specifically counter these dangers. Citizens were not given rights to ensure compliance — instead special institutions were set up to supervise adherence to data protection norms. Citizens could not decide on whether data concerning them was processed — at best they could merely rectify misleading or inaccurate information about themselves.

---

[3] Readers should also be aware of the European Union Telecoms Data Directive (97/6/EC) which came into force at the same time as the European Data Protection Directive. This is, in many ways, a version of the European Data Protection Directive which is specifically addressed at telecommunications companies. It deals with confidentiality of communications and requires Member States to prohibit listening, tapping, storage or other kinds of interception or surveillance of communications, by other users, without the consent of the users concerned, except when legally authorised. As we go to press the U.K. legislation to implement this directive has not been finalised. There are particular problems with the legislation since interception of e-mail is clearly within its scope and the directive, was designed for the monolithic European public telecommunications companies not for the deregulated United Kingdom where, according to construction of the Telecommunications Act 1984, everyone is actually operating under a government granted telecommunication licence every time they pick up the telephone or send an e-mail over the U.K. telecommunications network.
[4] This concept of the four ages of Data Protection was first outlined by Viktor Mayer-Schönberger of Vienna in his essay "Generational Development of Data Protection in Europe".

These early statutes avoided using well-known words like "privacy", "information", "protection of intimate affairs", and instead regulated "data banks" Complicated registration and licensing procedures were established. It was envisaged that only a few gigantic data banks would be established. Data security could be maintained by simple physical access controls. The legislation sometimes required a specific data protection official for each and every data bank.

7.06   However, the nightmare of a Big Brother world of huge centralised databases did not happen. Public concern about huge centralised databases worked against their creation. Also, the computer industry went down a different route with the creation of the minicomputer.[5] These allowed local departmental offices in government to have their own databases. Finally, the sharing of data between databases was found to be a difficult task. It was easy to corrupt accurate databases with bad data arising from incompatible data models or different data-collection procedures.

Later arrivals to the data protection debate (France, Austria, Norway) started to see things differently and produced Second Age legislation. These focused on the individual privacy rights of the citizen. Data protection was seen as the right of individuals to ward off society in personal matters. Their legislation became less linked to a particular stage of the technology. Existing individual rights were reinforced and linked to constitutional provisions. Instead of a licensing regime the legislation merely required registration of users of computers.

Two trends developed during the Second Age. As the number of computer systems increased, continental data protection commissioners not only investigated data protection offences and controlled enforcement but started to act like ombudsmen. Some data protection commissioners were turned into adjudicating bodies on how bureaucracy could legitimately interpret data protection laws.

7.07   But overall there was a growing awareness that citizens could not opt out of the databank society because government required a continuous flow of information from the individuals.

The Third Age of Data Protection developed from a realisation that data privacy decisions were rarely simple binary yes/no issues but required a degree of gradation. The individual should be able to determine how he/she would participate in society. This concept became known as informational self-determination.

The Fourth Age is where we are today. Some countries, forming the view that citizens needed to be protected against stupidly bargaining away their informational privacy rights, amended their laws to grant absolute protection and created no fault compensation for individuals.[6] But it was also appreciated that some personal data was normally considered more private than the rest and special protection was needed for this material and to protect against its misuse. Finally it was appreciated that codes of practice for various industry sectors could make data protection legislation relevant and

---

[5] Computers like the Digital Equipment PDP 8 and the PDP 11.
[6] *e.g.* recent amendments to German states' data protection laws (*e.g.* Section 20 of the Data Protection Act of the German state of Brandenburg and Section 7 (new) of the German Federal Data Protection Statute of 1990) introduced no-fault compensation for individual data protection claims thus expanding the Norwegian no-fault compensation model for data protection claims against credit reporting agencies (Section 40, Norwegian Data Protection Act).

lead to a better protection of citizen's rights. Thus, when the European Commission came to negotiate the creation of the European Data Protection Directive both sensitive personal data and codes of practice feature strongly in its provisions.

THE DATA PROTECTION ACT 1998

The DPA replaces the Data Protection Act 1984 in its entirety. It is bigger and more extensive than the 1984 Act it replaces. Whilst the DPA sets out the overall legal framework, much of the detail will be contained in secondary legislation. The DPA is divided into six parts and follows closely the structure of the Data Protection Act 1984. The terminology is changed to reflect the increased powers and status of the Data Protection Registrar under the new Act, who is now called the Data Protection Commissioner.

7.08

"Processing"

One major difference in the DPA when compared with the 1984 Act comes through the definition of "processing". This "processing" of information or data now means "obtaining, recording or holding the information or data or carrying out any operation or set of operations on the information or data, including:

7.09

    (a) organisation, adaptation or alteration of the information or data;
    (b) retrieval, consultation or use of the information or data;
    (c) disclosure of the information or data by transmission, dissemination or otherwise making available; or
    (d) alignment, combination, blocking, erasure or destruction of the information or data.

It is a very unusual use of the word "processing" but the significance is really that nothing falls outside of the scope of the DPA.

Manual Records

Manual files are now included within the scope of the legislation provided that they are part of what is termed a "structured filing system" so specific information relating to a particular individual is readily accessible. But the legislation only affects manual files after two transitional periods — the first period up until October 23, 2001 when all manual files are exempted from the provisions of the DPA and the second transitional period up until October 24, 2007 where only some of the data protection principles apply to manual files. Thereafter all the principles will apply.

7.10

Personal Data and the Data Controller

The DPA regulates the processing of information relating to living individuals. Section 1 of the DPA defines data as "information which:

7.11

    (a) is being processed by means of equipment operating automatically in response to instructions given for that purpose;

(b) is recorded with the intention that it should be processed by means of such equipment;

(c) is recorded as part of a relevant filing system or with the intention that it should form part of a relevant filing system; or

(d) does not fall within paragraph (a), (b) or (c) but forms part of an accessible record."

All information carried over the World Wide Web or as electronic mail will be data. As long as the data relates to an individual (including a foreign national or resident abroad) who can be identified from the data the DPA will apply. Accordingly, data about companies will not be caught. Personal data also includes data which relates to a living individual who can be identified from the data in conjunction with other information.

A data controller under the DPA is a person who alone or jointly determines the purposes for which personal data is processed. There can be more than one data controller.

Notification

7.12   The current system of registration is replaced with a similar system of notification.[7] This means that those persons falling within the DPA's ambit are required to notify the Commissioner of their "registerable particulars". The new system is intended to be a simplified less formalistic system and there are some exemptions from the requirement to notify.[8]

A data controller must notify the Commissioner of the registrable particulars and pay the prescribed fee. The registrable particulars are[9] basic items of information about the data controller such as name, address, description of data, purposes for which data is being processed, description of any recipient of the data and those countries outside the European Economic Area to which data may be transferred. In addition the data controller must give the Commissioner a general description of measures to be taken for the purpose of complying with the seventh data protection principle relating to security.[10]

It is an offence to process data without being included on the Commissioner's register.[11] In May 1996 U.S. Robotics (the U.K. based company now owned by 3Com) was fined £2,730 for not registering with the data protection registrar when holding customer information on its website.

It is certain that all U.K. based electronic commerce businesses will need to follow the notification procedure and multi-national businesses may need to comply with the notification requirements in several countries.

---

[7] Transitional Provisions mean that existing registrations under the 1984 Act continue to be valid until they expire.
[8] At the time of writing the details of the notification regulations, exemptions and fees are not yet available.
[9] Section 16(1) DPA 1998.
[10] Section 18(2)(6) DPA 1998.
[11] DPA, Section 21 1998.

EIGHT DATA PROTECTION PRINCIPLES

There are eight data protection principles with which a data controller must comply.   **7.13**
These are contained in Schedule 1 to the DPA. A breach of any of these principles can
lead to certain actions being taken by the Commissioner. The Commissioner can also
enforce the data protection principles against those who are exempt from registration.

Principle 1 — Data shall be processed fairly and lawfully

The first principle is of particular relevance to electronic commerce businesses. Personal   **7.14**
data shall not be processed unless one of the six conditions set out in Schedule 2 of the
DPA is met. The conditions most relevant to electronic commerce are:

(1) the data subject has given his/her consent to the processing;
(2) the processing is necessary for the performance or for entering into of a contract
     with the data subject.

The first principle also establishes the key principle that personal data shall be
processed fairly, regard being made to the method by which the data is obtained
including in particular whether any person is deceived or misled as to the purposes for
which the data is being processed. An electronic commerce business should give frank
and full information to the data subject of the use and purpose of any personal data
including any transfers or disclosures of the information unless it is obvious and also the
identity of the data controller. Additionally, a data subject should be provided with any
information which is necessary in the circumstances to enable the processing to be fair.
In the case of *Innovations (Mail Order) Ltd v. Data Protection Registrar* (September 1993),
the Data Protection Tribunal held that data subjects should be informed of any non-
obvious purpose for which the data were to be used before the personal data is used.
Where data is not obtained directly from the data subject the data controller must
ensure so far as practicable that the data subject is provided with the relevant
information.
In addition, Schedule 2 provides that processing may only be carried out where one of
the following conditions has been satisfied:

(1) the individual has given his consent to the processing;
(2) the processing is necessary for the performance of a contract with the individual;
(3) the processing is required under a legal obligation;
(4) the processing is necessary to protect the vital interests of the individual;
(5) the processing is necessary to carry out public functions;
(6) the processing is necessary in order to pursue the legitimate interests of the
     business (unless prejudicial to the interests of the individual).

Stricter conditions apply to the processing of sensitive data. This category includes
information relating to racial or ethnic origin, political opinions, religious or other
beliefs, trade union membership, health, sex life and criminal convictions. Where such
data is being processed not only must the controller meet the requirements of the
principles and Schedule 2, but processing is prohibited unless at least one of the
conditions in Schedule 3 can be satisfied.

Essentially the explicit consent of the individual will usually have to be obtained before sensitive data can be processed unless the data controller can show that the processing is necessary based on one of the criteria laid out in Schedule 3 of the Act.

Principle 2 — Data shall be obtained for specific and lawful purposes

7.15   This principle requires that all purposes for which a data controller holds data be specified in a notice either to the data subject or the Commissioner and that data is not used or processed in any manner incompatible with those purposes.

Principle 3 — Personal data shall be adequate relevant and not excessive

The third principle requires that personal data shall be adequate, relevant and not excessive in relation to the purpose for which the data is to be processed. Essentially this means that electronic commerce businesses should not obtain excessive and irrelevant data from customers and potential customers. Accordingly, if the electronic commerce business is only sending out information by electronic mail then postal address details or facsimile numbers may not be relevant.

Principle 4 — Personal data shall be accurate and where necessary kept up to date

7.16   A data controller will not be in breach of this principle if it has held inaccurate data when it has taken reasonable steps to ensure the accuracy of the data or if the data subject has notified the controller of the view that the data is inaccurate and the data indicates this fact.

Principle 5 — Personal data shall not be kept for longer than is necessary

Data controllers shall ensure that data is not kept longer than necessary by deleting data when it is not necessary. The data controller should give data a set period after which it is reviewed against the purposes given for holding the data.

Principle 6 — Personal data shall be processed in accordance with the rights of data subjects

A person contravenes the sixth principle only if:

(1) information is not supplied by a data controller to a data subject where data is being processed by a third party on behalf of data controller.
(2) the data controller does not comply with a notice requiring the controller to cease or not to process data likely to cause damage or distress.
(3) the data controller fails to comply with a notice not to process data for purposes of direct marketing.
(4) the data controller does not comply with a notice not to use data for automatic decision making.

Principle 7 — Measures to be taken against unauthorised or unlawful processing

7.17   This principle requires a data controller to take, amongst other things, reasonable steps to ensure the reliability of its staff which has access to personal data. Accordingly, an electronic commerce business must provide adequate security guarantees and ensure compliance with these guarantees. Where the processing of personal data is carried out by a data processor on behalf of a data controller the data processor must act under a written contract under which the data processor is to act only on instructions from the data controller and which imposes security obligations on the processor. An electronic commerce business which contracts with third parties such as computer bureaux, outsources certain operation to third parties, or engages a company to provide disaster recovery, should ensure that the contracts impose adequate technical and organisational guarantees to comply with the seventh principle and include appropriate warranties and indemnities.

Principle 8 — Personal Data shall not be transferred to a country outside the EEA unless there is adequate protection

The eighth principle prohibits the transfer of personal data to countries outside the European Economic Area[12] unless there is adequate levels of protection for the rights and freedoms of data subjects in relation to processing personal data. Many countries including the U.S. do not have equivalent data protection laws and it may be necessary for an electronic commerce business to transfer personal data to other countries for processing. **7.18**

In order to determine whether the level of protection afforded by a country is adequate, the circumstances of the transfer must be assessed. Consideration is given to the nature of the data, the country of origin and final destination, the purposes of processing, the security measures taken in respect of the data and the laws (if any) in force in the country. Adequacy is determined in the light of the "risk" involved in a particular transfer and does not necessarily depend on specific data protection/privacy legislation being in place.

The eight principle does not apply in the following situations:[13] **7.19**

(1) the data subject has given his/her consent to the transfer;

(2) transfer is necessary for performance of the contract between the data subject and a data controller or for taking steps at the request of the data subject with a view to his entering into a contract with the data controller;

(3) with respect to a contract between the data controller and a third person entered into at the request of the data subject in his/her interests, and the transfer is necessary for the performance or conclusion of such a contract;

(4) transfer is necessary for reasons of substantial public interest;

(5) transfer is necessary with respect to legal proceedings, legal rights or obtaining legal advice;

(6) transfer is necessary to protect the vital interests of the data subject;

(7) transfer of personal data on public register;

(8) transfer is made on terms of a kind approved by the Commissioner as ensuring adequate safeguards or the transfer is authorised by the Commissioner as being in manner ensuring adequate safeguards.

---

[12] The E.U. Member States and Norway, Iceland and Liechtenstein.
[13] DPA, Schedule 4.

7.20   The Commissioner has stated that she intends to take a pragmatic approach to the issue
of transferring personal data to overseas countries. This involves ensuring a high
standard of adequacy whilst not disrupting unnecessarily international commercial data
flows. Where a country does not have adequate protection there is likely to be
established model contract clauses[14] which guarantee the protection for personal data.[15]
As data subjects would not be able to assert their rights under a contract between the
controller and the controller/processor in the third country, an additional contract clause
between the data subject and the controller may be necessary.

The U.S., which prefers to leave regulation to industry, views the European data
protection directive as a classic demonstration of E.U. fondness for bureaucracy and
regulatory overkill. It has threatened to challenge the directive in the World Trade
Organisation (WTO) if it is ever used against U.S. companies.[16] In early October 1998,
three weeks before the law was due to come into force, talks between the E.U. and the
U.S. ended without concrete results. The U.S. continues to support self-regulatory
industry schemes[17] developed by U.S. business groups to address privacy issues rather
than Federal legislation. The U.S. approach is to have an organisation such as self-
regulating body police its members and deal with consumer complaints with serious
violations being reported to the relevant government agency.

Data Subject Rights

7.21   Data subjects have extensive rights under the DPA with which an electronic commerce
business need to comply. A data subject may write to an electronic commerce business
and ask to be supplied with a description, purposes and disclosures made of or a copy
of any personal data being held. Within forty days and on receipt of a single fee[18] an
electronic commerce business must respond to an individual's request.

A data subject has the right to prevent processing for the purposes of direct marketing
and, in certain circumstances, to prevent processing likely to cause him/her damage.[19]

An individual has the right to claim compensation where a data controller contravenes
certain requirements of the DPA. In the case of inaccurate data, an individual can apply
to the courts for correction, blocking, erasure or destruction.

Data subjects also have the right, subject to exceptions, not to have decisions made
about them which are based solely on automated processing.

Exemptions From the Act

7.22   There are exemptions to certain parts of the DPA. As with the Data Protection Act 1984,
there are exemptions for crime, taxation, health and social work, national security and
legal professional privilege. There are also some new exemptions which are unlikely to

---

[14] The CitiBank/German Railways agreement of February 1996 which was negotiated with the Berlin Data
Protection Commissioner is being cited as a useful model.
[15] The International Chamber of Commerce has drafted model contract clauses.
[16] See *Financial Times*, "**Regulators@odds**" — October 8, 1998.
[17] *e.g.* Truste, a non-profit organisation that has established principles of disclosure and informed consent for
online services.
[18] Maximum fee to be set by regulations. It was £10 under the Data Protection Act 1984.
[19] See para. 8.13.

be relevant to electronic commerce relating to confidential references, management forecasts and in respect of information by candidates in examination.

Enforcement

The Commissioner may issue an enforcement notice where a data controller has contravened the data protection principles. She may also issue an 'information notice' requiring the controller to provide her with information where she suspects a principle has been breached. Failure to comply with either notice is an offence.

7.23

Cookies

A cookie is a computer data storage program which enables a website to record a visitor's activities from his/her computer hard drive. The cookie is then available for subsequent access by the server itself or other servers to read the information stored and so analysing and publicising the viewing habits of the visitor to the server which enquires of the information recorded as a cookie. Under the original Netscape standard, cookies existed by default only for the duration of the actual web browsing session and could only be accessed by the web server and the web page that stored the cookie.[20] The original standard, however, and the subsequently revised cookie standards allow web servers to overwrite the defaults. A web server may extend the life-span of a cookie to several years. A web server may also set a cookie so that an almost unlimited number of other servers have access to the cookie information as well. This allows some companies to follow Internet users from website to website to collect information about the personal browsing habits of the visitor for advertising and marketing purposes. The website feeds the Internet user's browser a "cookie" and the browser being used by the Internet user automatically responds to this by giving out the information requested. This normally happens without Internet users knowing that their computers have been interrogated.

7.24

Many cookies are useful and, if asked, most Internet users are happy to accept cookies from any sites, since receiving cookies saves Internet users time and effort. These are the cookies which, for example, keep details of previous visits to the site and thereby save Internet users from having to re-register at websites every time they visit.

Early versions of the Netscape browser did not contain any facilities to notify Internet users before accepting a cookie. But concerns regarding privacy have led to improvements and now the current versions of both Netscape and Microsoft Internet Explorer contain user selectable options which allow users to be notified when a cookie is received. It has been said that merely being notified and allowing the Internet user to reject is not enough, and in consequence all browsers now contains an option which allows the user to automatically reject all cookies.

It is significant that the technology to capture this kind of information was developed and deployed in the U.S. which does not have the any data protection legislation. The gathering and use of personal data through the use of cookies is certainly an activity which may be within the scope of the DPA.[21]

---

[20] Netscape, Persistent Client State HTTP Cookies, Preliminary Specification (**http://www.netscape.com/newsref/std/cookie_spec.html**).
[21] See Computer Law and Security Report, Vol. 14, No. 3, 1998, p. 166. Article by Viktor Mayer–Schönberger.

PRIVACY ENHANCED TECHNOLOGIES

Principle 3 of the Data Protection Act 1998 says:

> "Personal data shall be adequate, relevant and not excessive in relation to the purpose of purposes for which they are processed"

7.25   While Internet users may be willing, in the course of an on-line session, to give the company a great deal of personal information, the company effectively has a duty to protect them from themselves and their generosity. There are new technological solutions to this problem which are being given strong support by European Data Protection Commissioners.

In 1995 the Information and Privacy Commissioner in Ontario Canada and the Registratiekamer in The Netherlands jointly produced a report called "Privacy-Enhancing Technologies: The Path to Anonymity" The authors argued that, at the present time, a person was almost always required to reveal his/her identity when engaging in a wide range of activities. Every time he/she used a credit card, made a telephone call, paid his/her taxes, subscribed to a magazine, or bought something at the grocery store using a credit or debit card, an identifiable record of each transaction was created and recorded in a computer database somewhere. In order to obtain a service or make a purchase (using something other than cash), organisations require that citizens identified themselves:

> "This practice is so widespread that it is simply treated as a given — an individual's identity must be collected and recorded in association with services rendered or purchases made. But must this always be the case? Are there no situations where transactions may be conducted anonymously, yet securely? We believe that there are and will outline a number of methods and technologies by which anonymous yet authentic transactions may be conducted."

7.26   The authors then developed their case for privacy-enhanced technologies. Their explanation is somewhat complex and we have instead compared it to a masked ball. At a masked ball the guest arrives at the ball and is identified as someone whom the host has invited to attend. He/she is dressed in a "mask" to hide his/her identity before entering the party. He/she has been authorised to participate in the party but nobody knows who he/she really is.

PETs perform the same function in an electronic environment. The user arrives at the system and encounters the "Identity Protector" which, once it has established that the user is authorised to proceed, gives the user a mask or "authorised pseudo-identity".[22] This may, in appropriate circumstances, be a different pseudo-identity each time the user connects to the system. Working through the Identity Protector, the user can enter into binding transactions. However, the user is in control of information regarding his/her true identity being passed onto the system; any attempts by the system to discover the true identity of the user are caught by the Identity Protector.

---

[22] This is a good application for a type of public key cryptosystem.

Since the European Commission is funding research in this area and the work is fully supported and encouraged by all the European Data Protection Commissioners, it is possible that shortly after the end of this decade privacy law and technology will come together to make it illegal in Europe to use Electronic Commerce systems which do not contain Identity Protectors.

There are serious issues which need to be addressed before such a situation could arise. Identity Protectors must not hinder the investigation of money laundering or serious tax evasion or terrorism or serious crime. PETs are not a fully worked out solution to the privacy problem. But they do provide a useful counter argument to an on-line vendor who claims that it must have personal information in order to authenticate a transaction.

JURISDICTIONAL DATA PROTECTION ISSUES

Many electronic commerce businesses will have several severs and databases in different countries. This can create difficulties in identifying which data controller is triable for any breach of data protection laws. It has been suggested that laws should be enacted to permit enforcement against internet service providers and internet access providers.[23]   **7.27**

Clause 5 of the DPA applies the requirements of the DPA to both U.K. data controllers established in the U.K. and also to data controllers established neither in the U.K. nor in any other EEA state but who use equipment in the U.K. for processing the data otherwise than for the purpose of transit through the U.K. Such non U.K. controllers must nominate a representative in the U.K.

The data protection rules which will apply will be those of the place of establishment of the data controller for whose purposes the processing is carried out. It is apparent, particularly for electronic commerce businesses, that a data controller may be established in more than on one Member State. Therefore, an electronic commerce business which is going to be holding data in a number of jurisdictions may have to comply with the data production laws for each relevant country.

Electronic commerce businesses which do not have a place of business in an E.U. Member State will not be caught by European data protection legislation notwithstanding that they engage in businesses with European consumers.

CONCLUSION

The Commissioner has made it clear that her officers have been reviewing websites and that some of these give her concern. It is clear that the DPA applies to information collected by electronic commerce businesses on the Internet as it does to any other method. The Commissioner has voiced concerns that the sites she has visited do not contain any notification of the uses and disclosures to be made of personal data as   **7.28**

---

[23] See E. France, 1997: "Can Data Protection survive?" in *Computers and Law — The Journal of the Society for Computers and the Law*, Volume 8, Issue 2.

required by the DPA. This may be because in the majority of cases the information is only to be used for obvious purposes such as permitting further direct contract by the electronic commerce business concerned (which does not have to be stated). In other situations there could be breaches of the DPA.

Another concern of the Commissioner was that in electronic commerce transactions notifications to data users is normally only given at the end or at the bottom of an on-line form. In non-electronic transactions, where disclosures are made on physical paper forms, disclosures are in prominent places such as near the signature on the form. The Commissioner has recognised that electronic commerce transactions are different. Where information is imported on to a form of a website it is immediately capable of being processed as personal data. When warnings are placed at the bottom of a form it is possible that they may not be seen or read by the user. The Commissioner therefore feels that indication as to the uses and disclosures of data should be given at the beginning of forms so that a user can decide on a fully informed basis whether to enter into the transaction or not. It is likely that the Commissioner's office will be preparing guidance notes on the use of data protection on electronic commerce transactions.

European electronic businesses must ensure that their websites are data protection complaint. A clear statement about the purposes for which personal data is obtained must be given. This may also require adding new terms and conditions to deal with data protection warnings and disclaimers to websites.

The growth of electronic commerce does raise a threat to the rights to privacy of individuals. The new DPA, with provision of increased rights to individual, does help to meet some of these threats. Nevertheless, it is necessary to develop technical means to protect the privacy of commerce business users. The use of security encryption methods and the development of the Internet protocol to improve confidentiality by classification of messages and better authentication of procedures is equally important. What is ultimately needed is a global model of data protection. The European model is an important step to protecting data but with the United States government favouring self regulation, an effective regime will only be found when there is a global solution to this transborder problem.

─── • 8 • ───

WEBVERTISING

"The advertising and promotional component of the web will far exceed the transactional"[1]

INTRODUCTION

Businesses have been quicker to realise the advertising and marketing potential of the Internet than they have in appreciating its potential as a world-wide trading medium. In 1997, it was estimated that businesses spent \$906.5 million[2] world-wide on "webvertising".

8.01

The opportunities for a business to advertise on-line fall into five broad categories: advertising in on-line publications; banner advertising[3]; website advertising incorporating the advertiser's brand name; linking a website with an e-mail address to facilitate to provision of data to the advertiser; and "spamming".

As a general rule, the legal issues that affect advertising in traditional media are of equal application and relevance to webvertising. The problem for electronic commerce businesses is applying national frameworks of laws and regulations to adverts that are disseminated to the world at large. In theory, a webvert is subject to the laws of every country in which it is accessed by an Internet user.

The Federal Trade Commission in the U.S. has been particularly aggressive in enforcing advertising laws against webvertisers. On May 6, 1998, the FTC published a proposal regarding the applicability of its consumer protection rules and guides to on-line advertising and commercial transactions in electronic media.[4] The proposal aims, for example, to clarify that the term "written" in the context of electronic media means information that is capable of being preserved in tangible form and read and that "mail" includes e-mail. Regulators in the U.K. and elsewhere in Europe are beginning to adopt a similar approach.

---

[1] Chief Executive of TicketMaster, *Wall Street Journal,* April 28, 1997.
[2] Figure provided by the Internet Advertising Bureau .
[3] See, for example, **www.nfl.com** and **www.capitalfm.com** and para. 8.23 (Linking).
[4] Interpretation of Rules and Guides for Electronic Media, Federal Register, Vol. 63, No. 87, 16 CFR Ch. 1.

LAWS REGULATING WEBVERTISING

8.02   U.K. webvertisers have to comply with a raft of domestic legislation. This includes the Trade Descriptions Act 1968[5]; the Consumer Protection Act 1987[6]; the Control of Misleading Advertisements Regulations 1988[7]; the Prices Act 1974; the Unsolicited Goods and Services Act 1971; the Trade Marks Act 1994; the Copyright, Designs and Patents Act 1988; the Data Protection Act 1984[8]; the Defamation Acts 1952 and 1996; the Obscene Publications Acts 1959 and 1964,[9] and the Lotteries and Amusements Act 1976.[10]

There will also be rafts of non-U.K. legislation which may be potentially breached by a webvert as a result of its global "reach". For example, in *United States v. Thomas*,[11] the operators of a pornographic electronic bulletin-board in California were convicted of criminal obscenity laws by a Federal court in Tennessee based on Tennessee standards of decency. The Court held that the material was "sent" to Tennessee and subject to local standards, despite the "sending" being electronic and the bulletin board being essentially accessible world-wide.

Jurisdiction is the most vexing issue affecting webvertising. Is the content of a website subject only to the law of the country of origin of the advertisement (which could be the place of business of the advertiser, or where its server is based), or subject to every foreign law where the advertisement is capable of being received? The strict legal position is the probably the latter, but this is recognised as impractical. At present there is no international unanimity on the issue. The general approach illustrated by existing cases[12] is that the laws of the countries of "publication" will apply; in other words, the countries in which there is evidence of "directed" activity.[13]

8.03   Simply placing information on a website will not, of itself, be treated as evidence of directed activity if there is something about that information which makes it clear that it is not targeted at consumers in a particular country. The language of the advertisement may be relevant, but not conclusive. The use of clear disclaimers may help to clarify who is included in the target audience. Disclaimers, such as *"This offer is only available for*

---

[5] Under the Trade Descriptions Act 1968 any person who, in the course of a trade or business, applies a false trade description to any goods, or supplies or offers to supply any goods to which a false trade description is applied, commits an offence. Offences under this Act are policed exclusively by Trading Standards Officers who are attached to Local Authorities.

[6] The Department of Trade and Industry's *Code of Practice for Traders on Price Indications* gives guidance in respect of the pricing requirements of the Consumer Protection Act and sets out what is good practice to follow in a wide range of different circumstances. If a Trading Standards Officer has reasonable grounds to suspect that a misleading price indication has been given, he has power under the Act to seize and/or detain goods or records which may be required as evidence in any court proceedings.

[7] S.I. 1988 No. 915 which implemented the E.U. Directive on Misleading Advertising 84/450 as amended by Council Directive 97/55 so as to include comparative advertising.

[8] See further Chapter 7.

[9] See para. 2.51 in Chapter 2.

[10] See further section 8.3 (On-line competitions).

[11] 1996 FED App. 0032 P (6th Cir.), II.C.2.

[12] For example, in 1996 Virgin Atlantic Airways was punished for putting a misleading advertisement on its U.K. server after it was discovered that they were quoting inaccurate fares and listing a fare that was no longer available in relation to flights from the USA. The US Department of Transportation fined the airline $14,000.

[13] For a detailed analysis see Chapter 4 "Jurisdiction".

consumers in X country", however, are likely to be construed narrowly and may be void in some countries.[14] One technical method of filtering web users is to use the standard JavaScript function called "get TimezoneOffset" which identifies the time zone in which potential customers are located. For example, a user whose computer responds as being in GMT plus three and a half hours is likely to be in Iran.

Impact of the Single European Market

Businesses using electronic communications for marketing face regulatory differences even within the E.U. itself. French laws,[15] for example, require all advertisements to be in the French language. It is also impossible to run a sales promotion campaign that carries a premium, free gift or sweepstakes lawfully across the E.U.[16] In theory, at least, the principles established by the Single European Market, whereby E.U. Member States are meant to recognise, through the principle of mutual recognition, the laws and regulations of the other Member States, should have avoided this problem.[17] However, the right of freedom to provide services is subject to a number of exceptions[18] and the advertising sector has particularly suffered from a lack of compliance with these rules.

8.04

In 1992, Yves Rocher,[19] the French cosmetics company, ran a mail order campaign across several countries. The German courts injuncted Yves Rocher on the grounds of unfair competition. The company took the case to the European Court of Justice which ruled that the German prohibition constituted an

> "obstacle to trade because it compels a trader either to adopt sales promotions schemes which differ from one Member State to another or to discontinue a scheme which he considers to be particularly effective".

More recently Polygram was prevented from launching CDs in Germany and thereby forced to abandon its cross-border campaign. The European Commission sent a reasoned opinion to the German authorities concluding that German legislation imposes

---

[14] See further Chapter 2, "Disclaimers".

[15] Code de la consommation, Law No. 93–949, July 26, 1993.

[16] See for example the survey recently published by FEDMA (the Federation of European Direct Marketing) and FAEP (the European Magazine Publishers Federation): "Sales Promotion Rules in the European Union", a country by country survey of sales promotion and advertising rules, self-regulation, privacy policy, codes of conduct and distance selling regulations for companies operation on-line. Also see f.n. below.

[17] See, for example, *Rewe-Zentral AG v. Bundesmonopolverwaltung fur Branntwein Case* 120/78 E.C.J. February 20, 1979 which concerned a rejection by the German authorities to the plaintiff's application for authorisation to import the alcoholic drink *Cassis de Dijon* from France on the basis that the drink did not contain the minimum alcoholic strength to comply with German rules. The E.C.J. ruled that there was no valid reason why, provided that they have been lawfully produced and marketed in one of the Member States, products should not be introduced into any other Member State; the sale of such products may not be subject to a legal prohibition on marketing.

[18] Articles 56 & 59 of the Treaty of Rome where restrictions can be justified on public policy, public security, public health or public interest grounds. See, for example, Case C-384/93 *Alpine Investments B.V. v. Minister van Financien* [1995] E.C.R. I-833, 45 where the decision of the Netherlands Government to impose a general measure prohibiting unsolicited calls for the purpose of selling financial services was challenged in the European Court of Justice on the basis that it constituted a restriction on free movement of services within the Community. The Court held that, while the Treaty applied to cold calling and accordingly the measure constituted a restriction, it was justified to protect investor confidence in national financial markets.

[19] See case C–126/91 *Schutzverband gegen Unwesen in de Wirtschafrt e. v. Yves Rocher GmbH* [1993] E.C.R. I-2361.

a disproportionate restriction on promotional gifts and discounts and requesting it to withdraw the relevant legislation failing which the Commission would refer this case to the European Court.

8.05   In an attempt to solve these problems, the Single Market Directorate (DGXV) published a Green Paper in 1996.[20] Having invited comments on proposals to improve the ability to disseminate marketing and advertising materials across borders without ensuring compliance with all the laws across the E.U., it has issued a follow-up Communication[21] in which it proposed criteria to clarify the laws on the fundamental E.U. principles of country of origin and proportionality.[22] The Committee of Government Experts, established under the Green Paper, is focusing on national regulations on sales promotions and price discounts and will thereafter address premiums and other sales promotion issues.

Content Standards

8.06   Whilst it is impractical to obtain legal clearance in every jurisdiction throughout the world electronic commerce businesses can adhere to some general principles to minimise the risk of infringing against the advertising regulations of other countries. Legal and trade mark clearance should be sought in target countries and in countries in which the electronic commerce business has a presence or assets. Appropriate disclaimers should be used to exclude non-target countries from the invitation. Other practical considerations include: how costly it would be to change a webvertisement; whether a competitor would be likely to be able to prove actual damage; and whether the authorities in a given country are likely to take a "laissez-faire" approach.

Contractual and Liability Issues

8.07   The risk that an electronic commerce business could incur liability for breach of a foreign advertising regulation makes it even more essential for contracts with advertising agencies to lay down clear lines of responsibility for ensuring legal compliance of advertising material. Third party rights will need to be licensed for both the territories of interest and the medium of the Internet, which is not a use for which consent would necessarily be implied.

The degree of control exercised by an electronic commerce business over material posted on or linked to their website may in itself give rise to liability.[23] Permitting third parties to post material onto its website could leave the website owner responsible for any such material that contains defamatory or otherwise illegal matter. Clear terms and conditions of access and use should be displayed. Open forum discussion areas pose particular risks of libel for the site owner and webvertisers should consider whether, for this reason, discussions via e-mail would be preferable.

---

[20] Green Paper on Commercial Communications in the Internal Market, May 1996.
[21] Follow up to the Green Paper on Commercial Communications in the Internal Market, March 4, 1998.
[22] Defined in Article 3b of the Treaty which provides that any action by the Community shall not go beyond what is necessary to achieve the objects of this Treaty.
[23] For further information see Chapters 2 and 3.

SELF-REGULATION

Throughout the E.U., regimes of self-regulation complement the legal frameworks on   **8.08**
matters such as misleading advertising and unfair competition. Although the structures
vary, each country's self-regulatory system is based on the principles enshrined in the
International Chamber of Commerce's Code of Advertising Practice.[24] The Code states
that all advertising should be legal, decent, honest and truthful, and respect the cultural
differences of the given country. Regulatory systems are generally founded on rules of
best practice drawn up, supported and enforced voluntarily by the country's advertising
industry itself.

In 1992 the European Advertising Standards Alliance (EASA) was formed to support
and co-ordinate the roles of the self-regulatory bodies across Europe. Its members now
include 24 bodies from 20 countries, including the whole of the E.U., Switzerland,
Turkey and the Czech, Russian, Slovak and Slovenian Republics. It also has corresponding members in New Zealand and South Africa. EASA's role in handling cross-border
complaints is now recognised in various E.U. directives and communications. The
decisive factor in identifying a cross-border complaint is that the complaint comes from
a different country from that of the media in which the advertisement appears. The
country of origin of the advertiser or the advertisement is irrelevant.[25] The Alliance has
developed a procedure to enable cross-border complaints concerning webvertisements
to be dealt with on country of origin basis.[26]

The British Codes of Advertising and Sale Promotion

In the U.K. the Committee of Advertising Practice (CAP) is the body responsible for   **8.09**
devising and enforcing the Codes. The scope of the Codes is broad, applying to
advertisements and promotions in all non-broadcast electronic media,[27] wording introduced in 1995. The Advertising Standards Authority, the independent body responsible
for investigating complaints of breaches of the Codes, has applied them to Internet-
related activities on a number of occasions, usually resulting in the webvertiser agreeing
to amend its website to comply with the ASA's recommendations and to consult the
CAP copy advice team on future site content. The ASA regularly reviews websites for

---

[24] June 1997 edition available on **www.iccwbo.org/Commissions/Marketing/advercod.htm**.
[25] See **www.easa-alliana.org**. The Alliance publishes reports on cross-border complaints in its newsletter,
Alliance Update and may issue an 'Euro Ad Alert' to it members.
[26] See **www.easaalliance.ocq/easaa.html**. This is in line with Commission policy on mutual recognition
and home country control in measures such as the *Television Without Frontiers* Broadcasting Directive under
which a Member State may only impose more restrictive rules on broadcasters under its own jurisdiction.
[27] See **www.asa.org.uk/** Advertisements and promotions in broadcast media are regulated by the Independent Television Commission (ITC) and Radio Authority Codes of Practice and implemented by the Broadcast
or Radio Advertising Clearance Centres as appropriate (BACC and RACC) through a pre-clearance system.
The ITC and Radio Authority are obliged to draw up these Codes by the Broadcasting Act 1990. An
advertisement on the Internet which includes anything other than text or other non-representational images
could be characterised as a "licensable programme service" under s.46 of the Broadcasting Act 1990. Pictures,
whether moving or not, could be subject to ITC regulation. The Government view is that this legislation was
not intended to apply to the Internet and it is working with the ITC and other bodies to formulate a specific
policy for the Internet. This is most likely to take the form of self-regulation as the ITC consider that it would
be impractical for it to operate a licence system for web sites. However, the advent of digital broadcasting and
web TV will raise further issues in this regard.

breaches of the Codes and has established a working group to examine how the regulatory regime should apply to webvertisements.

Although the Codes lack the force of law, certain sanctions do apply. An electronic commerce business may be asked by the ASA to withdraw or amend the advertisement. The complaint, together with the names of the advertiser and its agency, will be published in the ASA's Monthly Report. If an advertiser fails to comply with an ASA ruling, trade sanctions or a withdrawal of further advertising space may be invoked by CAP members. As an ultimate deterrent, the Director General of Fair Trading under the Control of Misleading Advertisements Regulations 1988 can subject flagrant and persistent abusers of the Codes to legal proceedings. The ASA may also ask the relevant Internet Service Provider to assist it in enforcing any adjudication.

Other Initiatives

8.10   The International Chamber of Commerce (ICC) has launched a new voluntary set of guidelines on webvertising setting out principles for 'responsible commercial communications' via electronic networks.[28] The guidelines state that the legality of a webvertisement should be determined by reference to the laws of the country in which it originated. However, the ICC points out that there is no international unanimity as to whether country of origin or country of destination applies, certain countries may, therefore, claim jurisdiction over messages posted on-line from abroad. The guidelines also fail to address what happens if a webvertiser in one country posts an advertisement on a website where the server is located in a different country. The ICC has also published model contract clauses to ensure the adequate protection of privacy in transborder data flows.[29] The Direct Marketing Association has also devised a code on marketing on the Internet to complement the existing frameworks.

COMPARATIVE ADVERTISING

8.11   Comparative advertising — where an advertisement implicitly or explicitly refers to a competitor or to goods or services offered by a competition — is another area where webvertisers are at risk because different countries have traditionally applied disparate rules. Whilst the U.S. (and to a lesser extent the U.K.)[30] have encouraged comparative advertising on the basis that it is in the interest of consumers to be better informed, most E.U. countries have taken the opposite approach, regarding it as unfair competition. The result has been that a lawful comparative webvertisement in one Member States is likely to breach the rules in another.

---

[28] See **www.iccwbo.org/Commissions/Marketing/Internet—Guidelines.html**.
[29] See para. 7.18 in Chapter 7.
[30] U.K. laws permit comparative advertising subject to the voluntary codes and the laws on trade marks, intellectual property, consumer protection and defamation. Under the Trade Marks Act 1994 comparative advertising is permitted provided that the use of the third party's trade mark is "in accordance with honest practices in industrial and commercial matters, and does not without due cause take unfair advantage of, or is not detrimental to, the distinctive character or repute of the registered trade mark. The Act also permits descriptive comparisons concerning the kind, quality, value or other characteristics of goods or services provided the use is in accordance with honest practices.

With a view to harmonising the laws in the E.U., the Commission has adopted a Directive on Comparative Advertising[31] as an amendment to the 1984 Misleading Advertising Directive.[32] The provisions have to be implemented into the national laws of the Member States by April 23, 2000. The drafting is somewhat ambiguous, however, and it is not clear whether the Directive sets maximum or minimum standards to be applied to comparisons in advertisements. The Directive states that comparative advertising shall be permitted when the following conditions are met[33]:

- it is not misleading

- it compares like with like

- it objectively compares one or more material, relevant, verifiable and representative features of those goods or services

- it does not create confusion in the market place

- it does not discredit or denigrate a competitor

- for products with a designation of origin, it relates in each case to products with the same designation

- it does not take unfair advantage of the other mark or product; and

- it does not present goods or services as reproductions or imitations of goods or services bearing a protected name or trade mark.

The U.K. Government's current position is that it will not be necessary to amend existing laws; its intention is merely to adopt the Directive by means of an amendment to the Misleading Advertising Regulations.[34]

PRIVACY ISSUES FOR MARKETING ON THE NET

The ability to collect data through on-line survey marketing and browser technology has obvious advantages for on-line marketers. At the same time it raises privacy concerns for regulators. Responsible web marketers who wish to stave off greater regulation are now looking to third party organisations to certify their sites as compliant with developing privacy standards. The Council of Better Business Bureau in the U.S. (the equivalent of the U.K.'s ASA) has launched its own on-line privacy initiative that will allow compliant sites to display its seal of approval.

8.12

Unlike the U.S., however, European laws grant individuals access to and extensive rights over data kept about them. In the U.K., the Data Protection Act 1998 (DPA)[35]

---

[31] 97/55 published in O.J. L290 Vol. 40, 23.10.97.

[32] 84/450.

[33] Article 3a.

[34] See n.7, above.

[35] For further details see Chapter 7. See also the Telecommunications (Data Protection and Privacy) Regulations 1998 which implements the Telecoms Data Protection Directive 97/66 and prohibit the sending of unsolicited faxes to consumers without consent and allow individuals to "opt-out" from receiving unsolicited direct marketing telephone calls.

places even greater responsibilities on companies that collect and process data for marketing purposes. Companies have to obtain consumers' consent and provide them with certain information before processing their personal data. In practice, express consent is not be required unless the data is "sensitive". However, as well as the name and address of the company collecting and processing the data, companies have to ensure that consumers are aware of the categories of potential recipients of their data, whether provision of the data is obligatory or voluntary, and of the existence of rights of access to and rectification of the data.

8.13   Security rules mean that, where data is requested during a visit to a company's website, the provider should be informed that its data may not be secure during transmission from one server to the other. A notice in the following form posted on to the web pages where date is requested should suffice:

> "Whilst we have taken all reasonable steps to ensure that the information you provide will be kept secure from unauthorised access, the Internet is not a secure environment. We cannot guarantee that the information will be secure during transmission to our web server".

One of the new rights provided to consumers under the DPA is an explicit right to object in writing to data being used for direct marketing purposes. Data subjects have a right to 'opt-out' of having their data used in this way and controllers must cease such use within a reasonable period of receiving a request to do so.

The DPA also prevents data being transferred to countries outside the EEA unless those countries have adequate data protection laws in place or the individual has consented.[36] This is extremely relevant for any company wishing to collect U.K. data and transfer it to, for example, the U.S. whose data protection laws still operate on a self-regulatory basis. Subject to guidance expected to be issued by the Data Protection Commission, current thinking is that steps would first need to be taken to obtain consent through contractual provisions or permission from the U.K. Data Protection Commissioner. To ensure that the consent satisfies all the requirements of the Act, the request would have to make it clear that the data is to be transferred to a non-EEA country whose data protection laws may be less stringent. The request should also name the country to which the data will be transferred and, if it is the case, that the transfer will be effected via the Internet.[37]

Children On-line

8.14   The Council Recommendation on the Protection of Minors and Human Dignity in Audio-visual and Information Services[38] is the first legal instrument at European level on the content of information services in electronic media. It aims to provide guidance for

---

[36] Subject to transitional provisions for processing.
[37] The International Federation of Direct Marketing Associations has adopted its own set of principles governing the protection of personal data in the framework of on-line service.
[38] COM (97) 570 adopted by the E.U. Council on May 28, 1998. This follows the Commission's Green Paper on the subject (COM (96) 483) and its Communication on Illegal and Harmful Content on the Internet (COM (96) 487.

Member States on issues such as parental control and the development of self-regulation with the objective of enabling minors to make responsible use of on-line services.

The U.S. is, however, ahead of the E.U. on the protection of children on-line. The Children's On-line Privacy Protection Act requires commercial website operators to provide clear notice of their information collection practices and obtain parental consent prior to eliciting personal information from children under the age of 13. It would also allow parents to access and check such information and curtail its use. While website operators are concerned at the logistics of contacting parents and verifying their consent before data is collected, the contrary view is that the burden should be on the party who wants the information. The final draft of the bill has not been finalised, but it is expected to be in force before 2000.

ADVERTISING TO CHILDREN

Many countries place outright bans or heavy restrictions on advertising to children. In the U.K. these arise under both the voluntary codes and statute. However, this is another area where the disparity of laws within the E.U. constitutes a barrier to trade. The ban introduced in Greece in 1994 on toy advertising on TV until after 10 pm is currently under investigation by the Commission while the attempts by Norway and Sweden to block trans-frontier broadcasts containing children's advertising have met with disapproval from, respectively, the EFTA Court and the European Court of Justice.[39] This means that any advertiser broadcasting from outside a E.U. country where advertising to children is banned should be able to advertise legally within those countries. In Flanders, Belgium, there is a prohibition on all T.V. advertising to children for a period of five minutes before and after children's programming. In Greece, toy advertising is prohibited on television until after 10 p.m., a measure which so far the Commission is being encouraged to investigate on the basis that it is an infringement of the Treaty. Sweden has a ban on all T.V. advertising to children under the age of 12, and has (unsuccessfully) sought to impose the same rules on its MS partners within the Council of Ministers. Spain operates a de facto ban on the advertising of "war" toys on T.V. Norway disallows advertising to children on television, but has recently lost an important test case in the EFTA Court in which it lost the contention that it also had the right, in pursuance of the advertising prohibition, to block transfrontier broadcasting from other MS of material which included children's advertising. The law governing this case in the EFTA Court is identical to E.U. law.

The Advocate General of the European Court of Justice (ECJ) gave his Opinion on September 17, 1996 on three joint cases concerning Sweden's ban on advertising aimed at children under 12 and advertising which was deemed to be misleading under Swedish law. Advocate General Jacobs said that Sweden had no right to ban advertisements broadcast from another MS. The Advocate General's Opinion was confirmed in 1998, and the judgment is now being examined on the Swedish national courts. In October 1994, the Greek Government adopted legislation that imposed an absolute ban

8.15

---

[39] European Court of Justice (EFTA) on advertising to children.

on the advertising of toys on Greek television between 0700 hrs and 2200 hrs. The ban, claimed as a measure to protect children and families against disputes thought to arise from purchase requests prompted by T.V. advertising, was in fact a trade protection measure designed to restrict toy imports. In this respect the ban was very successful: toy manufacturers trading internationally have lost 40 per cent of their turnover of advertised brands in Greece since 1994. Greek broadcasters have lost advertising revenue by a similar proportion and children's programming has consequently suffered.

The Toy Industries of Europe (TIE) complained to the European Commission under the procedure laid down by Article 169 of the Treaty on November 4, 1994, claiming that the ban was a violation of Articles 30 and 59 of the E.U. Treaty. The Commission has so far failed to endorse the complaint, despite sending the Greek Government an informal letter of notice ("pre-169") in January 1996 and a formal notice in March 1997. The TIE has made an official compliant to the E.U. Ombudsman about the case, which it sees as demonstrative of the Commission's failure to perform its duties. A paper written by the Commission on T.V. toy advertising was presented to the E.C. Expert Group on Commercial Communications in October 1998.

TELEMARKETING ON THE INTERNET

8.16   Electronic commerce business find that the Internet is the perfect tool for sending advertising messages to and soliciting contracts with consumers and businesses by electronic mail. Targets can be reached anywhere in the world for very little cost. While direct mail is tolerated by most national legal systems, provided it does not constitute harassment, spamming[40] raises new issues of cost and inconvenience for the recipient.[41]

The Distance Selling Directive[42] will place some of the existing requirements of the voluntary and trade codes of practice on a statutory footing. It contains similar provisions to the Telecoms Data Protection Directive,[43] although it also applies to mail and other forms of communication. The Directive requires Member States to ensure that the express prior consent (*i.e.* an "opt-in" system) of consumers is obtained for all uses of faxes or automated calling machines as a means of communications. All other means of distance marketing communications, unsolicited or not, including electronic mails, traditional mail-shots and calls, will only be able to be used where there is no clear objection from the consumer. Consumers will have to be given the opportunity to register his/her objection to receiving such communications. Options include either an

---

[40] See further section 2.4.
[41] See *Cyber Promotions Inc. v. America Online Inc.* (1996) C.A No. 96–2486 and 96–5213 which concerned unsolicited e-mails sent to AOL members which AOL intercepted. The Court held that there is no right under the US Constitution to send unsolicited e-mails over the Internet to members of a private company and AOL was therefore entitled to block these transmissions. And in *CompuServe Inc. v. Cyber Promotions Inc.* (1997) case No. C2-96-1070 the defendant sent unsolicited e-mails to the plaintiff's subscribers and modified their equipment to circumvent the block set up by CompuServe. CompuServe alleged that this constituted the tort of trespass and that Cyber's activities devalued their system and were granted an injunction.
[42] See section 2.2 and the Government's Consultation Paper of June 1998 which set out various options for implementing the Directive.
[43] See n.37 above.

opt-in or an opt-out system. Whichever form of communication is used, the identity of the supplier and the commercial aim of the communication will have to be stated at the outset.

ADVERTISING REGULATED GOODS AND SERVICES

Certain types of advertising are particularly problematic in other jurisdictions. Electronic commerce businesses must therefore be alert to the potential sensitive of the global audience to whom they offer their products. Section 2.7 deals with some of the products which are commonly sold on-line. With particular reference to webvertising two sectors have received particular attention in recent months, namely tobacco and alcohol advertising.

8.17

Tobacco Advertising

On July 6, 1998 the Tobacco Advertising Directive[44] was adopted. The proposal for a Europe-wide ban, which has been in the pipeline for nine years, will lead to a general European ban on all forms of advertising and sponsorship (excluding television advertising which is already covered by the "Television without Frontiers" Directive[45]). The first implementation date is July 30, 2001, although one and two year deferments will be allowed for press and sponsorship respectively, with a further transitional period of three years for exceptional global event sponsorship. By October 1, 2006 all the provisions of the Directive are required to be in force in their entirety.

8.18

The ban will apply to all forms commercial communications or sponsorship which have the direct or indirect effect of promoting a tobacco product, including the use of any distinctive features of tobacco products such as trade marks or logos. None of the exemptions will be relevant for webvertisers. Member States may also implement stricter rules at Member State level if this is considered necessary for health protection.

Alcohol Advertising

This is another area where E.U. rules on television alcohol advertising, contained in the Broadcasting Directives,[46] have allowed countries to adopt stricter rules than those laid down in the Directives.[47] This had led to various countries, most notably France, banning alcohol advertising altogether. The French "Loi Evin" has been the subject of much controversy, particularly surrounding the France World Cup 1998, due to the large fall in media revenue that it has caused. As a result, the Confederation of Common Market Brewers and the European Confederation of Spirits Producers lodged complaints with the European Commission which is considering whether to refer the case to the

8.19

---

[44] Directive 98/43 relating to the advertising and sponsorship of tobacco products. O.J. L213/9.
[45] Directive 89/552. The ban was extended to teleshopping programmes by the revised broadcasting Directive of June 1997 (97/36).
[46] The *Television Without Frontiers* Directive 89/552 and 97/36.
[47] Under the Directives, alcohol advertising (defined as products containing more that 1.2 per cent of alcohol by volume) cannot be aimed at minors, and cannot give the impression that the consumption of alcohol can lead to enhanced performance or increased success.

European Court of Justice. In its opinion, these national measures constitute a restriction on trade. Alternatively, it may introduce a separate proposal to harmonise the laws on alcohol advertising.

On-line promotions

8.20   Most countries regulate sales promotion schemes, including free prize draws and prize competitions, fairly vigorously.[48] In the U.K., the rules on chance promotions and skill competitions are set out in the Lotteries & Amusements Act 1976. Under the Act, all lotteries[49] which do not constitute gaming are unlawful unless they fall into one of the limited exemptions laid down under the Act, none of which are particularly suitable for advertisers and promoters of commercial products.

In countries where free prize draws are permissible promoters have developed the concept of the "no purchase necessary" route of entry. However, on-line promotions raise new issues, in particular as to what constitutes a payment to enter a promotion given the on-line cost to the entrant, and what special precautions need to be taken to guard against a finding that an entrant has paid to enter.

The peculiarities of the Internet must be taken into account in all on-line promotional rules. For example, it is sensible to restrict eligibility into Internet promotions to residents of countries where legal clearance has been obtained and to include choice of law and jurisdiction clauses in the rules which form the contract between the promoter and the entrants. A number of other special promotional rules will also need to be considered in light of the complexities inherent in the on-line environment.

LINKING AND FRAMING

8.21   More companies are taking advantage of the Internet to increase sales by promoting their own offerings, or for sponsorship or advertising revenue. It is not surprising then, that the question of how to protect the commercial value of websites has become the subject of recent legal claims both in the U.S. and the U.K. A clear answer is yet to emerge on whether traditional proprietary rights such as copyright and trade mark rights can be used to control information published to the world via the Internet. A frequent argument against such rights being enforceable on the Internet is that it stifles the free flow of information that up to now has been the Internet's unique characteristic. Those who hold this view assert that publication on the world wide web implies a licence to use and, perhaps most controversially, a licence to create links to other sites.

Linking is a feature of the Internet that is fundamental to its operation. For many commercial site operators seeking to reach as large an audience as possible, the ability to be found by search engines is all-important. Hyperlinks between sites are also commonplace. Hyperlinks are electronic pointers in a web page to other sites (or portions of

---

[48] See further para. 2.43 in Chapter 2 (Gaming).
[49] Lotteries are not defined under the 1976 Act but the courts have established the following criteria:-A lottery is the distribution of prizes by chance where the persons taking part, or a substantial number of them, make a payment or consideration in return for obtaining their chance of winning a prize. *Per* Lord Widgery C.J. in *Readers Digest Association Ltd v. William* 1976 3 All E.R. 737.

other sites) on the Web. A user may transfer from one site to another by clicking on highlighted text in the original site. Linking has benefits such as increasing the potential audience of a site but can also bring undesired results. The link may be to a specific item on the other site and cause browsers to bypass information or advertising that the site owner would have wished all visitors to the site to see. This could potentially diminish the ability of the site to convey the desired message. It could also affect the potential advertising revenue from the site if it carries third party adverts or affects sponsorship arrangements.

Recent cases in the U.S. and U.K. courts have tested the ability of site operators to object to unauthorised links on the basis that hyperlinks on the web may infringe copyright, trademark or related business reputation rights.   **8.22**

The *Shetland Times* case[50] is the closest there is to a U.K. authority on the subject. This case considered whether the creation of unauthorised links constitutes a breach of copyright. It is a case under Scottish law but the decision of the court was based on copyright legislation common to England, Scotland and Wales. The interim decision of the court found that the linking was a breach of copyright, on the grounds that it constituted an infringement of copyright in a cable programme as defined by the Copyright, Designs and Patents Act 1988. This basis is somewhat artificial because, on a straightforward analysis, linking does not actually involve copying. The case settled before the Court of Appeal. The case does, however, provide an indication of the attitude of the U.K. courts on the question of copyright infringement by hypertext links.

The U.S. courts have also seen claims for breach of copyright, trademark dilution and unfair competition as a result of unauthorised linking. Again, a case is yet to go to full trial leaving the law in an uncertain state. In the *TicketMaster v. Microsoft* case,[51] TicketMaster have asserted that a formal agreement was necessary before another company could offer a link to its site. TicketMaster had sought such an agreement with Microsoft. When no agreement was reached in negotiations, Microsoft decided to create an unauthorised link in any case. TicketMaster claim that the unauthorised link affected the value of its own sponsorship by companies such as MasterCard and diverted browsers from its pages containing advertising. It also claims that Microsoft was able to attract advertising to their site because of the link to the TicketMaster content — a Seattle event guide. TicketMaster's Chief Executive puts his argument in simple terms: **8.23**

> "The advertising and promotional component of the web will far exceed the transactional — why should they (Microsoft) get the benefit of the advertising when the money is mine?"[52]

Interestingly the claim does not mention copyright infringement but is based on claims of misrepresentation of a business link between the parties, trademark dilution and unfair competition. Until the issue is finally resolved, "deeplinking" into the website of a third party is to be avoided. Linking to a third party's home page may be less risky.

Another recent U.S. claim resulted from the use of so-called framing technology which operates so that the title of the page and other windows (often containing advertising)   **8.24**

---

[50] *Shetland Times Limited v. Wills*, (1997) F.S.R. 604 (OH).
[51] (1997) US case No. 97–3055 DDP.
[52] *Wall Street Journal*, April 28, 1997.

remain static while the user browses linked sites through the frames. The URL of the linked site is often obscured. In the case of *Futuredontics, Inc. v. Applied Anagramatics*,[53] Futerdontics (whose on-line dental referral pages were referenced by the defendant's link within a frame) claimed breach of copyright and unfair competition. The preliminary hearing did not dismiss the claim but did not grant an injunction as the Scottish court did in the *Shetland Times* case.

So, given the uncertain state of the law, what are the options open to an electronic commerce business which wishes to prevent or stop unauthorised linking or framing? Website operators may prevent hyper-linking in the first place by introducing a registration system with passwords so that only authorised users providing details when accessing via the home page will be given access. However, the technology may be expensive and the effect may be to reduce the potential audience. In the U.K. the site operator could threaten a copyright infringement action on the basis of the *Shetland Times* case. Although it is not settled law it may act as a sufficient deterrent. In addition, the Internet Service Provider (ISP) hosting the offending site could be notified. The ISP's contract with the website operator should give it the right to take action — which may include pulling the offending site altogether if it does not co-operate in the event of a legal challenge. Failing that, litigation is the only option but, given the current legal uncertainty, cannot be guaranteed to deliver the desired result. Early indications are, however, that the courts will protect the commercial interests of site operators marking the way for even more Internet promotion, advertising and sponsorship.

---

[53] (1998) 45 U.S.P.Q 2d (BNA) 2005.

— • 9 • —

TAXATION OF ELECTRONIC COMMERCE

> Walking to a voice that was music, the platinum terminal piping melodically, endlessly, speaking of numbered Swiss accounts, of payment to be made to Zion via a Bahamian orbital bank, or passports and passages and of deep and basic changes to be effected in the memory of Turing[1]

INTRODUCTION

The fact that trading is achieved electronically, rather than by other means should, in principle, make no difference from a tax point of view. The U.K. tax system (and other tax systems worldwide) are designed to tax trading whatever its form. The application of existing tax laws to electronic commerce is, however, not that straightforward. All the characteristics of electronic commerce mean that taxpayers, tax practitioners and tax authorities need to pay special attention to tax. This chapter explains how electronic commerce fits into the current U.K. tax system and identifies a number of issues that businesses may need to examine further. Inevitably, it deals with many complex areas of tax law only in summary.

9.01

The following paragraphs explain why the characteristics of electronic commerce make tax such a focus of attention.

Intangibility

Tax law has developed in response to, what are now, established methods of conducting business. Many tax provisions exist because of the significance physical structures have had and will continue to have in commerce. There is an element of maturity in such tax provisions and in related case law, reflecting, perhaps, that whatever can be done to make a profit from, for example, land and buildings has been tried (and taxed). In contrast, the intangible nature of electronic commerce places greater emphasis on, for example, how intellectual property is taxed. There has been concern for some time that the U.K. tax system could improve the way it deals with intellectual property.[2] In broad

9.02

---

[1] William Gibson, Neuromancer.

[2] The Intellectual Property Institute, London started a review of the taxation of intellectual property in 1995. More recently, the "Innovating for the future" consultation exercise concluded a rational and less complex system for the taxation of intellectual property is required (Joint D.T.I. and H.M. Treasury consultation document, March 1998).

terms, different categories of intellectual property have different treatments. The tax treatment of, for example, trademarks is different from that of patents. Electronic commerce places new focus on the intricacies and possible inadequacies of intellectual property taxation.

Flexibility

9.03   The flexibility of electronic commerce raises many issues. The scope for a business to adapt and evolve rapidly may mean that tax classifications change and with them the tax treatment of the business or aspects of it. What starts off as a trading business could evolve into an investment business. Different tax rules apply to these two activities, particularly regarding the deduction of expenses in computing taxable income. From a value added tax point of view it can be important to establish whether a business is supplying goods or services. What is supplied could be goods (such as a book) or it could be a service (the supply of information by electronic means). Electronic commerce brings these two categories closer together. The scope for someone to work at home or on the move will make it harder to decide whether workers are employed or self-employed. The Inland Revenue's preference is for individuals to be employees because tax is then deducted at source by employers under the 'Pay As You Earn' system. The scope for businesses to work together, means it is harder for a sole trader to recognise when his business has evolved into a trading partnership, which has tax consequences in addition to other legal consequences.

Many tax rules assume that a trade is of a permanent nature. However, the flexibility of electronic commerce will mean that, in tax terms, there may be a number of trades conducted by one business at one time and, indeed, there could be a succession of different trades. Tax practitioners may struggle to keep up with the tax compliance consequences of starting up and discontinuing a number of trades.

International

9.04   Electronic commerce will, inevitably, involve international considerations. A business based entirely in the U.K. with only U.K. employees, equipment, customers, distributors and suppliers, can make the safe assumption that is does not have to consider any overseas tax implications. Electronic commerce requires a business to understand, in more detail, when it faces exposure to overseas taxation and the prospect of double taxation. Double tax treaties provide rules to deal with a business trading from an office, factory or other permanent establishment overseas but make no express reference to, for example, web servers.

Anonymous

9.05   Characteristics of the recipient of a payment or of a supply can make a tax difference. The value added tax system, in particular, requires a business to identify whether or not a customer is a private customer or a business customer. The scope for anonymity with electronic commerce makes it harder to distinguish one sort of customer from another. The potential for anonymity also, inevitably, raises concerns with tax authorities that electronic commerce will be used as a means of tax evasion or money laundering.

Novelty

9.06   The current novelty of electronic commerce also adds to the need to pay particular attention to tax.

OVERVIEW

The following paragraphs provide an overview of the taxation of electronic commerce **9.07** and show that, in broad terms, electronic commerce is as subject to taxation as other forms of commerce. This can be seen clearly when the internet is used as a method of buying and selling goods, particularly in a domestic context.

9.08

Example
The Smith family have sold toys from their high street shop for many years. Mr and Mrs Smith continue to own and manage the family shop in partnership. In an attempt to compete with the large international and national toy retailers, the shop has recently been redesigned as a "childhood experience". The shop aims to create a nostalgic experience for parents and grandparents whilst retaining a magical atmosphere for children. Demand for toys can arise overnight particularly following the launch of a new film or other merchandising opportunity. Mr & Mrs Smith's son, Douglas Smith, discovered using the Internet that he could locate supplies of the latest toys, often before his family's usual suppliers could obtain such toys. Douglas therefore set up his own business. Using his family's contacts through the local Chamber of Commerce (and a copy of its e-mail address list), Douglas found several busy executives who were prepared to pay a premium price for new products for their children. Douglas conducts his business by e-mail and has built up an impressive customer list. He now employs a friend part time to research the toy market and identify new developments. Douglas works mainly from inside the family shop. He sits in the "New Millennium" section of the shop with his lap-top.
Mr and Mrs Smith pay U.K. *income tax* on their partnership profits. The Partnership is *VAT* registered. *PAYE* is operated on the wages paid to the shop assistants. *Business rates* are paid on the shop.
Douglas pays U.K. *income tax* on his profits. He is *VAT* registered and operates *PAYE* on the salary of his employee. He defers payment of *import duties* (and *VAT*) on toys imported from South East Asia under the duty deferment scheme.

The U.K. tax system is also, in broad terms, just as applicable when the internet is the source of the business, as well as the means to conduct business.

The following paragraphs look at:

- Taxation of trading profits
- VAT
- PAYE and national insurance
- Business rates
- Customs duties

There are various points in relation to the taxation of trading profits and VAT that require more detailed consideration. This is provided in paragraphs 9.41 *et seq.* and 9.72

et seq. below. Various tax issues related to starting a new business (and expanding it) are covered in paragraphs 9.50 *et seq.*

Taxation of trading profits[3]

9.09   Trade is defined to include "every trade, manufacture, adventure or concern in the nature of trade".[4] Trade is therefore widely defined and it appears that any commercial transaction[5] is taxable as a trade. A Royal Commission in 1955 identified six "badges of trade". Three badges emphasise trading in goods (the subject matter of the realisation, the length of the period of ownership of the property to be dealt in and supplementary work on or in connection with the property realised) but the remaining three badges (the frequency or number of similar transactions by the same person, the circumstances that were responsible for the realisation and motive) are of more general application. This chapter assumes there is a trade, although the versatility of the electronic commerce means there may be a number of borderline cases.[6]

Income tax is charged on the profits of:

- any person residing in the U.K. from any trade whether carried on in the U.K. or elsewhere, and

- any person, although not resident in the U.K., from any trade exercised within the U.K.

The profits of a profession or vocation are subject to U.K. income tax in similar circumstances.

Tax is charged under Schedule D.[7]

If a U.K. tax resident company carries on a trade it will pay corporation tax on its worldwide trading profits, not income tax. If a non-U.K. tax resident company conducts trade within the U.K. the profits will be subject to U.K. tax although the tax charged depends on whether or not the trade is conducted through a branch or agency. If it is corporation tax applies; if not, income tax.

Whatever business structure exists, the key issues are:

- is a tax resident involved? and

- in the case of a non-resident, is the trade carried on within the U.K.?

These issues are considered below together with what amounts to a branch or agency. There is also a summary of how tax on trading profits is administered. It will be apparent from the above that if someone is U.K. tax resident it will not, usually, serve

---

[3] The legislation relating to income tax corporation tax and capital gains tax including statutory instruments and supplementary mterials such as extra-statutory concessions and statements of practice is published in Butterworths Yellow Tax Handbook Parts I and II.

[4] T.A. [1988] s.832(1).

[5] Lord Radcliffe in *Edwards v. Bairstow and Harrison* 36 T.C. 207 at 230 and Lord Reid in *Ransom v. Higgs*, 50 T.C. 1 at 78.

[6] A profit motive is not essential (*Torbell Investments Ltd v. Williams* [1986] S.T.C. 397) but the impossibility of making profit may prevent there being a trade (*Religious Tract and Book Society of Scotland v. Forbes* (1896) 3 T.C. 415.

[7] Schedule D in T.A. [1988] s.18.

any useful purpose to argue a trade is conducted outside the U.K., in "cyber-space".[8] As. a tax resident, trading profits wherever arising fall to be taxed under Schedule D.[9] In the case of a non-resident, electronic commerce does offer scope to avoid a U.K. tax charge on trading profits, even though customers are based in the U.K. Even if a tax charge arises under domestic law, the non-resident may be able to claim the protection of a double tax treaty (see paragraphs 9.64 *et seq.*).

Tax resident

The following provides an outline of the U.K.'s approach to determining tax residency: **9.10**

(1) *Individuals:*

There is no statutory definition of a tax resident, although there are some statutory   **9.11** provisions involved in determining whether or not someone is U.K. resident.[10] The Inland Revenue's understanding of relevant law and practice is set out as regards individuals in its leaflet IR20. The following are the main rules:

- someone physically present in the U.K. for 183 days or more (ignoring days of arrival and departure) in a tax year (April 6 to April 5) is tax resident in that tax year;

- an individual who moves from abroad to live in the U.K. permanently or at least remain here for three years or more is accepted as tax resident from the date of arrival;

- an individual who visits the U.K. regularly who after four tax years has visits that average 91 days or more each tax year is tax resident from the fifth tax year;

- an individual coming to the U.K. for a purpose (*e.g.* work) that will mean he remains here for at least two years is treated as tax resident from the date of arrival until the date of departure;

- someone leaving the U.K. to work full time abroad under one or more contracts of employment can be treated as not resident from the day after departure[11];

- someone leaving the U.K. permanently or for at least three years can be treated as not resident from the day after departure[12];

- by concession[13] an individual may be treated as a non resident for part of a tax year (*i.e.* the period after arrival in the U.K. or the period before departure from the U.K.).

---

[8] However, in the case of a non-U.K. *domiciled* tax resident conducting a trade wholly abroad see paragraph 9.63 below.

[9] Tax is charged under Case I of Schedule D (Case II for professions or vocations). If a trade is carried on wholly abroad then profits are assessable under Case V not Case I (*Colquhoun v. Brooks* (1889) 2 T.C. 490).

[10] *e.g.* T.A. [1988] ss.334–336.

[11] Paragraph 2.2 of IR 20 sets out the conditions. In particular, visits to the U.K. must average less than 91 days a tax year.

[12] Paragraphs 2.8–2.10 of IR 20 set out the conditions. In particular, return visits must average less than 91 days a tax year.

[13] Extra-statutory concession A11.

Improvements in international travel, combined with developments in technology allowing someone to work wherever they are, mean many individuals living in the U.K. spend considerable periods outside the U.K. However, the above rules make it diffficult for someone to cease U.K. tax residency for income tax purposes without taking up permanent residence or full-time work abroad.

(2). *Corporations:*

9.12　A company incorporated in the U.K. is automatically tax resident in the U.K.[14] A company incorporated outside the U.K. is U.K. tax resident if the U.K. is the place where "central management and control" actually resides. This latter test of residency arises from case law.[15] Under this test a company is usually accepted as resident where the board of directors meet. This may well be different from the place of business operations and the countries in which directors and shareholders reside. The Inland Revenue, mindful, of the scope for board members to act as "little more than cyphers" for a controlling individual, will look to see where and by whom central management and control is actually exercised, rather than necessarily accept a company resides where its board meets.[16] The case law test is not easy to apply to directors located around the world who "meet" by international conference calls or video links. Until law or practice develops, boards of overseas companies that wish to remain non-U.K. resident are advised to meet in person and make decisions at a suitable location outside the U.K. If such an overseas company would be treated as resident in the U.K. under this case law test but as non-resident under the terms of an appropriate double taxation treaty then it will be treated as non-resident for all U.K. tax purposes.[17]

(3) *Partnerships:*

9.13　Trading partnerships are resident where the control and management of the trade is located.[18] This is the test and not the resident status of the partners in the partnership.

(4) *Trustees:*

9.14　A trust can also be used for trading. If all the trustees are non-resident, the trust will be accepted as non-resident. If all are U.K. resident, the trust will be U.K. resident.

Where trustees have mixed residence status they will be treated as U.K. residents if the settlor was resident, ordinarily resident[19] or domiciled[20] in the U.K. at any time when he settled property in the trust.[21] There are separate rules for capital gains tax purposes.

Trade within the U.K.

9.15　A non-U.K. resident is liable to U.K. tax on profits of a trade exercised *within* the U.K. If all that happens is trade *with* the U.K. (*i.e.* with U.K. customers) then this is insufficient to come within the tax charge. If a non-resident wishes to avoid U.K. tax then care must

---

[14] F.A. [1988] s.66.
[15] *De Beers Consolidated Mines Ltd v. Howe* 5 T.C. 198 at 212.
[16] S.P. 1/90.
[17] F.A. 1994, s.249.
[18] T.A. [1988] s.110.
[19] An individual is ordinarily resident in the U.K. if he is "resident here year after year" (Inland Revenue Inspectors Manual, I.M. 35).
[20] See para. 9.63.
[21] F.A. [1989] s.110.

be taken to limit what happens in the U.K., so as to avoid trading within the U.K. Someone visiting customers in the U.K. and signing sales contracts in the U.K. will be trading within the U.K., even if the goods or services are then provided from outside the U.K. The internet, of course, makes it easier to distribute information and solicit orders without visiting the U.K. The most important factor, however, is the place where contracts are made.[22] If this is the U.K. then there is trading within the U.K.[23] Even if sales contracts are made outside the U.K., the trade could still be exercised within the U.K. if there is sufficient connection in other ways to the U.K.[24]

If contracts are made outside the U.K. the interesting issue, in the context of electronic commerce, is the extent to which equipment sited in the U.K. creates an exposure to U.K. tax. The fact that there is equipment in the U.K. does not necessarily mean there is trading in the U.K. An overseas company can have a U.K. office (a representative office) without creating a U.K. tax liability.[25] It is the nature of what happens in the U.K. that is significant. The Inland Revenue attaches much importance to Lord Atkin's approach in the *Smidth (FL) & Co. v. Greenwood* case and has adopted as the principal criteria for determining whether there is trading in the U.K. The test of "where do the operations take place from which the profits in substance arise?" A non-resident company contracted overseas to provide the services of a property consultant who lived in the U.K. As his activities in the U.K. were the essential operations of the company it was subject to U.K. tax.[26] If a non-resident has equipment in the U.K. it is necessary to analyse the functions of that equipment and, by analogy with existing case law, determine if those functions amount to trading in the U.K.

The mere buying of goods in the U.K. (*i.e.* for sale abroad) does not amount to trading in the U.K.[27] If the equipment relays information to customers without any payment for that information then this not amount to trading in the U.K. The equipment could provide an electronic "shop window" in the U.K. For a non-resident trader and even the relaying of electronic enquiries from potential customers to the non-resident will not amount to trading in the U.K.[28] However, if a server in the U.K. provides information to paying customers then this could be considered an essential (and taxable) operation in the U.K. When services are provided by non-residents the Inland Revenue tends to give greater weight to the place where the service is provided (rather than the place where the contract is made).[29] In the case of transmission services the service is considered given where the transmission begins.[30] This is based on a case involving the relaying of telegraph messages, although in that case contracts were made in the U.K.[31]

9.16

If a non-resident uses an agent in the U.K. to accept orders or otherwise habitually make contracts on his behalf, then this also amounts to trading in the U.K. by the non-

---

[22] See Chapter 3.
[23] *Grainger & Son v. Gough*, 3 T.C. 462.
[24] *Firestone Tyre and Rubber Co. Ltd v. Lewellin* 37 T.C. 111, 142.
[25] *Smidth (FL) & Co. v. Greenwood*, 8 T.C. 193.
[26] *IRC v. Brackett* [1986] S.T.C. 521.
[27] *Sulley v. A.G.*, 2 T.C. 149.
[28] See the discussion on identifying profit producing activities in the Inland Revenue International Tax Handbook (I.T.H. 827).
[29] Inland Revenue International Tax Handbook, I.T.H. 826.
[30] *ibid.*
[31] *Erichsen v. Last*, 4 T.C. 422.

resident.[32] Even if contracts are made abroad, the use of a U.K. agent can bring the trading profits within the scope of U.K. tax.[33] Again, by analogy, if equipment belonging to independent Internet service providers or other third parties is used to make contracts in the U.K., or provides the service which is to yield a profit[34] then there is a risk that such activities come within the scope of U.K. tax, under domestic law.

9.17   In the case of a non-resident company trading in the U.K., the tax charged is corporation tax if the trade is carried on through a "branch or agency".[35] If there is no branch or agency then income tax applies but only at the basic rate. This is because the higher rate only applies to individuals. This distinction is, of course, easier to make if there is an office, other premises or appointed agent in the U.K. In the case of supplying goods over the internet, such a presence may well exist. If the internet is used to supply services this is less likely. It is difficult to see how independent internet service providers, routers and so on, can be categorised as a branch or agent, but the law is unclear. If there is a trade conducted in the U.K. by a non-resident company then, possibly, there must be a U.K. branch or agent?[36]

If care is taken over where contracts are made and where profit earning activities take place then both companies and other non-residents can avoid U.K. tax on trading profits. In practice though, there will no doubt be many who are oblivious to the significance of, in particular, the place of making contracts, who will as a matter of domestic law be conducting taxable trading in the U.K.

If the non-resident is based in a country that does not have a double tax treaty with the U.K., then tax liability is determined by the above rules. If there is a tax treaty then protection from U.K. tax may be provided if there is no "permanent establishment" in the U.K. This possibility is considered below in paragraph 9.66.

If a non-resident conducts trading activities wholly or partly in the U.K., double tax treaties also provide assistance in determining what profit gets taxed in the U.K. Domestic law has no express provisions dealing with this issue. The emphasis in case law on the place of making sales contracts suggests an "all or nothing" approach (so, if there is a U.K. sales contract, all the profit is taxable in the U.K. even if all or part of the performance of the contract occurs outside the U.K.). The Inland Revenue does, however, accept that an "Arm's length" principle applies under domestic law and so a non-resident can argue that economic activity outside the U.K. should be excluded from U.K. tax.[37]

Computation of trading profits

9.18   A trader must make a tax return in respect of the trade to the Inland Revenue and pay tax in accordance with the provisions of the Taxes Management Act 1970. Every individual, trustee (and personal representative) is obliged to deliver to the Inland Revenue by January 31 following the tax year a tax return incorporating the taxpayer's

---

[32] See, for example, *Erichsen v. Last* 4 T.C. 422.
[33] *Lovell and Christmas Ltd v. Taxes Commissioner* [1908] A.C. 46.
[34] *ibid.* 53.
[35] T.A. [1988] s.11(1).
[36] See the discussion in Inland Revenue International Tax Handbook, I.T.H. pp. 843 *et seq.*
[37] I.T.H. 857.

self-assessment. Tax is payable on account on January 31 during the tax year and July 31 following the tax year. The balance of tax payable is due on January 31 following the tax year. Self-assessment also now applies to companies.[38] There are procedures for the electronic lodgement of tax returns.[39] Taxpayers' records may, with limited exceptions, be kept as electronic capies of the originals.[40]

An electronic trader has to satisfy the same conditions as any other trader to deduct expenses in computing taxable profits. A deduction is not automatically available because it has been made in computing profits for accounts purposes. The main requirements are that the expenditure is:

(a) wholly and exclusively for the purposes of the trade[41];
(b) revenue expenditure not capital expenditure; and
(c) not expressly disallowed by statute.[42]

Some expenditure is expressly allowed as tax-deductible by statute provided conditions set out in the relevant statutory provisions are satisfied. There are several such provisions relevant to technology.[43]   **9.19**

If expenditure is of a capital nature then a deduction may still be available in computing taxable profits but under the capital allowances regime. Capital allowances are available on certain types of capital expenditure for the purposes of a trade. The full amount of a trading expense is deductible in computing profits. Although so-called 100 per cent allowances are available for some capital expenditure,[44] normally only a proportion of the capital cost is allowed. It is therefore generally better for expenditure to be tax-deductible as a trading expense. If the expenditure qualifies neither as a trading expense nor for capital allowances then no deduction in computing trading profits is available.

The above general principles are explained in more detail below (see paragraphs 9.41 *et seq.*) in respect of expenditure on computer software, trademarks, plant and machinery and goodwill.

VAT[45]

Europe (as defined for VAT purposes) has a common system of value added tax (VAT)   **9.20**
with a uniform basis of assessment.[46] Hundreds of millions of consumers throughout the European Community are familiar with VAT as an extra cost of buying goods and

---

[38] F.A. [1998] s.117.
[39] T.M.A. [1970] Schedule 3A and see SP1/97. The Inland Revenue's Business Support Team can provide additional information (telephone: 01274–539301).
[40] T.M.A. [1970] s.12B.
[41] T.A. [1988] s.74(1)(a).
[42] See, in particular, T.A. [1988] s.74 (general rules as to deductions not allowable), s.577 (business extertaining expenses) and s.827 (VAT penalties etc).
[43] See, for example, T.A. [1988] s.83 (patent fees etc and expenses), s.84 (gifts to educational establishments), s.120 (rent etc. payable in respect of electric line wayleaves) C.A.A. [1990] s.136 (allowances for expenditures on scientific research not of a capital nature, and on payments to research associations, universities etc.).
[44] C.A.A. [1998] s.1 (buildings and structures in enterprise zones) and s.137 (allowances for capital expenditure on scientific research).
[45] The legislation relating to VAT, including statutory instruments, E.C. legislation and supplementary materials is published in Butterworth's Orange Tax Handbook.
[46] See, in particular, the Sixth Council Directive (77/388/EEC).

services. Millions of business owners are familiar with VAT as an extra administrative burden.

From a U.K. perspective, VAT is charged on the following:

(a) on the supply of goods or services in the U.K.;
(b) on the acquisition of goods in the U.K. from other Member States; and
(c) on the importation of goods from places outside the Member States.

These charges, particularly the first, are wide in scope and mean that VAT is as applicable to electronic commerce as it is to other forms of commerce. Each of the above VAT charges is explained in more detail in the following sections together with an outline of how VAT is administered by a VAT registered business. All the characteristics of electronic commerce, particularly its international dimension make it likely that some of the more complex aspects of the VAT system will apply.

Supplies of goods or services in the U.K.

9.21   VAT is charged on:

(a) a supply;
(b) of goods or services;
(c) which is a taxable supply;
(d) made in the U.K.;
(e) by a taxable person;
(f) in the course or furtherance of a business.

Supply

9.22   Supply for VAT purposes is a word of the widest import.[47] A supply, for VAT purposes, does exclude anything done otherwise than for a consideration. If internet users are not charged then, as a general rule, there is no supply for VAT purposes. The activity is said to be outside the scope of VAT.

Consideration, however, also takes a wide meaning. Consideration can obviously be in the form of money but can be found in something other than money.[48] A barter transaction involves supplies by both parties for consideration. The exchange of information over the internet could involve supplies for VAT purposes. Case law suggests there must be a direct link between what is provided and the consideration received.[49] The central feature of consideration can be seen as reciprocity.

The wide definition of supply means many users of the internet may be involved in making supplies for VAT purposes without realising it. There can still be a supply even though no profit is made on a transaction.

Certain events are treated as supplies for VAT purposes. This includes the receipt of certain services from abroad. These are services described in Schedule 5 to the Value Added Tax Act 1994.

---

[47] Griffiths J. in *CEC v. Oliver* [1980] S.T.C. 73 at 74 and see VATA [1994] s.55(2)(a) ("supply" . . . includes all forms of supply).
[48] VATA [1994] s.19.
[49] Fox L.J. in *Apple and Pear Development Council v. CEC* [1985] S.T.C. 383, 389 and see also the same case at [1988] S.T.C. 221.

Schedule 5 Services, include:

- Transfers and assignments of copyrights, patents, licences, trademarks and similar rights;
- Advertising services;
- Services of consultants, engineers, consultancy bureaux, lawyers, accountants and other similar services, data processing and provisions of information (but excluding from this head any services relating to land);
- Banking, financial and insurance services (including reinsurance, but not including the provision of safe deposit facilities);
- Telecommunications services, that is to say services relating to the transmission, emission or reception of signals, writing, images and sounds or information of any nature by wire, radio, optical or other electromagnetic systems, including the transfer of assignment or the right to use capacity for such transmission, emission or reception.

If Schedule 5 services are received from abroad by someone in the U.K. who uses them for business purposes, then what is known as the "reverse charge" applies. The significance of this and other aspects of Schedule 5 services are explained below. The U.K. business customer must account for VAT as if it had made the supply. This mechanism ensures that U.K. suppliers are not unfairly disadvantaged as compared with non-U.K. suppliers. The Government is considering the possible extension of the reverse charge procedure to take account of the growth in services over the Internet. **9.23**

Goods or services?

If a supply is made the next step from a VAT point of view is to establish whether it is a supply of goods, or of services, or of neither. The latter category is outside the scope of VAT. There are complex rules to categorise supplies. Goods means tangible, moveable goods. If the whole property in goods is transferred there is a supply of goods. **9.24**

Other less obvious transactions amount to the supply of goods. The supply of any form of power, heat, or refrigeration is a supply of goods.[50]

It is the definition of services that is particularly wide. Anything which is not a supply of goods but is done for a consideration (including, if so done, the granting assignment or surrender of any right) is a supply of services.

VAT classification of software provides a useful introduction to the distinction between goods and services.[51] In the case of off-the-shelf software products (so called normalised products) if one price is charged for the package (*e.g.* containing the CD–ROM or floppy disks carrying the software and any brochures) this is treated as a supply of goods. However, H.M. Customs & Excise accept that if separate charges are made for the software and the carrier medium then two supplies are made; one of services and one of goods. If bespoke software is commissioned its supply is generally **9.25**

---

[50] Article 5 paragraph 2 of the Sixth Directive states "Electric current, gas, heat, refrigeration and the like shall be considered tangible property". The internet's use of electric current does not, however, turn supplies over the internet into supplies of goods.
[51] H.M. Customs & Excise Notice 702/4/94 (importing computer software).

treated as entirely a supply of services. The carrier medium element is ignored as incidental.

In the case of audio or video recordings, as a general rule, H.M. Customs & Excise consider there to be a supply of goods.

Unless the internet is used as the medium to buy goods then electronic commerce will invariably involve supplies of services.

9.26   H.M. Customs & Excise tried unsuccessfully to argue that the use of a computer ordering system changed the nature of the supply (of sandwiches) from that of goods to one of a supply of services.[52]

The distinction from the customer's point of view between receiving a supply of goods and receiving a supply of services does appear marginal in respect of many internet supplies. VAT legislation describes the transfer and assignment of copyright, patents, licences, trademarks and similar rights as supplies of services. The guidance issued by H.M. Customs and Excise makes it clear that this does not apply to transfers of normalised products by way of a physical medium. However, increasingly the computer disk, CD–ROM or other such medium is an immaterial part of the transaction. When copyright material is downloaded from a website it is clearly a supply of services and not of goods and yet the VAT treatment can be very different.[53]

Taxable supplies

9.27   Supplies of goods and services made for a consideration are categorised for the purposes of charging VAT as either taxable supplies or exempt supplies.

The standard rate of VAT in the U.K. is 17.5 per cent. There is currently a reduced rate of 5 per cent for supplies of domestic fuel and power. Some supplies are zero rated.[54] All these supplies are generally classified as taxable supplies. However, in the case of zero rated supplies, such as sales of books or children's clothing, the purchaser does not actually pay VAT because it is charged at 0 per cent. This categorisation (and also that of an exempt supply) is significant from the point of view of VAT registered businesses as explained below.

Goods exported outside the Member States are zero-rated, as are goods exported to a business customer in another Member State. H.M. Customs & Excise state that the storage and dissemination of textual information in non-printed formats (*e.g.* electronically) does not qualify for zero-rating.[55]

Certain categories of supply are expressly stated to be exempt from VAT.[56] Purchasers of domestic property and certain financial and educational supplies do not, therefore, pay VAT because these supplies are not taxable supplies on which VAT is charged. Electronic data services which provide financial news or share price movements are not exempt suppliers.

A taxable supply will, however, only be charged to VAT if it is made in the U.K., by a taxable person in the course or furtherance of a business. All these conditions must be

---

[52] *Emphasis Ltd* [1995] V.A.D.R. 419.
[53] Goods imported from outside the Member States are charged to VAT on entry into the E.C. In contrast, services supplied from outside the E.C. to a private customer are not subject to VAT.
[54] V.A.T.A. [1994] Sched. 8.
[55] H.M. Customs & Excise Notice 701/10/85 (printed and similar matter).
[56] V.A.T.A. [1994] Sched. 9.

met, otherwise the taxable supply will be outside the scope of VAT. There is no VAT charged on supplies that are outside the scope.

Made in the U.K.

In the case of goods, if there is no removal of the goods to or from the U.K., then the rule **9.28** to determine the place of supply is straightforward. A supply of goods is made in the U.K. if the goods are situated in the U.K. and it is made outside the U.K. if the goods are situated outside the U.K. The use of the internet as a means of buying and selling goods will not, in itself, alter where the goods are located and will not therefore alter the place of supply. It may, however, make it more likely that goods are removed to or from the U.K., with the access it provides to the international marketplace.

Goods removed to the U.K. are supplied in the U.K. if they are installed or assembled in the U.K. Also, as explained below, if goods are imported from outside the Member States and, in some cases, if the distance selling provisions apply[57] on goods brought into the U.K., there will be supplies made in the U.K.

Goods exported are as a general rule considered as supplies made in the U.K. (but as **9.29** mentioned above zero-rating can apply). However if, for example, goods are installed or assembled in the country to which they are removed, then the supply is made outside the U.K. and therefore outside the scope of U.K. VAT. If the goods are removed to another Member State and supplied there to someone who is not registered for VAT then the supply may be treated as made in that other Member State. This is under the local equivalent of the distance selling provisions (see further in paragraph 9.54 below).

The general rule for services is that they are supplied in the country where the supplier belongs.

A supplier belongs in the U.K. if:

(1) he has a U.K. business establishment or some other fixed establishment and no such establishment elsewhere;
(2) he has such establishments both in the U.K. and elsewhere but the U.K. establishment is the one most directly concerned with the supply; or
(3) he has no such establishments (in the U.K. or elsewhere) but his usual place of residence is in the U.K.

A company or other person carrying on business through a branch or agency in the U.K. is treated as having a U.K. business establishment. Any company incorporated in the U.K. will have a place of residence in the U.K. These rules raise similar issues to those discussed in the context of non-residents trading in or with the U.K. An establishment has been described as requiring "a sufficient minimum strength in the form of the presence of the human *and* technical resources necessary for supplying specific services".[58] It is therefore possible to argue that equipment on its own does not amount to a business establishment. Electronic commerce clearly provides scope either to avoid a U.K. establishment or to ensure that a non-U.K. establishment is most directly concerned with making the supply.

---

[57] See paragraphs 9.54 *et seq.*
[58] *Berkholz v. Finanzamt Hamburg — Mitte-Altstadt* [1985] 3 C.M.L.R. 667 (a case involving gaming machines on ferries).

9.30   The general place of supply rule for services is, however, altered in respect of certain types of supply. The reverse charge, mentioned above, involves treating certain supplies as made where the recipient belongs.[59] The place of supply of Schedule 5 services (see above) is where the recipient belongs in certain circumstances.[60]

There is a category of services that are treated as supplied where the services are performed. This category includes supplies of services that consist of cultural, artistic, sporting, scientific, educational or entertainment services.[61] Although such services could, on the face of it, be supplied electronically, the relevant statutory instrument makes it clear that such services are supplied where they are "physically carried out".[62]

There is a further special rule for telecommunication services. This term has the same meaning as for reverse charge purposes (see Schedule 5 above). This definition includes basic access to the Internet e-mail and Chatline facilities.[63] If the "effective use and enjoyment" of the telecommunication services takes place outside the E.C. then the supply is treated as made outside the U.K. More significantly, for suppliers of telecommunication services that belong outside the EC, supplies are treated as made in the U.K. to the extent that "effective use and enjoyment" of the telecommunication services takes place in the U.K.[64]

Taxable person

9.31   A taxable person is someone who is or is required to be registered for VAT purposes. (This aspect is considered in more detail in paragraph 9.52.)

In the course of furtherance of business

"Business" *includes* any trade, profession or vocation.[65] H.M. Customs and Excise suggest that, in VAT terms, business means any continuing activity which is mainly concerned with making supplies to other persons for a consideration.[66] Such activity must have a degree or frequency and scale and be continued over a period of time. Isolated transactions are not normally business for VAT purposes (in contrast to trading as defined for income tax and corporation tax purposes). If what would otherwise be a supply for VAT purposes (*e.g.* the supply of information over the Internet for payment) does not occur in the course or furtherance of a business, then VAT will not arise. However, what starts as essentially a hobby or recreation may, of course, develop into a business for VAT purposes.

Acquisitions of goods from other Member States[67]

9.32   VAT is also charged on the acquisition of goods from other Member States. A U.K. VAT registered business that receives goods from a business registered for VAT in another Member State will not be charged VAT by the supplier. Instead, it is the U.K. VAT

---

[59] V.A.T.A. [1994] s.8.
[60] S.I. 1992 No. 3121, para. 16 (and see paras 9.74 *et seq.* below).
[61] S.I. 1992 No. 3121, para. 15.
[62] See *British Sky Broadcasting Ltd v. CEC* [1994] VATTR 1.
[63] H.M. Customs & Excise Business Brief 22/97.
[64] See VAT Information Sheet 2/97.
[65] V.A.T.A. [1994] s.94(1).
[66] H.M. Customs & Excise Notice 700, para. 2.6 and see *CEC v. Lord Fisher* [1981] S.T.C. 238.
[67] V.A.T.A. [1994] s.2(1)(b).

registered business that must account for U.K. VAT. The rate of tax is the one applicable to those goods in the U.K. If the goods are normally zero rated then no VAT will be due.

Someone in the U.K. buying goods for non-business purposes would generally be charged VAT at the rate applicable in the supplier's member State. But in some cases, as explained in paragraph 9.54 below, a liability to register and account for U.K. VAT could arise instead.

An overseas supplier of goods in the U.K. may also have to register for U.K. VAT under the distance selling scheme. This applies if the overseas supplier is responsible for delivery of goods to persons who are not VAT registered. This possibility is also explained in more detail in paragraph 9.54 below.

Importation of goods from outside the Member States[68]

VAT is charged on the importation of goods from outside the E.C. Importation, for VAT purposes, has a special meaning, which is the act of bringing goods in from outside the E.C. This is in contrast to the *acquisition* of goods, which refers to bringing goods in from another Member State.

9.33

VAT on imports is charged at the same rate as if the goods had been supplied in the U.K., whether or not the person importing the goods is registered for VAT. VAT is charged in addition to any customs duty or other charges due. It is calculated last of all, on a value which includes such charges.

VAT on imports in the case of a U.K. [VAT registered] business is normally either paid outright on importation or later under duty deferment arrangements.[69]

There are special rules dealing with certain postal imports. A VAT registered business can account for VAT on consignments not exceeding £2,000 in the normal course of events on his VAT return (see below). This does not apply to Datapost packets not exceeding £2,000, on which VAT is due on delivery.[70]

Purchasers of goods over the Internet must therefore be prepared to deal with the payment of VAT (and other duties), even though the goods come from outside the E.C.

Input tax and output tax

In the U.K., a VAT registered business has to account to H.M. Customs & Excise for VAT it charges its customers (its output tax). If a customer is VAT registered and the supplies are for use in its business then the VAT it is charged is its input tax. A VAT registered person can, with some exceptions, reclaim input tax to the extent it relates to standard rated and zero rated supplies of that business (and certain other supplies.[71]) There is, however, no ability to recover input tax related to exempt supplies of that business or non-business activities.

9.34

Every VAT registered business has to submit regular VAT returns and account for any excess of output tax over input tax in relation to the return period. In this way, VAT is for most businesses an administrative exercise which involves passing on the cost of VAT to customers.

---

[68] V.A.T.A. [1994] s.2(1)(c).
[69] See further in paragraph 9.56.
[70] S.I. 1995/2518, reg. 122.
[71] V.A.T.A. [1994] s.26(2).

If input tax exceeds output tax then a repayment of VAT can be claimed by a VAT registered business. This will happen if the business makes only zero rated supplies to customers.

If a business only makes exempt supplies then it cannot register for VAT purposes and so cannot recover any input tax. If a business makes both taxable and exempt supplies then it is said to be partially exempt. Such a business is restricted in its ability to recover input tax. This is why the difference between making exempt supplies and zero rated supplies is important from the point of view of a business, although it makes little difference to the consumer.

It is the obligation of the supplier to charge VAT correctly.[72]

9.35   The VAT return has a section for accounting for VAT due on acquisitions. The same amount entered as VAT due on acquisitions can be recovered as input tax, subject to the restrictions on recovering input tax mentioned above.

VAT on imports can be recovered, subject to the normal rules, as input tax of the VAT registered business. It is claimed as input tax on the VAT return for the period in which the importation took place.

If a business with a turnover that is below the VAT registration threshold (see paragraph 9.52) imports goods for business purposes it can still opt to defer payment of VAT but it cannot recover VAT as input tax because it is not registered for VAT purposes.

In the case of overseas traders who are not registered for U.K. VAT, there is a system for obtaining refunds of VAT. There is one scheme for traders carrying on business in Member States and another for those in business in "third countries".[73]

A VAT registered business must (with limited exceptions) provide a tax invoice to every business customer.[74] Tax invoices provide the main evidence of input tax paid by VAT registered businesses. VAT records may be preserved by electronic means.[75]

Outside the scope

Some transactions are outside the scope of U.K. VAT, including:

- supplies other than for a consideration;
- supplies that are neither supplies of goods nor services;
- taxable supplies that are not made in the U.K.;
- taxable supplies that are not made by a taxable person or are not provided in the course or furtherance of a business.

Pay As You Earn

9.36   U.K. income tax is charged under Schedule E on the emoluments from any office or employment.[76] The Pay As You Earn (PAYE) system imposes a duty on an employer to account to the Inland Revenue once a month[77] for tax that the employer has (or ought to

---

[72] See further in paragraph 9.78.
[73] H.M. Customs & Excise Notice 723.
[74] See further in paragraph 9.77.
[75] See Notice 700, para. 8.1.
[76] T.A. [1988] s.19.
[77] Quarterly for certain employees.

have) deducted from payments to employees.[78] The PAYE system also imposes requirements on an employer in respect of reporting benefits in kind. Although, in theory, the main charge to income tax on employees is the charge under self-assessment, in practice most Schedule E tax is accounted for under the PAYE system. The PAYE system is also used to collect national insurance contributions. The following general issues should be noted:

Employed or self-employed?

There is often a strong preference on the part of some workers to be classified as self-employed because of the cash flow advantage and the greater scope to claim expenses as tax-deductible, although, in practice, the differences may be less worthwhile than imagined. In some cases, it may be advantageous to be an employee.[79] Nevertheless, technology now permits many work arrangements to be structured as instances of self-employment, rather than employment. There is no single test to establish whether or not someone is an employee. The full circumstances are considered. A useful approach is to ask if someone is in business on their own account.

9.37

Someone working from home (or where they choose), using their own equipment (PC, modem and so on) is clearly part of the way to establishing self employment.[80]

Who operates PAYE?

The PAYE system has evolved to try to ensure that whatever the payment arrnagements someone will operate PAYE on payments to an employee liable to take under Schedule E. An employer with a sufficient taxable presence in the U.K. must operate PAYE. An overseas company with a U.K. branch or agency will satisfy this requirement.[81] If the employee works for someone in the U.K. and the employer is outside the PAYE regulations the person for whom he works can be made to operate PAYE.[82]

9.38

Business rates

The U.K. has a system of business rates (non-domestic rating). In broad terms, occupiers of property used for business purposes pay amounts annually to the relevant local authority based on the rateable value of the property. The amount paid does not increase if the property is used to operate a 24 hour business (*e.g.* worldwide Internet trading).

9.39

Customs duties

Import duties are also (like VAT) E.C. regulated.[83] Duty is paid at the point of entry of goods into the E.C. according to the duties applicable under the H.M. Customs and Excise Integrated Tariff. The World Trade Organisation has ruled it will not impose

9.40

---

[78] T.A. [1988] ss.203 *et seq.*
[79] See, for example, T.A. [1988] ss.148 and 188(4) (tax free payments in connection with the termination of an employment).
[80] For more information on the relevant factors see Chapter 14 of Essential Law for the Tax Adviser published by The Chartered Institute of Taxation.
[81] *Clark v. Oceanic Contractors Inc.* [1983] S.T.C. 35.
[82] T.A. [1988] s.203C.
[83] Although the customs territory of the E.C. is different in some respects from that of the E.C. for VAT purposes (see H.M. Customs & Excise Notice 703).

customs duties on electronic transmissions.[84] Customs duties apply to goods. If goods are ordered electronically and delivered physically from outside the E.C. then customs duties will continue to apply at the appropriate rate for the product. However, "goods" supplied electronically from outside the E.C. will be treated as services and therefore be free of import duties. There are no plans to introduce additional import duties to electronic transmissions.

DIRECT TAXATION IN MORE DETAIL

The following paragraph considers miscellaneous points likely to be relevant to the taxation of the trading profits of electronic commerce.

Expenses

9.41   Many categories of expenditure related to conducting business electronically will be tax-deductible but, as illustrated in the following cases, care needs to be taken.

Trade marks

Royalties or periodic fees paid for the use of a trade mark in a trade should be tax-deductible against trading profits. This is on the basis they are revenue expenses incurred wholly and exclusively for the purposes of the trade.

However, in some cases, a licensee may instead have to claim a deduction against its total income (a so-called charge on income) rather than just against trading profits. As a condition for making such a claim, the licensee has to deduct tax from its payments and account for the tax deducted to the Inland Revenue. Payments subject to this regime are known as annual payments. Annual payments are explained further in paragraph 9.47. In broad terms, if the licensor provides services in connection with the trade mark then the annual payments regime should not apply.

Generally, the Inland Revenue does not expect the cost of creating a trade mark to be claimed as a tax deduction. The expectation is that a trade mark is an enduring asset and so expenditure on creating it is capital expenditure. No capital allowances are available for trade marks.

In contrast, fees paid and expenses incurred registering a trade mark (or renewing a registration) are tax-deductible. This is because of an express statutory right to a tax deduction.[85]

If it is clear that a trade mark will have a limited life then there may be scope to claim the creation costs as revenue expenditure. Revenue treatment may allow a 100 per cent deduction in the year of expenditure or, perhaps more likely, spread over the anticipated life of the trade mark.

Computer software

9.42   The Inland Revenue has published its views on the U.K. tax treatment of expenditure on computer software.[86] In response to concerns, a new provision was introduced into the Capital Allowances Act 1990 to provide for capital allowances on capital expenditure on a right to use or otherwise deal with computer software.[87]

---

[84] Declaration on global electronic commerce.
[85] T.A. [1988] s.83.
[86] Tax Bulletin November 1993.
[87] C.A.A. 1990, s.67A.

In summary, the position is as follows:

- software acquired under licence:

  — regular payments akin to a rental are revenue expenditure and the timing of deductions will be governed by accounting practice;

  — a lump sum payment for software expected to have a useful economic life of less than two years will be accepted as revenue expenditure (possibly also if, it will be useful, for a longer period but still provides only a sufficiently transitory benefit) and the timing of deductions will be governed by accounting practice;

  — a lump sum payment for software as a capital asset of the licensee's trade (*i.e.* it has a sufficiently enduring nature) will qualify for capital allowances.

- equipment acquired as a package:

  — the expenditure between hardware and software should be apportioned;

  — capital allowances under the ordinary plant and machinery rules will be due on the expenditure on hardware;

  — the treatment of the balance will depend on the above considerations.

- Software owned outright: whether the expenditure is capital or revenue depends on the economic function of the software in the trade as it does for licences acquired for lump sums.

Plant and machinery

There is no statutory definition of plant and machinery. As indicated above, expenditure on computer hardware, telecommunications and other equipment will generally qualify for capital allowances under the plant and machinery rules, although assets incorporated into a building or structure may fail to qualify. Plant is that with which the trade is carried on rather than the setting or premises in which it is carried on. There is a statutory list of assets that are treated as forming part of a building and are therefore excluded from qualifying as plant and machinery. The excluded assets include "mains services and systems of . . . electricity". However, it should be possible to establish that the following are plant:

9.43

- electrical systems provided mainly to meet the particular requirements of the trade or provided mainly to serve particular machinery or plant used for the purposes of the trade;
- powered systems of ventilation, air cooling or air purification; and any ceiling or floor comprised in such systems;
- computer and telecommunication systems (including their wiring or other links);
- sprinkler equipment and other equipment for extinguishing or containing fire;
- expenditure on the provision of pipelines or underground ducts or tunnels with a primary purpose of carrying utility conduits.[88]

---

[88] C.A.A. [1990] Schedule AA1 Tables 1 and 2, *Cole Bros Ltd v. Phillips* [1982] S.T.C. 307 and *Hunt v. Henry Quick Ltd* [1992] S.T.C. 633.

Goodwill

9.44   In commercial terms, goodwill is the value of a business over and above its net asset value. This is recognised as a capital asset for tax purposes. Expenditure on goodwill on, for example, the acquisition of a business as a going concern is therefore capital expenditure. Goodwill is not in itself within the categories of expenditure that qualify for capital allowances.

Traditionally, goodwill has been particularly associated with the location of business premises (*e.g.* public houses, restaurants, retail shops, cinemas, petrol stations). In such cases the value of the property interest will be taken to include goodwill. Electronic commerce will involve a greater emphasis on "free" goodwill, which is separate from the value of any premises and arises from how the business is carried on, not where it is carried on.

It may be possible to achieve a revenue deduction for expenditure on goodwill, if instead of acquiring goodwill outright, regular payments are made for the use of goodwill for a defined period.[89]

Withholding tax

9.45   There are a number of circumstances in the U.K. tax system in which the payer of an amount is obliged to deduct or withhold tax from the payment made and account for this to the Inland Revenue. In the context of electronic commerce there are two withholding situations in particular that could be relevant if customers are asked to pay recurrent fees.[90] Neither of these concerns apply to one-off fees.[91]

So the payment of a once only fee for the use of a software program will not be subject to withholding tax. The two possibilities in respect of regular fees are:

Royalties where owner abroad

9.46   Tax at the basic rate of income tax should be deducted from a payment of royalties to use a copyright if the owner of that copyright's usual *place of abode* is not within the U.K.[92] Copyright for this purpose does not include a cinematograph film or video recording or the sound-track of such a film or recording, so far as it is not separately exploited. There is no requirement to withhold tax if the payment is for the use of copyright that has been exported for use outside the U.K. Place of abode is usually taken to be the equivalent of place of residence for tax purposes.[93] Unless the website is designed to provide for the operation of the withholding tax mechanism it may be impossible for the user to comply with his statutory obligation and pay a net amount. Statute provides that any agreement to pay gross is void. If a double tax treaty applies this may reduce or remove the obligation to deduct tax.[94]

---

[89] *Ogden v. Medway Cinemas Ltd* (1934) 18 T.C. 691.
[90] Any royalty or other sum paid in respect of the user of a patent (sections 348(2)(a) and 349(1)(b) T.A. [1988]).
[91] Although if a non-U.K. resident sells rights relating to a U.K. patent for a capital payment then a withholding tax obligation may arise under T.A. [1988] s.524.
[92] T.A. [1988] s.536.
[93] Inland Revenue Inspector's Manual I.M. 4005.
[94] S.I. 1970 No. 488 reg. 6.

Annual payments

A withholding tax regime also applies to certain regular payments known as annual **9.47** payments, that are charged to tax under Schedule D Case III. Someone contracting over the internet for merchandising rights, for example, could encounter this requirement.

Payments for the use of registered designs, know how and trade marks could all come within the annual payments regime. If the receipt forms part of the trading profits of the recipient, then the regime will not apply. An important ingredient in identifying an annual payment is that the receipt is pure income profit of the recipient. If the recipient has to do something to earn the payment (for example providing goods or services) then the annual payment regime should not be relevant.[95] Someone who sold the right to use a secret process in return for a share of profits found themselves within this regime.[96]

If an annual payment is involved, then the following categories of payer may or will be obliged to deduct tax at the basic rate of income tax:

- a payment made by an individual for bona fide commercial reasons in connection with the individual's trade, profession vocation[97];
- payments made by non-individuals (*e.g.* companies, and trustees).[98]

Digital cash

The receipts of a trade can take the form of money's worth as well as money.[99] In broad **9.48** terms, arguments by a trader that non-cash receipts (*e.g.* digital credits) should not be taken into account for tax purposes are unlikely to succeed. The Inland Revenue's approach will be to value such assets. If there is some restriction on the realisation of a non-cash item, then this may reduce its value but it is not an argument that it has no value.[1]

Non-business use

Non-business use of an asset will either prevent or restrict the ability to claim a tax- **9.49** deduction or allowance in computing trading profits. This must be borne in mind when claiming deductions for, for example, computer equipment and software. In the case of claiming a trading deduction, if the trader had some other purpose in mind than a trade purpose at the time of buying, for example, a software package then a trading deduction should not be claimed. Even if there is a subsidiary non-trade purpose, this duality of purpose, prohibits a trading deduction. If, fortuitously, fortunately, accidentally or incidentally there is a non-trade benefit, expenditure may, however, still be deductible.[2] If duality of purpose is a potential problem, then separate payments should be made in respect of the distinct elements.[3]

---

[95] *Campbell v. IRC* (1968) 45 T.C. 427.
[96] *Delage v. Nuggett Polish Co. Ltd* (1905) 92 L.T. 682.
[97] T.A. [1988] s.347A.
[98] T.A. [1988] ss.348 and 349.
[99] *Gold Coast Selection Trust Ltd v. Humphrey* (1948) 30 T.C. 209.
[1] *Ibid.*; Viscount Simon at 240.
[2] *Mallalieu v. Drummond* [1983] S.T.C. 124, 129 (and see also (1983) S.T.C. 665).
[3] *Murgatroyd v. Evans-Jackson* (1967) 43 T.C. 501.

Capital allowance claims are not, however, prejudiced by a duality of purpose. Instead, the capital allowance claim is reduced by the appropriate percentage of non-business use.

STARTING A BUSINESS

The following paragraphs deal with various tax issues that arise on starting a business.

Choice of structure

9.50   A business can be conducted by a sole trader, a partnership or through a legal entity such as a company or trust.

The choice of business structure involves a careful consideration of legal, tax and commercial issues. Electronic commerce may have an impact on legal and commercial considerations. From a tax point of view the issues to consider are likely to be those that apply to anyone starting a business and, in particular, the tax issues relevant to whether or not to incorporate a business.[4]

The amount of tax payable and when it is paid will vary according to the type of business structure. The main tax point to appreciate is that a company is likely to achieve a tax deferment rather than a tax saving. The main rate of tax is now less than the higher rate of income tax.[5] This tax difference encourages reinvestment of profits by companies. However, at some stage shareholders will want to benefit from their investment in the company. It is then that additional tax will probably be payable. If the shareholders receive income (*e.g.* salaries, dividends) then income tax is likely to be payable. If shares are sold then capital gains tax liability may arise.[6]

There are a number of detailed tax points that may be relevant in particular cases. As examples:

- the difference in the national insurance contributions payable on the earnings of a sole trader or partner in contrast to those payable by an employer and employee on employment earnings;
- a company may provide a more attractive pension arrangement for its directors, then would be available to a sole trader or partner;
- an unincorporated business may offer more scope to utilise losses that arise in the trade (whether trading or capital losses). (Losses of a company cannot be set off against the income or grains of shareholders);
- there are, in broad terms, more methods of reducing tax on capital gains (*e.g.* on a sale of a business) available to individuals than there are to companies (see further below).

---

[4] Buttersworths Business Tax Service Part II. 3 (Incorporate a business).
[5] In the 1998/1999 tax year the higher rate of income tax is 40 per cent. In the 1998 financial year the main rate of corporation tax is 31 per cent and in the financial year 1999 30 per cent.
[6] Certain transactions in securities may be subject to income tax and the avoidance provisions in T.A. [1998] Part xvii Chapter 1 apply (Cancellation of tax Advantages from certain transactions or securities).

Tax registrations

There are several tax compliance issues that need to be addressed by new businesses: **9.51**

Notice of liability to Income Tax or Corporation Tax

If a trader has not received a tax return in respect of a tax year, he must notify his Inspector of Taxes by October 5 following the end of the tax year that he is so chargeable.[7] On receiving a tax return the individual is required to make a self assessment. This involves completing the self employment or partnership supplementary pages as appropriate and returning the tax return by no later than January 31 following the end of the tax year. If the tax return is submitted by September 30 following the end of the tax year then the Inland Revenue can be asked to calculate the tax due. Each tax return when received by the Inland Revenue, should be accompanied by a Tax Return Guide which gives instructions on how to complete the tax return and supplementary pages. There are help sheets and leaflets that provide additional information.[8]

There is an equivalent obligation on a company to notify when it is chargeable to corporation tax, although the notification period is twelve months from the end of the company's accounting period.[9] In practice, soon after a company is incorporated, the Inland Revenue will send a letter to the company, asking for basic information on the company, including details of its accounting period.

VAT

It is vital to consider VAT from the outset. A trader is obliged to register for VAT if his   **9.52** turnover exceeds certain registration limits. Ignorance of the legislation is no excuse for failure to register.[10] A trader will usually become liable to be registered at the end of any month where the value of taxable supplies made in the previous 12 months exceeds the prescribed threshold.[11] If H.M. Customs and Excise can be convinced that turnover in the next 12 months will not exceed a prescribed limit then it should be possible to avoid registration.[12] Alternatively, if turnover in the next thirty days is expected to exceed a prescribed limit then, again registration is compulsory.[13] It should be remembered that turnover should be taken to include zero rated, standard rated and other positive rate supplies. H.M. Customs & Excise must be notified within thirty days of any of the compulsory registration events happening. The standard registration form (or forms in the case of group or partnership registrations) must be used.[14]

---

[7] T.M.A. [1970], s.7.

[8] These are available from the Inland Revenue Order Line, the telephone number for which for the 1997/1998 tax year was 0645–000404 (facsimile number 0645–000604) (open seven days a week between 8 a.m. and 10 p.m.). The help sheets and leaflets include SA/BK3: *Self Assessment. A Guide to keeping records for the Self Employed*; IR220: *More than one Business*; IR222: *How to calculate your taxable profits*; IR227: *Losses* and IR229: *Information from your Accounts*.

[9] T.M.A. [1970], s.10, Self assessment for companies begins for accounting periods ending or after July 1, 1999; see F.A. [1998] s.117.

[10] *Neal v. CEC* [1988] S.T.C. 131.

[11] From April 1, 1998: £50,000.

[12] From April 1, 1998: £48,000.

[13] From April 1, 1998: £50,000.

[14] These must be ordered from the relevant local VAT Office. In many cases, VAT registration has been delegated to Newry VAT Office. There is an automated VAT registration form ordering system operated by Newry VAT Office (telephone 0345–112114).

A business that makes only zero rated supplies (who would normally be a repayment trader) can apply for exemption from registration. It is still necessary to notify liability to register. Exemption should be claimed in an accompanying letter.

If a business has turnover below the registration threshold it is possible to register voluntarily for VAT purposes. It is also possible to register for VAT as an intending trader, provided suitable documentary evidence can be provided to show that taxable supplies will, eventually, be made. There is a VAT leaflet which explains the registration provisions in more detail.[15]

9.53   There are significant penalties for late notification of the liability to register for VAT.

A business faced with compulsory VAT registration may consider arrangements to split the business into two or more separate activities, with a view to each activity falling below the VAT registration threshold. This is particularly attractive when the business has relatively small amounts of input tax. However, such arrangements should be approached with caution. H.M. Customs & Excise have powers to counteract the maintenance or creation of any artificial separation of business activities.[16] In determining whether any separation of business activities is artificial, regard should be had to the extent to which the different persons carrying on those activities are closely bound to one another by financial, economic and organisational links.[17]

A business that provides only exempt supplies may find it is obliged to register if it receives services from abroad that come within the reverse charge regime. If the value of such supplies exceeds the registration limits then there is a requirement to register and account for VAT on the deemed supplies.

9.54   An overseas business may have to register for U.K. VAT under the distance selling provisions. Equivalent provisions apply in other Member States. Each Member State has its own distance selling threshold.[18] Once the value of distance sales by a business exceeds this threshold, the business must register in the U.K. and account for tax in respect of all further sales made. The threshold is calculated by reference to sales made during a calendar year. Distance selling applies when a business registered for VAT in another Member State supplies goods, and is responsible for their delivery, to any non-VAT registered person in the U.K. In addition to private individuals this will include public bodies, charities and businesses that are not registered for VAT. There is scope to register for VAT even if distance sales are below the threshold. The VAT registration procedure is similar to that described above. A different VAT registration application form is used.[19]

There is another basis on which VAT registration could occur. In broad terms, this applies to businesses not registered for VAT but which acquire goods direct from a VAT registered supplier in another Member State. Such goods are known as acquisitions and the recipient of such goods must register for VAT in the U.K. if the total value of the goods exceeds the registration threshold.[20] This limit is based on acquisitions made in a

---

[15] Notice 700/1 "Should I be registered for VAT?"

[16] VATA [1994], Schedule 1 paras 1A and 2.

[17] VATA [1994], Schedule 1 para. 1A(2).

[18] In the U.K. this is set out, 100,000 ECU: equivalent to about £70,000.

[19] Form VATA 1A. The H.M. Customs & Excise Notice 700/1A/97: "Should I be registered for VAT? — Distance Selling" provides more information.

[20] From April 1, 1998: £50,000.

calendar year. Registration is also obligatory if there are reasonably grounds for believing that the value of acquisitions to be made in the next thirty days will exceed this same limit. The registration procedure is similar to those mentioned above. There is a different VAT registration form to complete.[21] There is VAT Notice which explains the arrangements in more detail.[22]

PAYE

As soon as the business has employees (or payments are planned, if a company, to directors) then the business must register for PAYE. The business should contact its local tax office to find out which office deals with PAYE for the business. The Inland Revenue will provide the business with a package of documents to enable it to operate PAYE.

9.55

Duty Deferment

A VAT registered business (and certain others) may enter into a duty deferment arrangement with H.M. Customs & Excise. This defers the time of payment of VAT, customs duties and certain other duties due on importation of goods (or the removal of goods from, for example, a customs warehouse). A guarantee from a bank or insurance company is required.[23]

9.56

Tax incentives

The following are tax incentives that may be relevant when establishing a business:

Pre-Trading Expenditure

If a person incurs expenditure for the purposes of trade within seven years before the trade begins, such pre-trading expenditure can be claimed as a revenue deduction once the trade begins.[24] It is important that the person incurring the pre-trading expenditure is also the person who then starts the trade.[25]

9.57

Pre-trading capital expenditure, which qualifies for capital allowances, is dealt with similarly. Such expenditure, incurred for the purposes of a trade by a person about to carry it on, is treated as incurred when the trade commences.[26] If an asset originally acquired for private purposes (*e.g.* a personal computer) is subsequently brought into business use, it is the market value at the time that is eligible for capital allowances.

There is also scope to recover VAT incurred before a business is registered for VAT purposes. VAT incurred for the purpose of the business, on services, in the six months prior to the date of registration, may be recovered. VAT on goods (*e.g.* stock and office equipment) still retained by the business at the date of registration.[27]

Initial Allowances

The capital allowances regime does provide for 100 per cent initial allowances in some circumstances. These allowances are available to existing businesses as well as new businesses. Such allowances are, in particular, available for capital expenditure on

9.58

---

[21] Form VAT 1B.
[22] H.M. Customs & Excise Notice 700/1B/97: "Should I be registered for VAT? — Acquisitions".
[23] Further information is available from the Central Referment Office (telephone 01702–367425).
[24] T.A. [1988] Sub-section 401.
[25] Tax Bulletin (Issue 5) November 1992.
[26] C.A.A. [1990], s.83(2).
[27] See further in H.M. Customs & Excise Notice 700, para. 4.09.

industrial or commercial buildings (including hotels) in enterprise zones.[28] First year allowances equivalent to 100 per cent of expenditure may also be made available from time to time.[29]

An enhanced allowance in the first year, less than 100 per cent, may also be available from time to time.[30]

Trading Losses

9.59   The amount of a trading loss is calculated according to the same principles, as apply in calculating profits. If loss arises in the first four years of the business the loss may be carried back and set off against income for the three years before that in which the loss arises.[31] This provision only applies to individuals. This provision is in addition to the normal provision that a trading loss can be set off against general income of the relevant tax year and the preceding year.[32] It is also possible to set a trading loss in a tax year against chargeable capital gains realised in that year.[33]
If relief cannot be given under the above provisions then the loss may be carried forward and set against future profits of the relevant trade.[34] As a general rule if the trade discontinues then relief for losses is lost.

It is important that the trade is carried on on a commercial basis and with a view to the realisation of profit. If not, the loss will not be accepted as a trading loss for the above purposes.[35] A company can set off trading losses against profits (including capital gains) in the same accounting period and preceding three years.[36] It may also carry forward the loss and set it against trading income of the same trade in succeeding accounting periods.[37]

Enterprise Investment Scheme

9.60   The Enterprise Investment Scheme (EIS) comprises various reliefs. EIS reliefs are only relevant in the case of a trade carried on by a company which issues new shares for cash. There are various detailed conditions to be met by the company and the subscriber.[38] In outline, the reliefs available, if conditions are satisfied, are as follows:

- 20 per cent income tax relief on the amount invested;
- capital gains tax exemption on a disposal of EIS shares;
- a reinvestment relief for gains on assets where the proceeds of disposal are reinvested in EIS shares; and

---

[28] There are Enterprise Zones in Inverclyde, Sunderland, Lanarkshire, Dearne Valley, East Midlands, East Durham and Tyne Riverside. An Enterprise Zone designation lasts for 10 years. C.A.A. [1990], Section 1(1).
[29] Certain expenditure on plant and machinery for use in Northern Ireland incurred in the period from May 12, 1998 to May 11, 2002 attracts a first year allowance of 100 per cent (F.A. [1998], Section 83).
[30] Certain expenditure incurred from July 2, 1998 to July 1, 1999 qualifies for a 40 per cent first year allowance (F.A. [1998], s.84).
[31] T.A. [1998], s.381.
[32] T.A. [1998], s.380.
[33] F.A. [1991], s.72.
[34] T.A. [1998], s.385.
[35] T.A. [1998], s.384(1).
[36] T.A. [1998], s.393A.
[37] T.A. [1998], s.393.
[38] T.A. [1998], ss.289 *et eq.* and T.C.G.A. [1992] ss.150A *et seq.*

- a loss on a disposal of EIS shares may be set against income tax or capital gains tax.

There is an Inland Revenue publication which explains the EIS scheme in more details.[39] Particular points to note are:

- the business activity of the EIS company must be carried on wholly or mainly in the U.K. for at least three years after the relevant share issue;
- The EIS company must carry on a qualifying trade. Certain activities are excluded, unless they form an insubstantial part of the trade. From the point of view of electronic commerce, receiving royalties or licence fees could prevent the trade from qualifying.[40]

Interest Relief

Tax relief for certain payments of interest. These include interest on loans to buy into a partnership.[41]

9.61

Other Relevant Reliefs

A loss on the disposal of unquoted shares in a trading company or holding company of a trading group can be set off against income if various conditions are met.[42]

9.62

Non-domiciled Entrepreneurs

A non-U.K. domiciled individual who is resident in the U.K. benefits from the remittance basis of taxation. In broad terms, capital gains arising on non-U.K. assets are not subject to U.K. tax on capital gains until all proceeds are remitted to the U.K.[43] Similarly, income arising from non-U.K. sources is also taxed on a remittance basis.[44] In the case of a U.K. resident individual owning a business overseas it is, however, difficult to establish such a business as a non-U.K. source of income because the "head and brains" or the organisation will normally be in the U.K.[45] Domicile from income tax and capital tax purposes is a general law concept. Domicile is not the same as nationality or residence. The Inland Revenue's approach is broadly speaking, to ask where someone has their permanent home.[46] Someone born outside the U.K. can, live in the U.K. for a considerable time without establishing a U.K. domicile. From an inheritance tax point of view, a non-U.K. domiciled individual is only subject to inheritance tax on U.K. assets. There is, however, a different test of domicile for inheritance tax purposes.[47]

9.63

Non-domicile individuals may prefer to conduct their business through non U.K. incorporated companies. The shares in such companies will be non U.K. assets for

---

[39] I.R. 137.
[40] T.A. [1998] s.29(2)(e).
[41] T.A. [1998], s.362.
[42] T.A. [1998], ss.573 *et seq.*
[43] T.C.G.A. [1992], s.12.
[44] T.A. [1998], ss.19 and 65.
[45] *Ogilvie v. Kitton*, S.T.C. 338.
[46] I.R. 20, para. 5.
[47] I.H.T.A. [1984], s.267 — "The 17 Year rule".

capital gains tax and inheritance tax purposes. Such a company could be U.K. tax resident under the central management and control test and pay corporation tax on its worldwide profits.

However, if the company is operated so as to be a non-U.K. resident and no part of its business is conducted in the U.K. then profits can arise free of U.K. tax (and, possibly, free of any tax if the company operates from a "tax haven").[48]

GOING INTERNATIONAL

9.64   Preceding paragraphs have explained the scope of U.K. taxation in respect of electronic commerce. The emphasis has been on electronic commerce conducted by U.K. residents and on the tax aspects of conducting that business in the U.K. However, the nature of electronic commerce makes it likely that overseas tax will have to be considered. Although U.K. tax residents are, in broad terms, are taxable in respect of worldwide income and capital gains, this does not mean that overseas tax issues can be ignored.

All the tax compliance issues raised in respect of starting a new business in the U.K. could apply equally in respect of a business conducted in another jurisdiction. The other jurisdiction could stake its claim to tax on trading profits within its territory, just as the U.K. does in respect of non-resident trading in the U.K. A U.K. based business could have employees in one or more other jurisdictions, which would be subject to the local equivalent of pay as you earn and national insurance contributions. In some territories, tax withholdings are needed on payments to other categories of workers, not just employees. Similarly capital assets held in other jurisdictions could be subject to local taxes on capital gains. There may be local business rates or other property taxes to pay in respect of any interest in land and buildings in other jurisdictions. As explained, in the case of goods sold in other Member States, local VAT may be payable under the distance selling provisions. If there is a place of business overseas that provides goods or services then the local equivalent of VAT clearly needs to be considered.

Although the U.K.'s approach to the taxation of electronic commerce provides a good guide to the overseas tax issues that are likely to arise, tax legislation does vary significantly from one jurisdiction to another and detailed local advice is likely to be needed.

As explained in relation to the taxation of trading profits in the U.K., in addition to taxing U.K. residents on worldwide trading and profits, the U.K. also taxes non-residents on income arising from trade within the U.K. If a U.K. company, with overseas activities, encounters the same approach to taxation in the country in which it is trading, then clearly there will be double taxation. The overseas jurisdiction will seek tax on the trading profits arising in its jurisdiction and the U.K. will expect U.K. tax to be paid on those profits. Similarly, a U.K. tax resident employee who works overseas, could face taxation on his salary in both the U.K. and an overseas jurisdiction. Double taxation is recognised internationally as objectionable and tax systems adopt various approaches to try to avoid or minimise the incidence of double taxation.

---

[48] See paras 9.80 *et seq.* regarding the use of offshore companies by U.K. domiciled and resident individuals.

In some jurisdictions there are significant exemptions from tax on overseas income. In the U.K. two approaches can be identified to deal with double taxation:

(1) double taxation agreements;
(2) unilateral relief (*i.e.* credit for foreign tax paid against the U.K. tax liability or deducting foreign tax in computing business profits).

Both of the above is considered further below and, in particular, the opportunities available under double taxation agreements to avoid or reduce overseas taxation.

In practice, if a U.K. tax resident is conducting business in a country with which the U.K. has a double tax treaty then there are significant protections available.

Double taxation agreements

The Inland Revenue proudly announced in 1996 that the U.K. was the first country to enter into double taxation agreements with over 100 countries. The Government can enter into arrangements with other governments with a view to affording relief from double taxation pursuant to statutory authority.[49] The usual approach is for a treaty to follow the latest model treaty devised by the OECD.[50] Relevant provisions in the latest model treaty ("the Model") are considered, as follows[51]:   **9.65**

Permanent Establishments and the Taxation of business profits

The concept of a permanent establishment is vital in determining the right of one government (in tax treaty terms known as a contracting state) to tax the profits of an enterprise of the other contracting state. Under Article 7 of the Model a contracting state cannot tax the profits of an enterprise of the other contracting state unless it carries on its business through a permanent establishment situated therein. A permanent establishment is a fixed place of business through which the business of an enterprise is only or partly carried on. The Model confirms that a permanent establishment includes especially a place of management, a branch, an office, a factory, a workshop and certain places of extraction of natural resources (*e.g.* mines). This gives the impression that some sort of premises are required. However in certain instances, it is sufficient for the facility to comprise machinery or equipment. In the context of electronic commerce it is this latter possibility that it is of particular concern. Various comments in the OECD commentary on the Model are also relevant, including: **9.66**

"the place of business may be situated in the business facilities of another enterprise. Equipment constituting the place of business [does not have] to be actually fixed to the soil on which it stands. It is enough that the equipment remains on a particular site. If the place of business was not set up merely for a temporary purpose, it can constitute a permanent establishment, even though it existed, in practice, only for a very short period of time because of the special nature of the activity of the enterprise or because, as a consequence of special circumstances . . . it was prematurely liquidated".

"The activity [of the permanent establishment] need not be of a productive character".

[49] T.A. [1988], s.788.
[50] The Model Double Taxation Convention was adopted on April 29, 1977 and revised on July 23, 1992.
[51] Model Tax Convention on Income and Capital: Report of the OECD Committee on Fiscal Affairs, 1992.

"Where tangible property such as facilities, industrial, commercial or scientific (ICS) equipment . . . or intangible property such as patents, procedures and similar property, are let or leased to third parties through a fixed place of business . . . this activity will, in general, render the place of business a permanent establishment".

". . . a permanent establishment may . . . exist if the business of the enterprise is carried on mainly through automatic equipment, the activities of the personnel being restricted to setting up, operating, controlling and maintaining such equipment".

9.67   Previously, the main concern has been over gaming and vending machines. In broad terms, a permanent establishment may exist if the enterprise which sets up the machines also operates and maintains them for its own account. This remains the case even if the machines are operated and maintained by an agent dependent on the enterprise. The Model does list a number of activities which are treated as exceptions to the general definition of a permanent establishment. The common characteristic of these activities is that they are, in broad terms, preparatory or auxiliary activities. These exclusions allow, for example, a representative office to escape classification as a permanent establishment. This assumes the representative office will restrict its activities to, for example, collecting information and promoting business but not actually conducting it. If electronic commerce involves siting equipment in other jurisdictions, for the purpose of routing information only, rather than processing it, then it should be possible to argue that there is no permanent establishment. This is on the basis that although there is a fixed place of business it is solely for the purpose of carrying on, for the enterprise, an activity of a preparatory or auxiliary nature. Similarly, the acquisition of telecommunications capacity in a country perhaps through leasing telephone lines, should also be considered preparatory or auxiliary.

If a permanent establishment is found to exist then under the Model only so much of the profits as is attributable to that permanent establishment can be taxed in the other contracting state. Again, the commentary on the market provides guidance how this principle operates.

Independent Personal Services

9.68   A separate provision of the Model is concerned with professional services and other activities of an independent character. This excludes industrial and commercial activities and also services performed as an employee. Professional services is taken to include independent scientific, literary, artistic, educational or teaching activities as well as the independent activities of lawyers, accountants and so on. Some electronic commerce may fall within this provision rather the definition of business profits. The Model provides a similar protection to that available for business profits.[52] Income derived by a resident of one contracting state in respect of professional services is taxable only in the state of residence, unless he has a fixed based regularly available to him in the other contracting state for the purpose of performing his activities. If he has such fixed base, the income attributable to that fixed base may be taxed in the other state. It is not clear to what extent (if at all) the definition of a fixed base differs from that of a permanent

---

[52] *Ibid.*, Article 14.

establishment. The OECD commentary gives two narrow examples of a fixed base (a physician's consulting room and the office of an architect or a lawyer).

Dependent Personal Services

The Model provides an important exemption in respect of employment income.[53] An employee who is a resident of one contracting state can avoid taxation in another contracting state if, in outline:

9.69

- the employee is present there for no more than 183 days in the relevant tax year;
- the remuneration is paid by or on behalf of an employer who is not a resident of that other state; and
- the remuneration is not borne by a permanent establishment or a fixed base which the employer has in the other state.

Royalties

Under the Model, royalties are taxed only in the country of residence of the beneficial owner of royalties.[54] However, in practice, many agreements provide for the state in which the royalty arises to charge tax up to a specified level. Under the Model, royalties is defined to include payments of any kind received as consideration for the use of, or the right to use, any copyright of literary, artistic or scientific work. Various examples are given (*e.g.* patents, trademarks and so on). The definition does not refer specifically to computer software. The commentary on the royalties article contains a discussion on the difficulties of determining where the boundary lies between software payments that are properly to be regarded as royalties and other types of payment (*e.g.* commercial income or a capital gain).[55] If royalties are paid in connection with rights effectively connected with a permanent establishment or a fixed base then the relevant provisions (*e.g.* business profit or independent personal services) apply, rather than the royalties article.

9.70

Unilateral relief

If a double tax treaty does not apply then unilateral relief is available. Relief from income tax and corporation tax shall be given in respect of tax paid overseas by allowing that tax as a credit against income tax or corporation tax.[56] The alternative is to deduct the foreign tax in computing the profits of the business.[57]

9.71

VAT POINTS TO WATCH

Many types of business have special VAT rules that apply to them. The following paragraphs address some issues that are likely to be relevant to a wide range of electronic commerce businesses. In particular, this includes looking in more detail at the

9.72

---

[53] *Ibid.*, Article 15.
[54] *Ibid.*, Article 12.
[55] The commentary was revised following the OECD Ministerial Conference in October 1998.
[56] T.A. [1998], s.790.
[57] T.A. [1998], s.811.

differences in VAT liability that arise on supplies of goods and services to customers outside the U.K. and some administrative issues.

Supply of goods to non-U.K. customers

9.73   It is assumed that the goods in question would be standard rated if supplied to a customer in the U.K. As a general rule, if the goods are supplied to someone in the U.K. then it makes no difference if the customer receives the supply for the purpose of a business carried on by him or for private purposes; the supply remains standard rated. If goods are exported to a place outside the E.C. then it, similarly, makes no difference to what use the goods are put. The export of goods outside the E.C. to both business and private customers is zero-rated. However, if goods are removed to another Member State then zero-rating only applies if the goods are acquired in that Member State by a person who is liable for VAT in accordance with the laws of that Member State (the equivalent of the VAT charge on acquisitions described in paragraph 9.32 above). In other cases, either U.K. VAT is charged or, the supplier has to charge local VAT (under the local equivalent of the distance selling provisions described in paragraph 9.54).

Table 1: Supply of goods by a U.K. VAT registered business

VAT liability	Place (and circumstances)
0%	Goods exported outside E.C.
0%	Goods removed to another Member State and acquired by a VAT registered business
Rate applicable in other Member State	Goods removed to another member State and supplier is registered there under distance selling rules
17.5%	Goods removed to another member State in other circumstances.

Note: It is assumed that the supply of goods to someone in the U.K. would be standard rated (17.5 per cent).

If goods are exported outside the E.C. then the U.K. VAT registered business must possess evidence of such export to claim zero-rated treatment. The involvement of the internet as the means of selling goods for export should not make it any harder to obtain such evidence.[58] In the case of supplies to other Member States, the supply may be zero-rated if:

---

[58] Notice 703: Exports and removals of goods from the U.K.

- the customer's E.C. VAT registration number is included on the tax invoice;
- the goods are sent or transported out of the U.K. to another E.C. Member State and;
- commercial documentary evidence is obtained that the goods have been removed from the U.K. (There is a time limit for obtaining this.)

It is the first of these requirements that may, in particular, cause a practical problem. It is usual to ask the customer for their VAT number. If the number provided is not in the published format for the relevant Member State, it would no doubt be rejected by the trader (or his computer program). Provided all reasonable steps have been taken to ensure the customer is VAT registered and to obtain his VAT number H.M. Customs & Excise state they will not hold the U.K. supplier liable to account for VAT if it turns out the number is invalid.[59]

Supply of services to non-U.K. customers

It is assumed that the services supplied would be standard rated if supplied to a customer belonging in the U.K. Again, as a general rule it makes no difference if a customer in the U.K. uses the services for business purposes or private purposes, the supply remains standard rated.

9.74

Schedule 5 services

If services are supplied to a customer belonging outside the U.K. it is important to distinguish, in particular, supplies of a description within paragraphs 1 to 8 of Schedule 5 to the Value Added Tax Act 1994 ("Schedule 5 services") from other services.

9.75

Examples of Schedule 5 services were given in para. 9.22. It is important to realise that the transmission of images and games and so on which are not copyright will probably not come within any of the items in Schedule 5 and so will not be a Schedule 5 service. However, if an Internet package is provided for a single inclusive price (*e.g.* covering access to information pages, on-line shopping, games fora etc.) then there is a single supply that falls within Schedule 5.[60]

Melbourne Agreement[61]

The Melbourne Agreement permitted the supply of telecommunications capacity by public telecommunications authorities and similar operators to other such authorities to be zero-rated. This aspect of the Melbourne Agreement has, however, been superseded by the new place of supply rules for telecommunications services.[62] U.K. providers who fall under the provisions of the Melbourne Agreement do not have to account for the reverse charge on such services.[63]

9.76

If services are supplied that are not Schedule 5 services, then U.K. VAT at the standard rate applies, regardless of where the customer belongs and whether or not the supply is for business or private purposes.

---

[59] *Ibid.*
[60] Business Brief 22/97.
[61] The final acts of the World Administrative Telegraph and Telephone Conference in 1988 in Melbourne.
[62] See para. 9.30 above.
[63] VAT Information Sheet 2/97, para. 7.1.

If Schedule 5 services are supplied to a customer belonging outside the E.C. then the supply is outside the scope but with a right to recovery of input tax. If the services are supplied to a customer belonging in another Member State then the supply is only outside the scope of VAT if made for the purposes of a business carried on by the customer. The local equivalent of the reverse charge should apply. Otherwise, the supply is standard rated.

Table 2: Supply of Schedule 5 services (other than telecommunications services) by a U.K. VAT registered business to a customer belonging in a place outside the U.K.

VAT liability	Place (and circumstances)
OTS	Outside the E.C.
OTS	Another Member State where supply received for customer's business
17.5%	Another Member State in other circumstances

Note: OTS means outside the scope of U.K. VAT.

There is again a practical issue of identifying whether or not an EC customer is in business. VAT registration numbers are the best evidence and should always be requested. If a VAT number is not available then alternative evidence of business status is acceptable. Unfortunately, for an electronic trader, the examples of alternative evidence given by H.M. Customs & Excise[64] are of documents, such as business letterheads which will not be available in an interest transaction.

Tax invoices

9.77   A VAT invoice must contain certain prescribed information. A VAT invoice does not have to be in writing. The requisite particulars can be recorded in a computer and transmitted by electronic means.[65] Various conditions must be met. H.M. Customs & Excise must be given at least one month's notice in writing of what is planned and comply with any general regulations in existence and such requirements as H.M. Customs and Excise may impose in any particular case.

VAT inclusive or exclusive prices?

9.78   The amount paid for a supply includes VAT. In other words, consideration is a tax inclusive amount.[66] If a price is shown and no reference is made to VAT then the usual implication is that the price is VAT inclusive. This implication may be displaced by the

---

[64] Notice 741: "VAT: Place of supply of services". See para. 9.04.
[65] V.A.T.A. [1994] Schedule 11 para. 3(1).
[66] V.A.T.A. [1994] s.19.

circumstances in which the price is quoted. Care must therefore be taken to ensure that in contract law it is clear whether a price is VAT exclusive or inclusive.

ANTI-AVOIDANCE

The U.K. currently has no general anti-avoidance provision.[67] A taxpayer is therefore able to organise his affairs, provided it is in a lawful manner, so as to minimise or avoid tax. In the House of Lords in *IRC v. Duke of Westminster*, Lord Tomlin states:

> "Every man is entitled if he can to order his affairs so that the tax attaching under the appropriate Acts is less than it otherwise would be. If he succeeds in ordering them so as to secure this result, then, however unappreciative the Commissioners of Inland Revenue or his fellow taxpayers may be of his ingenuity, he cannot be compelled to pay an increased tax".[68]

9.79

There has also been a tradition of interpreting tax legislation in such a way as to place a burden on the tax authorities to show that a taxpayer fell fairly within the scope of the charge in question. The development of the Ramsay principle provides a general method of counteracting artificial tax planning schemes but this has its limits.[69]

U.K. tax legislation does, however, contain a significant number of highly effective provisions to counteract tax avoidance.[70] There are a number of provisions aimed at counteracting tax avoidance through transactions involving shares and other securities. There are also wide ranging anti-avoidance provisions related to the sale by an individual of income derived from his personal activities and in respect of so-called artificial transactions in land. The following paragraphs consider the anti-avoidance provisions that apply and other approaches that can be taken by the Inland Revenue to counteract attempts by a U.K. resident to escape the charges to tax on trading profits explained in paragraph 9.09 above.

A U.K. resident individual is charged to tax under Schedule D Case I on a trade if it is conducted wholly in the U.K. or partly within the U.K. and partly outside. If the trade is conducted wholly outside the U.K., it is still taxed but under Case V instead of Case I. A U.K. tax resident company will similarly pay tax under either Case I or Case V. If a non-U.K. resident company conducts a trade, then it will only be within the scope of U.K. tax to the extent that trade is conducted within the U.K. There is the potential with electronic commerce for a trade to be conducted wholly outside the U.K. A company is a legal entity, separate from its shareholders, directors and employees. Therefore, U.K. tax resident individuals may well be able to avoid the usual tax charges by arranging for a trade to be conducted by a non-tax resident company. There are a number of tax haven

9.80

---

[67] On October 5, 1998 the Inland Revenue published a consultative document, "A General Anti-Avoidance Rule for Direct Taxes". It examines the advantages a general anti-avoidance rule would have in countering tax avoidance, in relation to the corporate sector, and considers how it might be framed. The document builds on the work of the Tax Law Review Committee report, "Tax avoidance" (November 1997). H.M. Customs & Excise is due to publish its own report.

[68] 19 T.C. 490 at 520.

[69] *Ramsay (W.T) Ltd v. IRC* [1981] S.T.C. 174; *Furniss v. Dawson* [1984] ST.C. 153.

[70] T.A. [1988] ss.703 *et seq.*

jurisdictions that offer no or low tax regimes and so, in principle, there is a tax planning opportunity. However, in practice, it is difficult to achieve tax savings.

Example

Douglas sells toys (see para. 9.08). One of Douglas's customers suggested Douglas sets up a British Virgin Islands incorporated company, with Jersey resident directors. The suggestion is that in this way Douglas does not have to pay any tax on his business profits. There was no suggestion that Douglas should work from Jersey; Douglas would continue to work in the U.K. but would use the offshore company's name.

However, another of Douglas's customers, a tax lawyer, warned Douglas that at best he would not save tax and at worse Douglas would commit a criminal offence and incur significant tax penalties and interest.

In the case of an individual owning an offshore company there are the following obstacles to avoiding U.K. tax:

- an overseas incorporated company can still be U.K. tax resident;
- an overseas company may have a taxable trade in the U.K.;
- the arrangement may be ignored as a sham;
- income (and capital gains) arising in the offshore company may be deemed that of a U.K. resident and taxed accordingly.

In the case of a company owning an offshore company or an interest in it there are also the controlled foreign company provisions to consider. Transactions may also be subject to adjustments under transfer pricing provisions.

This chapter assumes that a taxpayer would only consider attempting to reduce his tax liabilities through lawful measures (*i.e.* tax avoidance). If a taxpayer tried to reduce his tax liabilities in a way that is not lawful, this is tax evasion. A tax evader faces criminal prosecution and, in particular, imprisonment. His advisers and associates may also find they have committed criminal offences[71]

Company residence

9.81   As explained above, an overseas incorporated company can nevertheless be U.K. tax resident under the central management and control test. It is relatively straightforward to find individuals in tax haven jurisdictions who will act as directors of a company. If such individuals act as mere cyphers for the U.K. resident shareholder then the company will be U.K. tax resident. It will then be subject to tax on its worldwide profits. Circumstances can, however, be imagined in which the non-U.K. resident directors do exercise central management and control outside the U.K. Electronic commerce offers the potential to make this easier to achieve, as more of the trading process is automated. The U.K. resident individual will then more clearly have a relationship with the company as, say, a shareholder, rather than as a shadow director. Nevertheless, in

---

[71] *R. v. Charlton* [1996] S.T.C. 1418, CA.

practice, some risk is likely to remain that the presence of a key individual in the U.K. will make an offshore company U.K. tax resident.

U.K. branch or agency

Corporation tax is charged on non-resident companies trading through a branch or agency in the U.K. If someone is involved in the U.K. in the trading activities of an offshore company, that person may create a taxable branch or agency.[72]   **9.82**

Sham transactions

It is unlikely that an arrangement will be overturned as a sham transaction but this remains a possibility in extreme circumstances.[73] In which case, the use of the offshore company would be ignored and the trade taxed as if the company did not exist.   **9.83**

Deemed income

The most formidable obstacle for individuals to overcome is that of Section 739 of the Income and Corporation Taxes Act 1988 and related provisions.   **9.84**

Section 739, unusually for a statutory provision, contains a preamble to explain the aim of the legislation when introduced in 1936. The preamble reads:

> ". . . this section shall have effect for the purpose of preventing the avoiding by individuals ordinarily resident in the U.K. of liability to income tax by means of transfers of assets by virtue . . . of which . . . income becomes payable to persons resident or domiciled outside the U.K."

The statutory provisions are drafted in wide terms and have been interpreted widely by the Courts.

Briefly, if by virtue of a transfer of an asset or assets income is payable to a non-U.K. resident then a tax charge will arise on an individual ordinarily resident in the U.K. if:

- the individual is the transferor of the asset and has power to enjoy that income (power to enjoy is widely defined);
- the individual is the transferor of the asset and is entitled to receive a capital sum connected with the transfer, or
- the individual, is not the transferor of the asset, but receives a benefit from the asset.

If the main tax charge under Section 739 is not to apply then the transferor must accept that neither he (nor any spouse) can have power to enjoy the income of the offshore structure either directly or indirectly. The benefit of the offshore structure must belong to someone else. If this is acceptable then there may be scope to accumulate profits tax free offshore. However, if a U.K. resident wishes to benefit from the profits of the offshore company then a tax charge is very likely to arise under this anti-avoidance provision.

---

[72] *IRC v. Brackett* [1986] S.T.C. 521.
[73] *Snook v. London & West Riding Investments Ltd* [1967] 2 Q.B. 786.

Example

A U.K. tax resident chartered surveyor (Mr. B) set up a Jersey trust in 1974 for the benefit of the mother of their two children. The trustees incorporated a Jersey company, (D Ltd) the directors of which were two Canadians and a Jersey advocate. The intention was for the offshore structure to share in the profits of a property development in Jersey. The property development did not, however, go ahead.

Mr. B. had retired from private practice but continued to earn fees as a property consultant. Following discussions (outside the U.K.) with the directors of D Ltd it was agreed that D Ltd would start a consultancy business. It would employ Mr. B to give advice to its clients. When Mr. B was asked for business advice he would refer the potential customer to D Ltd. D Ltd would agree to provide the advice and would deal with administrative matters (invoices and payment of expenses).

Mr. B received some remuneration from the company. The balance of the fees was retained by D Ltd. These funds accumulated tax free in D Ltd.

D Ltd bought properties from Mr. B at what were believed to be market value prices. These purchases were made at a time when there had been a collapse in the U.K. property market and so probably could not be sold on the open market.

The contract of employment between Mr. B and D Ltd is the transfer of an asset for the purposes of T.A. (1988) s.739. Mr. B had power to enjoy the income of D Ltd because of the benefits he received from D Ltd: namely the provision of liquidity, payments of salary and also the discharge of Mr. B's moral obligations to provide for his children and their mother.

As Mr. B was permanently resident in the U.K. and his activities constituted the esssential operations of D Ltd's trade, D Ltd was carrying on a trade in the United Kingdom thorugh a U.K. branch or agency. The profits of the offshore structure therefore fell to be taxed in the U.K.

(*IRC v. Brackett* [1986] S.T.C. 521.)

Deemed gains

9.85 If the offshore company realises a chargeable gain, rather than a trading profit, then another anti-avoidance provision may apply. The gains of certain non-resident companies can be apportioned to its shareholders and deemed to be their gains and taxed accordingly.[74]

Controlled foreign companies

9.86 A controlled foreign company (CFC) is one which is not U.K. resident but is controlled by U.K. residents, whether individuals or companies, and which is taxed in its country of residence at a lower level (as defined) than in the U.K. The CFC legislation[75] exists to prevent the accumulation of income in such lower tax jurisdictions. U.K. resident companies with an interest in a CFC can be charged to tax on their share of the chargeable profits (less any creditable overseas tax). There are exceptions from the CFC

---

[74] T.C.G.A. [1992], s.13.
[75] T.A. [1988] ss.747–756, Schedules 24–26.

regime. It may be difficult for some electronic businesses to come within the exceptions, in particular, for permitted businesses.

Transfer pricing

Legislation exists to counteract the manipulation of prices by associated businesses.[76] In broad terms, if a U.K. trader sells goods at less than market value or buys goods at more than market value from an associated business, then the prices can be adjusted to market value. The provisions apply to the transfer of rights, interests or licences and the giving of business facilities of whatever kind. The introduction of self-assessment has led to a change in emphasis and restructuring of the legislation. Taxpayers will soon have to use the arm's length principle in making their returns.[77] The complexity of some electronic commerce transactions may make it difficult to apply the arm's length practice.

9.87

In addition to the above statutory provisions, double taxation agreements contain transfer pricing rules and mutual agreement procedures for resolving disputes between tax authorities.[78]

CONCLUSION

As always, it remains vital to have a correct and complete understanding of the background facts, in order to provide a full tax analysis of any electronic commerce.

9.88

There are potential tax pitfalls with electronic commerce. Traders may not realise the need to register for VAT in other Member States (under the equivalent of the distance selling provisions or otherwise) or an equivalent to VAT in other territories. The internet does not necessarily offer the best VAT treatment. Information bought in book form is zero rated for VAT purposes, in contrast to receiving an electronic supply of information from a U.K. supplier on which VAT is charged at the standard rate. There are potential practical problems obtaining the necessary information from customers to ensure the correct VAT treatment or other tax treatment. At a governmental level, developing countries are concerned at the potential loss of revenue if there is a move from importing goods (on which import duties are raised) to importing intangibles. Governments are concerned about the scope for tax evasion.

Electronic commerce does provide scope for legitimate tax planning. The Government accepts that betting and gaming duties may be avoided by establishing, for example, "virtual casinos" outside the U.K. on the Internet. The place of supply rules for VAT purposes create planning opportunities. It is in the interest of private customers to buy Schedule 5 services (excluding telecommunications services) from suppliers outside the E.C. There remains a competitive advantage purchasing Internet packages from outside the E.C. Developments in technology will, no doubt, make it easier to receive other services from businesses outside the E.C.

---

[76] T.A. [1988] s.770, to be replaced by s.770A.
[77] F.A. [1998], ss.108 *et seq.*
[78] The OECA publishes "Transfer Pricing Guidelines for Multinational Enterprises and Tax Administrations."

Diagram: Using the VAT Place of Supply Rules to Provide a VAT Free Service to a U.K. Private Customer

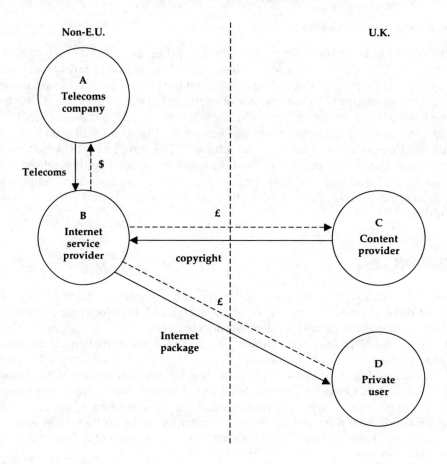

	Supply	Comment
9.89	A to B	This supply is outside the scope of U.K. VAT.
	C to B	This is a supply of Schedule 5 services and is outside the scope of U.K. VAT. If D bought the copyright material direct from C he would be charged VAT unless he bought, it say, in book form from C).
	B to D	This is a supply of Schedule 5 services and is outside the scope of U.K. VAT. The reverse charge does not apply to private customers. If D bought his internet package from a U.K. service provider he would be charged VAT)

There are likely to be a number of changes to the U.K. tax system as electronic **9.90**
commerce develops. The changes made to Schedule 5 from July 1, 1997 in respect of
telecommunication services show the commitment of U.K. and European tax authorities
to avoid significant tax distortions.

The Government is now consulting on moving towards a simpler system or intellectual property taxation, essentially following the accounting treatment for relieving
intellectual property expenditure and taxing proceeds.[79] There is also consultation on
simplifying the taxation of royalty payments. In place of the current variable treatment
the aim is to allow as many payments as possible to be made gross and to align
withholding tax rules with the terms of double tax treaties.[80] The Government is also
involved in initiatives to clarify the meaning of permanent establishment and, in
particular, whether a web server could be a permanent establishment. As harmonisation
continues some intra-Member State VAT difficulties should disappear.

The Inland Revenue and H.M. Customs & Excise have published a joint paper on U.K.
tax policy regarding electronic commerce.[81] The broad policy principles are neutrality,
certainty and transparency, effectiveness and efficiency. In broad terms, the Government
does not believe any major changes in existing tax law (or new taxes) are necessary to
achieve these policy principles. This was also a conclusion of the OECD Ministerial
Conference in Ottawa on October 7–9, 1998. Many tax aspects of electronic commerce
will be monitored by the U.K. and other Governments as electronic commerce develops,
particularly tax compliance issues, to ensure that existing taxation principles continue to
work.

---

[79] Pre-Budget Report H.M. Treasury November 1998 "Steering a stable course for lasting prosperity" para.
3.33.
[80] *Ibid.*, para. 3 33.
[81] Inland Revenue Press Release 128/98 and H.M. Customs & Excise News Release 25/98.

INDEX

(All references are to paragraph numbers)